W9-BCN-682

MAR   2008

The Intellectual Foundation of Information Organization

Digital Libraries and Electronic Publishing
William Y. Arms, series editor

Gateways to Knowledge: The Role of Academic Libraries in Teaching, Learning, and Research, edited by Lawrence Dowler, 1997

Civic Space/Cyberspace: The American Public Library in the Information Age, Redmond Kathleen Molz and Phyllis Dain, 1999

Digital Libraries, William Y. Arms, 1999

From Gutenberg to the Global Information Infrastructure: Access to Information in the Networked World, Christine L. Borgman, 2000

The Intellectual Foundation of Information Organization, Elaine Svenonius, 2000

The Intellectual Foundation of Information Organization

Elaine Svenonius

The MIT Press
Cambridge, Massachusetts
London, England

© 2000 Massachusetts Institute of Technology

All rights reserved. No part of this book may be reproduced in any form by any electronic or mechanical means (including photocopying, recording, or information storage and retrieval) without permission in writing from the publisher.

This book was set in Sabon by The MIT Press and was printed a.·d bound in the United States of America.

Library of Congress Cataloging-in-Publication Data

Svenonius, Elaine.
 The intellectual foundation of information organization / Elaine Svenonius.
  p. cm—(Digital libraries and electronic publishing)
 Includes bibliographical references and index.
 ISBN 0-262-19433-3 (hc.: alk. paper)
 1. Information organization. 2. Bibliography—Methodology. 3. Cataloging.
 I. Title. II. Series.
 Z693.S92 2000
 025.3—dc21   99-41301
                                                      CIP

10 9 8 7 6 5

To the memory of
my mother and father

Contents

Preface

Instant electronic access to digital information is the single most distinguishing attribute of the information age. The elaborate retrieval mechanisms that support such access are a product of technology. But technology is not enough. The effectiveness of a system for accessing information is a direct function of the intelligence put into organizing it. Just as the practical science of engineering is undergirded by theoretical physics, so too the design of systems for organizing information rests on an intellectual foundation. The topic of this book is the systematized body of knowledge that constitutes this foundation.

Much of the literature that pertains to the intellectual foundation of information organization is inaccessible to those who have not devoted considerable time to the study of the disciplines of cataloging, classification, and indexing. It uses a technical language, it mires what is of theoretical interest in a bog of detailed rules, and it is widely scattered in diverse sources such as thesaurus guidelines, codes of cataloging rules, introductions to classification schedules, monographic treatises, periodical articles, and conference proceedings. This book is an attempt to synthesize this literature and to do so in a language and at a level of generality that makes it understandable to those outside the discipline of library and information science.

A book on the intellectual foundation of information could be written in several ways. It is therefore useful to state the scope of this one, contrasting what it is not about with what it is about. First, it is not a how-to-do-it cookbook of methods used to organize information. The techne or practical skill of information organization is a function of changing technology, whereas its intellectual foundation, which encompasses theory, is relatively impervious to change. To ground the discussion of theory, however, particular devices and stratagems used by different technologies are introduced by way of example. Thus, general statements involving abstractions are frequently followed by a detail or a graspable image.

The book does not focus primarily on how users seek information but rather on the design of organizing systems. Systems for organizing information must be designed with the user in mind, but sometimes overlooked is that the objectives and principles that undergird these systems constitute a hypostatization of users' needs. The specifications relating to user satisfaction that are embodied in these objectives and principles have been developed and refined over a period of 150 years. They are not only historically determined but also empirically warranted. Moreover, they are more stringent than can be imagined by most users or, for that matter, inferred from most studies of information seeking behavior.

This book is not primarily about how the computer is used to organize information, although the topic is discussed, since recognizing the impact of technology on information is unavoidable. The digital revolution has affected how information is embodied and what is used to organize it. It has forced a general reexamination of how the carriers of information are identified and described. Using automation to achieve the objectives of systems for organizing information has opened avenues of research and development that have significantly enriched the body of knowledge that constitutes the intellectual foundation of information organization.

The book is not written for the novice who is about to begin a job as a cataloger and wants an instant understanding of its mysteries. It is not a catechism of rules, a compendium of practice, or a training manual. Instead, the book takes a scholarly approach and looks at the rules used to describe information entities — not to spell them out but to consider their intellectual source and grounding or lack thereof. It looks at principles that have been used to guide systems design, asks why decisions were made as they were, and considers problems that were encountered and overcome. Oriented thus, the book is directed toward two groups of people: those who are interested in information organization as an object of scholarly investigation and those who are involved in the design of organizing systems.

This book does not enumerate various systems for organizing information, though meritorious features of these are referenced by way of example, but strives to express what these systems have in common — to speak in terms of generalities rather than particulars. One of its central aims is to look at information organization holistically and thereby to raise discourse about it to a level general enough to unify the presently compartmentalized approaches for achieving it. Specifically, it endeavors to integrate the disparate disciplines of descriptive cataloging, subject cataloging, indexing, and classification. A difficulty in carrying out this aim, and indeed in writing the book, has been to reconcile different ways of referring to similar concepts, principles, and techniques. To deal with this difficulty — and to limit jargon generally — an effort has been made to eschew where possible discipline-specific terminology and to resist the temptation of inventing new terminology.

Finally, this book is not an idiosyncratic view on how to organize information effectively. Rather, it reflects practice and theory as developed within the discipline of library and information science. It adopts a particular conceptual framework that views the process of organizing information as the use of a special language of description, called a *bibliographic language*. This framework is rooted in a tradition that originated nearly a hundred years ago and has been used since then by theorists to introduce rigor, unification, and generality into theorizing about information organization.

The book is divided into two parts of five chapters each. The first part is an analytic discussion of the intellectual foundation of information organization. Chapter 1 introduces and defines what is meant by an *intellectual foundation* and the concepts of *information* and *document*. It establishes a conceptual framework that identifies the central purpose of systems for organizing information: bringing like things together and differentiating among them. It considers the function of principles in the context of systems design and concludes with an illustration of some of the problems encountered in the design of organizing systems.

The second chapter looks at one of the cornerstones of the intellectual foundation of information: the objectives of systems designed to retrieve information. It reviews their history from Antonio Panizzi (1850), through Charles Ammi Cutter (1876) and Seymour Lubetzky (1957), to the 1998 International Federation of Library Associations and Institutions (IFLA) *Functional Requirements for Bibliographic Records*. An additional objective is postulated and an argument made for it on the basis of literary and use warrant. The degree to which the objectives can be operationalized is discussed as well as arguments pro and con their necessity.

Chapter 3 deals with ontology, the information entities mandated by the objectives, which include documents and sets of documents formed by the attributes of work, edition, author, and subject. It discusses the function of these entities in information organization and the problems that attend their definition. A distinction is made between conceptual and operational definitions. The latter, expressed in set-theoretic terms, are needed for uniformity and precision in bibliographic description and for automating aspects of organizing information.

Chapter 4 conceptualizes the organization of information as the use of a special purpose bibliographic language. This conceptualization has several advantages, two of the most important being that it unifies the traditional subject and author-title approaches to information organization and enables the development of a bibliographic-specific linguistic theory. Bibliographic languages are classified in terms of the objects they describe — whether works (information per se), documents (carriers of information), or subjects — and are categorized in terms of their components (that is, vocabulary, semantics, and syntax). The chapter concludes with a discussion of the rules governing the use of these languages and the form and function of the bibliographic descriptions created by their application.

Another foundation cornerstone consists of the principles or directives that guide the construction of bibliographic languages. This is the topic of Chapter 5. Five principles are explicated: user convenience, representation, sufficiency and necessity, standardization, and integration. These are discussed from the point of view of their origin, usefulness, internal conflict, and viability in a multimedia environment.

The second half of the book moves from generalities to particulars. It presents an overview of three bibliographic languages used to organize information — work languages, document languages, and subject languages — and looks at these languages in terms of their vocabulary, semantics, and syntax.

Chapter 6 looks at the languages used to describe works, illustrating these using the work language developed within the *Anglo-American Cataloging* tradition, which is the most sophisticated language so far developed. A distinction is drawn in the vocabulary of this language, which names attributes, entities, and relationships among these, between metadata that are derived and metadata that are assigned: the former provide the means to find information, and the latter provide the normalization required to organize it. The role of syntax in disambiguating vocabulary and ordering bibliographic displays is discussed, as is the role of semantics in matching the natural language of users with the normalized system vocabulary. Discussed as well are the relationships expressed in bibliographic work languages — membership, inclusion, equivalence, aggregation, sequence, and commentary — with respect to their definition and function.

Chapter 7 focuses on document languages, using *AACR2R* as a fodder for examples and problems. Document languages are the languages used to describe space-time embodiments of information. The traditional metadata used to describe these embodiments relate to the physicality of documents — how they are produced and accessed. Document description is beset with problems generated by new media, including the following:

• The problem of classifying these media, which has given rise to the subproblems of format integration and multiple versions;
• The problem of deciding what physical characteristics of nonbook media should or can be described in bibliographic records;
• The problem (brought to the fore by documents in digital form) of how to organize entities that lack essential descriptive attributes, because they are unstable or in flux; and
• The political and technological problem of creating stable, standard document identifiers.

Subject languages are more advanced than work and document languages. Three chapters are devoted to them. Chapter 8 begins by distinguishing the two main types of subject languages: alphabetic-subject languages and classification languages. The Dewey Decimal Classification (DDC) is used as an example of the latter, and the Library of Congress Subject Headings (LCSH) as an example of the former. Each is the most widely used language of its type. The bulk of the chapter deals with the first steps taken in designing a subject language: the selection and classification of its vocabulary. These steps are discussed in terms of the techniques used to accomplish them, the obstacles encountered, and the degree to which they are or can be automated.

Chapter 9's topic is subject-language semantics — the structures used to normalize subject-language vocabulary, first by disambiguating them and then by establishing relationships of meaning among them. Structures for disambiguation belong to the referential semantics of a subject language and include domain specification, parenthetical qualifiers, scope notes, and hierarchical displays. Structures for establishing meaning relationships belong to the relational semantics of a subject language and include equivalence, related terms, and hierarchical links. Referential and relational structures are discussed with reference to their possible automation and to problems in their definition and use.

Chapter 10 deals with subject-language syntax. It introduces the topic through an historical introduction and then illustrates different types of syntax through a brief overview of the DDC, LCSH, and Preserved Context Indexing System (PRECIS). The second half of the chapter is devoted to problems and issues that arise in designing a subject-language syntax: term-string synonymy, citation order, regularity versus complexity, automation, precoordination versus postcoordination, and natural versus artificial syntax.

An Afterword speculates on the continuing development of bibliographic languages as reflected in trends toward formalization and automation.

Finally, I'd like to share a personal word about why this book was written. It was motivated first by the conviction that the intelligent organization of information is of paramount importance not only for the scholarly community but also for individuals, commerce, and society in general. Second, the principles, objectives, and techniques that have been developed to organize information within the field of library and information science constitute a body of knowledge with wide application, not the least of which is the organization of information in digital form. The writing of this book has been an attempt to report on these principles, objectives, and techniques at a level of generality and from a conceptual stance that will facilitate the transfer of ideology and technology across disciplinary boundaries, with the aim ultimately of informing the practice of information organization in the electronic age and advancing that part of information science that seeks to base information organization on an intellectual foundation.

Acknowledgments

This work has come about as a result of many years of association with those engaged in theoretical scholarship in the organization of information. Their influence has fanned an excitement kindled when in the Graduate Library School at the University of Chicago I learned to look at the organization of information as an object of study. I have been inspired by the interest of my students and gained insights by their questions and ideas. I feel fortunate to have been able to talk with many of the fine minds of the twentieth century who have contributed significantly to the disciplines of cataloging, classification, and indexing, both in this country and abroad, especially in India. I feel particularly fortunate for the recent conversations I have had with Seymour Lubetzky, whose principled thinking, even at age 100, is remarkable to behold.

As to the actual writing of the book, my first thanks must go to Dorothy McGarry, who willingly shouldered the burden of reading chapters as they were produced, catching me up on details, asking for clarifications, and being always and wonderfully encouraging. And then thanks go to a few of the people who reviewed the book in manuscript form for MIT Press — Barbara Tillett and Ed O'Neill. Their constructive suggestions were very welcome indeed as I was struggling to produce a better product. Thanks also to Richard Fackenthal, Helen Schmierer, and Boyd Rayward, all of whom read parts of the book and gave me reactions and points of view I found I needed. A special thanks to Bhagi Subramanyam for her bibliographic and moral support at the end of my labors. Thanks finally to the staff at MIT: copyeditors Deborah Cantor-Adams and Rosemary Winfield, who conferred elegance on my writing; Erica Schultz, who flawlessly composed the text; and acquiring editor Doug Sery, who started me on what proved to be a difficult journey and cheered me along the way.

The Intellectual Foundation of Information Organization

1

Information Organization

Introduction

A system for organizing information, if it is to be effective, must rest on an intellectual foundation. This intellectual foundation consists of several parts:

- An ideology, formulated in terms of purposes (the objectives to be achieved by a system for organizing information) and principles (the directives that guide their design);
- Formalizations of processes involved in the organization of information, such as those provided by linguistic conceptualizations and entity-attribute-relationship models;
- The knowledge gained through research, particularly that expressed in the form of high-level generalizations about the design and use of organizing systems; and
- Insofar as a discipline is defined by its research foci, the key problems that need to be solved if information is to be organized intelligently and information science is to advance.

Conceptual Framework

It is useful to begin by establishing a conceptual framework to ensure that the discussion does not become idiosyncratic and at the same time to bootstrap it to the level of theory. The conceptual framework adopted here looks at the organization of information in an historico-philosophical context. Its salient feature is that information is organized by describing it using a special-purpose language.

Historical Background

The relevant historical background is the tradition of Anglo-American descriptive and subject cataloging during the last century and a half. While some form of systematic information organization has been practiced since 2000 B.C.E.,[1] its modern history is usually regarded as beginning in the middle of the last century with Sir Anthony Panizzi's plan for organizing books in the British Library.[2] In the period following Panizzi, the groundwork was laid for the major bibliographic[3] systems in use in libraries today: the Dewey Decimal Classification (DDC), the Library of Congress Classification (LCC), the Universal Decimal Classification (UDC), the Library of Congress Subject Headings (LCSH), and the Anglo-American Cataloguing Rules (AACR). Though strong, particularly in their ideologies, these systems were jolted in the twentieth century by information explosions, the computer revolution, the proliferation of new media, and the drive toward universal bibliographic control. How they have withstood these jolts, where they have remained firm, where they have cracked, and where cracked how they have been repaired or still await repair is a dramatic — and instructive — history for those interested in organizing information intelligently.

Santayana wrote that "when experience is not retained . . . infancy is perpetual. Those who cannot remember the past are condemned to repeat it."[4] To be so condemned would not be all bad, since reinventing what has been done in different times and circumstances reinvigorates a discipline, rids it of routinized procedures and ways of thinking, and energizes it by the influx of new ideas and new terminology. Nevertheless it is instructive — especially given the recent interest and activity directed toward organizing digital information — to understand certain features of traditional bibliographic systems. Two features in particular are worth considering. One is the solutions these systems have provided to the problems that obstruct efficient access to information. While today some access problems are caused by the new technology, others — such as those that stem from the variety of information, the many faces of its users, and the anomalies that characterize the language of retrieval — have been around a long time. For instance, whether users search library shelves or the Internet, some will retrieve too much, some too little, and some will be unable to formulate adequate search requests. The thought that has gone into addressing problems like these, cumulated over a century and a half — particularly the thinking that deals with rationales for why things are done as they are — provides, independent of time and place, an informed context for systems design.

A second feature that makes traditional bibliographic systems worthy of continued interest is the vision expressed in their ideologies. A system's effectiveness in organizing information is in part a function of an ideology that states the ambitions of its creators and what they hope to achieve. The systems produced during the second half of the nineteenth century, a period regarded as a golden age of organizational activity,[5] were ambitious, full-featured systems designed to meet the needs of the most demanding users. Some would argue that they were too ambitious — that there was no need to construct elaborate Victorian edifices since jerrybuilt systems could meet the needs of most users most of the time.[6] However, good systems design begins by postulating visionary goals, if only to make users aware of the extent to which compromises are being made. The bibliographic systems of the past (in their ideologies, at least) reflect what can be achieved by intelligent information organization.

Philosophical Background
Relevant to the intellectual foundation of information organization are the points of view embraced by three philosophical movements that have permeated academic and popular thinking during the twentieth century: systems philosophy, the philosophy of science, and language philosophy.

Systems Philosophy
A philosophy of ancient origin, general systems theory was resurrected by Ludwig von Bertalanffy in the mid-twentieth century in an attempt to stop-gap what he perceived to be an increasing fragmentation of knowledge.[7] General systems theory is a philosophical expression of holistic or big-picture thinking. Its credo encompasses a belief in purpose as opposed to chance processes, a way of looking at phenomena in terms of their organization and structure, and a conviction that general laws and principles underlie all phenomena. From this philosophy derives the practice of systems analysis, which in its most general form is the analysis of an object of study, based on viewing it as a system whose various parts are integrated into a coherent whole for the purpose of achieving certain objectives.

Systems thinking was introduced into the discipline of information organization by Charles A. Cutter in 1876.[8] Dubbed the great "library systematizer,"[9] Cutter was the first to recognize the importance of stating formal objectives for a catalog. He recognized as well the need to identify the means to achieve these objectives and principles to guide the choice of means when alternatives were available. Since Cutter's time, systems thinking has assumed a variety of different expressions, tending to become more elaborate and increasingly formalized, as, for instance, in its articulation in the form of conceptual modeling. However expressed, the ultimate aim of systems analysis is to determine and validate practice. Why certain methods, techniques, rules, or procedures are adopted to the exclusion of others in the practice of organizing information requires explanation. One way to provide this is to show that a particular element of practice can be viewed as part of a system and as such contributes to fulfilling one or more of the system's objectives.[10] An improvised practice, one that is adventitious and not rationalized with respect to the big picture, is ineffective, inefficient, and, by definition, unsystematic.

Philosophy of Science

Scientific methodology has been a central focus for philosophical inquiry for nearly a century. In the first part of the twentieth century, the dominant philosophy of science was logical positivism, whose credo was expressed by the principle of verifiability. This principle states that to be meaningful a proposition must be capable of verification. A proposition to be verified must have concepts that can be operationalized, which means (in effect) interpreted as variables and defined in a way that admits of quantification.

To the extent that problems encountered in the organization of information are definitional in nature, solutions to them can be approached by introducing constructive or operational definitions. An example of such a definition relating to information organization is the dual precision-recall measure created by Cyril Cleverdon in the mid-1950s. The measure was introduced to quantify the objectives of information retrieval. Precision measures the degree to which a retrieval system delivers relevant documents; recall measures the degree to which it delivers all relevant documents.

Defining concepts operationally enables a discipline to advance, the most frequently cited illustration of which is Einstein's use of them in his analysis of simultaneity.[11] The power of operational definitions resides in their ability to provide empirical correlates for concepts in the form of variables, which, in turn allows variables to be related one to another.[12] For instance, quantifying the objectives of information retrieval in terms of the precision and recall variables makes it possible to establish propositions about the impact of various factors — such as specificity of indexing, depth of indexing, and vocabulary size — on retrieval effectiveness. Propositions that express relationships among variables are "scientific" in the sense that they represent high-level generalizations about the objects of study. This gives them an explanatory function: if verified, they assume the character of laws; if in the process of being verified, they have the status of hypotheses.

While some aspects of the philosophy of science are abstruse, its dictates are clear enough: quantify and generalize. To a greater or lesser degree all the social sciences have struggled to follow these dictates. In their striving for scientific respectability, they have pursued empirical research and undergone quantitative revolutions. Library "science" self-consciously embraced a scientific outlook in the 1930s at the Chicago Graduate Library School. This school, established for the express purpose of conducting research, had considerable influence on the field through its brand of scholarship, which encompassed theory, forced definitional clarity, and questioned assumptions.[13] Increasingly since the 1930s, understanding of the information universe and, in particular, how it is organized and navigated has been pursued through "scientific" research.

Language Philosophy

Interest in language has dominated two twentieth-century philosophies. The first was the already mentioned logical positivism, which was a linguistic form of radical empiricism. Its principle of verifiability — which states that a proposition to be meaningful must be capable of being verified — is a linguistic principle.[14] The philosophy of logical positivism was countered in the middle of the century by another language philosophy, the Wittgensteinian philosophy of linguistic analysis.[15] A major tenet of this philosophy was that the meaning of a word is its use and this use is governed by rules much like the rules that govern moves in games. As there are many different special-purpose uses of language, so there are many different language games.

The act of organizing information can be looked on as a particular kind of language use. Julius Otto Kaiser, writing in the first decade of the twentieth century, was the first to adopt this point of view.[16] Kaiser developed an index language, which he called *systematic indexing,* wherein simple terms were classed into semantic categories and compound terms were built using syntax rules defined with respect to these categories. Similar points of view have been adopted by theorists since Kaiser, mostly in the context of organizing information by subject but applicable as well to organizing by other attributes, such as author and title. The advantage to be gained by looking at the act of organizing information as the application of a special-purpose language is that linguistic constructs such as *vocabulary, semantics,* and *syntax* then can be used to generalize about, understand, and evaluate different methods of organizing information.[17] Another advantage is that these constructs enable a conceptualization that can unify the heretofore disparate methods of organizing information — cataloging, classification, and indexing.

Philosophical movements constitute the backdrop against which scholarly disciplines develop. The impact of systems philosophy on the discipline of information organization is apparent insofar as this organization is regarded as effected by a system that has purposes and whose design is guided by conceptual modeling and the postulation of principles. It is apparent as well in the discipline's increasing reliance on operational definitions, in its use of algorithms for automating aspects of organization, in frameworks it establishes for empirical research, and in generalizations that build theory.

Information and Its Embodiments

Like *meaning* and *significance,* terms with which it is allied, *information* has many senses, nuances, and overtones. This makes reaching agreement about a general definition of the term difficult. Some special-purpose definitions of the term have relatively fixed meanings. The best known of these is the one that is used in information theory, which associates the amount of information in a message with the probability of its occurrence within the ensemble of all messages of the same length derivable from a given set of symbols.[18] A definition like this, however, is too particular for use in discourse about organizing information. What is needed is one more consonant with common usage, one that implies or references a person who is informed. The definition used in this book is developed in the next chapter, but as first approximation a gloss on a general dictionary meaning will do. One definition of *information* is "something received or obtained through informing."[19] Informing is done through the mechanisms of sending a message or communication; thus, *information* is "the content of a message" or "something that is communicated."

Defining *information* as the content of a message is specific enough to exclude other definitions — for instance, the definition that equates information with "a piece of fact, a factual claim about the world presented as being true."[20] This definition, which is positivistic in nature, conceptualizes *information* narrowly. Certain types of knowledge may be restricted to facts or true beliefs, but to apply such a restriction to information in general would rule out the possibility of false information or information that is neither true nor false, such as the information in a work of art or a piece of music, which when conveyed "informs" the emotions. Factual claims about the world constitute only a small subset of information broadly construed as the content of a message or communication.

Information is sometimes defined in terms of data, such as "data endowed with relevance and purpose."[21] A datum is a given; it could be a fact or, at a more elemental level, a sense perception. Either might be endowed with signatory meaning simply by focusing attention on it, as a certain smell is indicative of bread baking. While data in the form of sense perceptions and raw facts have the potentiality to inform, it cannot be rashly assumed that all information could be reduced to these. It is not possible, at least not without wincing, to refer to *The Iliad, The Messiah,* or the paintings in the Sistine Chapel as data, however endowed. The messages they convey represent highly refined symbolic transformations of experience,[22] different in kind from data.

While message content is probably a good approximation of what information systems organize, not all message content falls under the purview of such systems. The content contained in ephemeral messages — such as the casual "Have a nice day!" — lies outside the domain of information systems. For the most part, these domains are limited to messages whose content is (1) created by humans, (2) recorded,[23] and (3) deemed worthy of being preserved. The question of which messages fall into the latter category is sometimes begged by equating "worthy of being preserved" with what libraries, information centers, archives, and museums in fact collect. The collective domain of all systems for organizing information — all message content created by humans, recorded, and deemed worthy of being preserved — has been likened to the "diary of the human race."[24] The purpose of these systems is to make this diary accessible to posterity.

The term *document* is easier to define and is used in this book to refer to an information-bearing message in recorded form.[25] This usage is warranted both by the information-science literature and by common usage.[26] *Webster's Third* gives as meanings of *document*:

• a piece of information
• a writing (as a book, report, or letter) conveying information
• a material having on it (as a coin or stone) a representation of the thoughts of men by means of some conventional mark or symbol.[27]

The first two of these meanings are particularly apt in that they explicate *document* with respect to *information*: "a piece of information" and "conveying information." The second is limited in that it instances "a writing," whereas in contemporary bibliographic contexts documents include not only messages using alphanumeric characters but also those expressed using sounds and images.

The third meaning of *document* introduces the concept of *material*. This underscores a distinction of great importance in the literature of information organization, one that is referenced repeatedly throughout this book: information is an abstract, but the documents that contain it are embodied in some medium, such as paper, canvas, stone, glass, floppy disks, or computer chips. Potentially any medium can serve as a carrier of information. While some media make information immediately accessible to the senses (for example, paper), others require an intermediate mechanism (such as a computer chip, a microfiche, or a compact disc). Organizing information to access it physically requires not only descriptions but also its material embodiments and the mechanisms needed for retrieval.

The distinction between information and its embodying documents is so important in the literature of information organization it warrants a brief history. It is claimed to have been recognized as early as 1674 by Thomas Hyde.[28] Certainly Panizzi in the middle of the nineteenth century acknowledged it implicitly in the design of his catalog and in certain passages of his writing.[29] Julia Pettee in 1936 formulated the distinction explicitly, referring to a particular message content as a *literary unit* and its embodiment in a medium as a *book*.[30] In 1955 S. R. Ranganathan introduced the distinction, presenting it as the dichotomy between expressed thought and embodied thought: the former he referred to as a *work*, the latter as a *document*.[31] In the 1960s, the significance of the distinction was brought to popular attention as a result of Seymour Lubetzky's eloquent juxtaposition of the work versus the book.[32] He regarded a work as the intellectual creation of an author. A work is what in the preceding paragraphs has been characterized as (1) information, (2) the disembodied content of a message, or (3) expressed thought. It is a kind of Platonic object. A book, by contrast, is a particular physical object that embodies or manifests the work. One work can be manifested in many physical objects, and, conversely, one physical object can manifest several works.

Because of its centrality, the distinction between information and its embodiments has invited terminological confusion in the form of synonyms and near synonyms. *Literary unit, (message) content, expressed thought,* and *text* have been used either coextensively or as operationalizations of *work. Manifestation, expression, edition, version, publication,* and *carrier* have been used somewhat ambiguously to refer either to a slightly altered form of an original work, to its physical embodiment, or to both. In this book, *work* is used in the Ranganathan and Lubetzkian sense to indicate a particular disembodied information content. Ranganathan's term *document*, rather than Lubetzky's *book*, is used to indicate a material embodiment of information — at least for the most part. Exceptions are made when citing the literature and introducing further distinctions.

Purposes, Principles, and Problems

In 1674 in the Preface to the *Catalogue for the Bodleian Library,* Sir Thomas Hyde lamented the lack of understanding shown by those who never had the opportunity to make a catalog:

"What can be more easy (those lacking understanding say), having looked at the title-pages than to write down the titles?" But these inexperienced people, who think making an index of their own few private books a pleasant task of a week or two, have no conception of the difficulties that rise or realize how carefully each book must be examined when the library numbers myriads of volumes. In the colossal labor, which exhausts both body and soul, of making into a alphabetical catalog a multitude of books gathered from every corner of the earth there are many intricate and difficult problems that torture the mind.[33]

Three centuries and many myriads of "books" later, the problems that torture the mind when attempting to organize information have increased exponentially. It has never been easy to explain why colossal labor should be needed to organize information. If not the most successful, at least the most passionate attempt to do so was made by Panizzi when before a Royal Commission he defended his plan for organizing books in the British Library (1847–1849). Many members of the Commission did not understand the plan and, not understanding it, found it too complicated. The most celebrated of the commissioners, Thomas Carlyle, went so far as to accuse Panizzi of trying to enhance his reputation by building a catalog that was "a vanity of bibliographical display."[34] And this despite his reputation as a leading intellect of the time.

Organizing information would seem to be no different from organizing anything else. The assumption that this is the case has led to attempts to interpret it as a routine application of the database modeling techniques developed to organize entities like the employees, departments, and projects of a company. But there are important differences. One that is particularly important, because it is at the root of many of the complexities unique to organizing information, is that two distinct entities need to be organized in tandem and with respect to each other: works and the documents that embody them.

Organization can take many forms. Its prototypical form is classification. Classification brings like things together. In traditional classifications, like things are brought together with respect to one or more specified attributes. Any number of attributes can be used to form classes of documents embodying information, such as same size or color, same subject, or same author. However, the most important attribute for a system whose objective is to organize information is the attribute of "embodying the same work." No other attribute can match it in collocating power because documents that share this attribute contain essentially the same information. Organizing information if it means nothing else means bringing all the same information together.

Normally bibliographic systems that organize information in documents do more than bring together *exactly* the same information; they aim also to bring together *almost* the same information. This introduces further complexity, particularly in trying to understand what is meant by "almost the same information." Intuitively the concept is simple to grasp. A work like *David Copperfield* may appear in a number of editions, such as one illustrated by Phiz, one translated into French, and another a condensed version. Because they are editions of the same work, they share essentially, but not exactly, the same content, differing only in incidentals such as illustrations, language, size, and so on. But the attempt to operationalize the intuitive concept in a code of rules — to draw a line between differences that are incidental and those that are not — runs into definitional barriers: What is a work? What is meant by *information*?[35]

Once editions containing almost the same information are brought together, their differences then need to be pinpointed. Panizzi insisted on this in his defense before the Royal Commission: "A reader may know the *work* he requires; he cannot be expected to know all the peculiarities of different *editions;* and this information he has a right to expect from the catalog."[36] He then went on to argue for a full and accurate catalog, one that contained all the information needed to differentiate the various editions of a work. The task of differentiation has its mind-torturing challenges and can create what to an outsider might seem like a display of bibliographic vanity. But imagine the hundreds of editions of the Bible that might be held by a library. Not only must salient differences be identified, but they must be communicated intelligibly and quickly. Intelligible communication in part is accomplished by arranging records for the different editions in a helpful order. The placing a given edition in its organizational context within the bibliographic universe is not unlike making a definition: first one states its genus (the work to which it belongs) and then, in a systematic way, its differentia.

The essential and defining objective of a system for organizing information, then, is to bring essentially like information together and to differentiate what is not exactly alike. Designing a system to achieve this purpose is subject to various constraints: it should be economical, it should maintain continuity with the past (given the existence of more than 40 million documents already organized), and it should take full advantage of current technologies.

In addition to constraints, certain principles inform systems design. Principles are desiderata that take the form of general specifications or directives for design decisions. They differ from objectives in that objectives state what a system is to accomplish, while principles determine the nature of the means to meet these objectives. An example of a principle used to design the rules used to create a bibliographic system states that these rules collectively should be necessary and sufficient to achieve system objectives. Others are that rules should be formulated with the user in mind, they should ensure accuracy, they should conform to international standards, and they should be general enough to encompass information in any of its embodiments.

What makes the labor of constructing a bibliographic system colossal are the problems that are encountered in the process of doing so. A major source of problems is the infinite and intriguing variety of the information universe. These kinds of problems are frequently definitional in nature: defining *work,* for example, is difficult because it amounts to defining *information.* Does *The Iliad* in the original Greek consist of the same information (represent the same work) as an English translation of it? Do two different English translations represent the same work? (The answer to these questions is usually yes.) Does translation to another medium abrogate workhood? Does a film version of *Hamlet* contain the same information content as its textual counterpart? (The answer to this kind of question is usually no.) Are two recordings of a symphony, one a CD and the other a video, the same work? (Here the answer seems to be pending.) The dictum that "the medium is the message"[37] suggests that there is significant value added (or subtracted) when an original work is adapted to another medium, so that information that is to be organized is a function of its symbolic expression. The definition of *work* has become the focus of recent attention, which is hardly surprising since it is important to come to grips with the meaning of information. This is something that needs to be grasped, since how information is defined determines what is organized and how it is organized.

Another significant source of problems in organizing information stems from the need to keep pace with political and technological progress. An example of how technological progress poses problems is the invention and proliferation of new media, which has required bibliographic systems to generalize their scope from books to any kind of media that can carry information. An example of political progress requiring adaptation is the rise of internationalism, which has required these systems to extend their reach from local to universal bibliographical control. Political problems are for the most part settled through international agreements and the establishing of standards but are addressable technically at a systems level. An example is the problem that arises from a conflict between two principles — that of universal standardization and that of user convenience. Different cultures and subcultures classify differently, use different retrieval languages, and subscribe to different naming conventions. The technical problem to be solved is how to provide for local variation without abrogating the standards that facilitate universal bibliographical control.

The most dramatic twentieth-century event to affect the organization of information is, of course, the computer revolution. It has changed the nature of the entities to be organized and the means of their organization. It has provided solutions to certain problems but spawned a host others. One of the new problems relates to the nature of digital documents. A traditional document, like a book, tends to be coincident with a discrete physical object. It has a clearly identifiable beginning and end; the information it contains — a play, novel, or dissertation — is delimited by these; it is "all of a piece."[38] By contrast, a digital document — such as a hypertext document or a connected e-mail message — can be unstable, dynamic, and without identifiable boundaries.

Documents with uncertain boundaries, which are ongoing, continually growing, or replacing parts of themselves, have identity problems. It is not possible to maintain identity through flux ("One cannot step twice into the same river").[39] A single frame is not representative of a moving picture. A snapshot cannot accurately describe information that is dynamic. This is not simply a philosophical matter, since what is difficult to identify is difficult to describe and therefore difficult to organize.

The oldest and most enduring source of problems that frustrate the work of bibliographic control is the language used in attempting to access information. In a perfectly orderly language, each thing has only one name, and one name is used to refer to each single thing. Philosophers and linguists have idealized such languages. Leibniz, for instance, imagined a language so free from obscurities that two people involved in an argument might resolve their differences simply by saying "Let us calculate."[40] Such languages are artificial: they do not exist in nature. Natural languages are rife with ambiguities and redundancies; their robustness depends on these. But at the same time they cause problems when attempting to communicate with a retrieval system. It can happen, for instance, that a work is not found because it is known by several names and the user happens on the wrong one. Or a deluge of unwanted information may be retrieved because the user has entered a multivocal search term, one naming several different works, authors, or titles. It would seem that the most colossal labor of all involved in organizing information is that of having to construct an unambiguous language of description — a language that imposes system and method on natural language and at the same time allows users to find what they want by names they know.

2

Bibliographic Objectives

The first step in designing a bibliographic system is to state its objectives. Other design features — such as the entities, attributes, and relationships recognized by the system and the rules used to construct bibliographic descriptions — are warranted if and only if they contribute to the fulfillment of one or more of the objectives.

Traditional Objectives

Panizzi, writing in the middle of the nineteenth century, indirectly referenced bibliographic objectives when he argued in favor of the need for a catalog to bring together like items and differentiate among similar ones. It is Cutter, however, who in 1876 made the first explicit statement of the objectives of a bibliographic system.[1] According to Cutter, those objectives were

1. to enable a person to find a book of which either
   the author
   the title   } is known
   the subject
2. to show what the library has
   by a given author
   on a given subject
   in a given kind of literature
3. to assist in the choice of a book
   as to its edition (bibliographically)
   as to its character (literary or topical).

Cutter formulated his objectives based on what the user needs and has in hand when coming to a catalog. The first objective, the *finding objective*, assumes a user has in hand author, title, or subject information and is looking for a known document. The second objective, the *collocating objective,* assumes a user comes with similar information but needs a set of documents, such as the set of all documents by a given author, on a given subject, or in a given genre. The third objective, the *choice objective,* assumes a user is faced with a number of similar documents and needs to make an effective choice from among them, such as from among several editions of a work.

Cutter's list of objectives is likely the most cited text in the bibliographic literature.[2] These objectives stood respected and unchallenged for seventy-five years until 1960, when they were revised by Lubetzky to bring to the fore the distinction between the work and the book (a distinction implicit in Cutter's choice objective) and to affirm the primacy of information content as a classifying attribute. In Lubetzky's revision, these objectives read as follows:

First, to facilitate the location of a particular publication, i.e., of a particular edition of a work, which is in the library.

Second, to relate and bring together the editions which a library has of a given work and the works which it has of a given author.[3]

Lubetzky's objectives, modified slightly to mention search criteria, were formally adopted at a Conference on Cataloging Principles held in Paris in 1961. That modified version reads:

The catalogue should be an efficient instrument for ascertaining
1. whether the library contains a particular book specified by
   (a) its author and title, *or*
   (b) if the author is not named in the book, its title alone, *or*
   (c) if author and title are inappropriate or insufficient for identification, a suitable substitute for the title; and
2. (a) which works by a particular author and
   (b) which editions of a particular work are in the library.[4]

Because the scope of the Paris Principles was intentionally restricted to organizing documents by author and title, its objectives statement does not include a choice objective, and it does not formulate an objective governing organization by subject. It is only a partial statement of what a bibliographic system aims to achieve.

In 1997, the bibliographic objectives were once again modified, this time to modernize their wording and rationalize current bibliographic practice.

Under the aegis of the International Federation of Library Associations and Institutions (IFLA) a study group reformulated the objectives:

1. to *find* entities that correspond to the user's stated search criteria (i.e., to locate either a single entity or a set of entities in a file or database as the result of a search using an attribute or relationship of the entity);

to *identify* an entity (i.e., to confirm that the entity described in a record corresponds to the entity sought, or to distinguish between two or more entities with similar characteristics);

to *select* an entity that is appropriate to the user's needs (i.e., to choose an entity that meets the user's requirements with respect to content, physical format, etc., or to reject an entity as being inappropriate to the user's needs);

to acquire or *obtain* access to the entity described (i.e., to acquire an entity through purchase, loan, etc. or to access an entity electronically through an online connection to a remote computer).[5]

The IFLA objectives statement differs from that of the Paris Principles in several ways. First, it restores the choice objective, substituting *select* for *assist in the choice of*. Second, it generalizes vocabulary to make the objectives pertinent to a global, nonbook, digital environment. It does this by dropping references to libraries, replacing *books* with the more generic term *entities*, and removing the restriction of search criteria to author, title, and subject. Third, it resolves an ambiguity that attaches to the traditional finding objective, which could be variously interpreted to mean (1) finding the location of a document in a database, (2) identifying a document, or (3) ascertaining whether the document is available.[6] It does this by replacing the generic finding objective by three more specific objectives.

The IFLA statement is both timely and relevant in its generalization to embrace nonbook materials and information agencies other than libraries, in its modernization of terminology, and in its resolution of ambiguity. However, another change it makes is somewhat problematic — the collapsing of the traditional finding and collocating objectives. The traditional *finding objective* specifies that what is to be found is a particular known document, while the traditional *collocating objective* specifies that what is to be found is a set of documents, defined by criteria such as author, work, and subject. The first IFLA objective integrates these into a single finding objective. While this is logical and introduces a certain elegance of expression, at the same time it diminishes the importance of the concept of *collocation*. This concept is well entrenched in bibliographic discourse. It is particularly useful for the emphasis it gives to what in the first instance is the primary act of information organization — bringing like things together. Both for its set-forming connotations and its ties to tradition it is too valuable to lose.

Also, in breaking with tradition, the first IFLA objective does not specify the sets of entities to be found but relegates this task to an accompanying entity-attribute-relationship model. This is problematic from a database design point of view. In the design of a database objectives should determine ontology and not vice versa, since for any given set of objectives, alternative models can be developed for alternative purposes. Moreover, a statement of objectives should embody a hypostatization of user needs. It should state just what it is that users need to find.

For the purposes of this book, the first IFLA objective will be amended to reintroduce the finding-collocation distinction, as follows:

1. To *locate* entities in a file or database as the result of a search using attributes or relationships of the entities:
1a. To find a singular entity — that is, a document (finding objective)
1b. To locate sets of entities representing
All documents belonging to the same work
All documents belonging to the same edition
All documents by a given author
All documents on a given subject
All documents defined by other criteria.[7]

Sufficiency of Objectives

Though objectives are postulated, they can still be evaluated insofar as they are intended to reflect user needs. They can be evaluated with respect to their sufficiency and necessity. A nontraditional position, one peculiar to this book, is that the four objectives as stated (to find, identify, select, and obtain) are in fact not sufficient. A fifth objective is needed — a *navigation objective*. Nearly half a century ago, Pierce Butler implied the existence of such an objective when he characterized *bibliography* as "the means by which civilized man navigates the bibliographic universe."[8] The metaphor is apt in its depiction of a user roaming from point A to point B and so on to reach a destination — the desired document. The argument for explicitly recognizing a navigation objective has two parts: the first is drawn from research into users' information-seeking behavior, and the second from analyses of traditional codes for bibliographic description.

Some users come to a search for information knowing exactly what they want. But other users do not quite know or are unable to articulate the object of their search,[9] and yet they are able to recognize it immediately when they find it. Such users expect guidance. Bibliographic systems have traditionally met this expectation. An example is the guidance provided by a classification used to order books that are stored on the shelves of a library. Walking through library stacks (a microcosm of the bibliographic universe) and browsing, a user may suddenly come across just the right book and credit this luck to serendipity. But such a finding would be serendipitous only if the books were shelved in random order, whereas in fact they are ordered according to a rigorous system of semantic relationships, which like an invisible hand guides the seeker to his "lucky" find.

Another reason for postulating a navigation objective is that the bibliographic codes of rules used to organize documents assume its existence. Ideally, for each rule in a code, it should be possible to point to an objective that warrants it. Actual code construction, however, is frequently less than ideal, and rules sometimes are introduced in a Topsy-like fashion, without due regard to objectives. Many of these rules are unwarranted, but some actually have a legitimate purpose, in which case the objectives themselves can be questioned. Among rules with a legitimate purpose are those that establish bibliographic relationships. Such rules can be found in codes both for author-title description and for subject description. They include rules that specify relationships between works as well as relationships between names of work attributes, such as authors and subjects. Work-work relationships include generalization relationships *(is a subclass of)*, the aggregation relationships *(is a part of)*, and various associative relationships *(is a sequel to, is an adaptation of, is an abridgment of, is described by)*. Relationships among names of work attributes include equivalence, hierarchical, and associative relationships. The aim of the rules setting up these relationships is to map the bibliographic universe — that is, to facilitate navigation.[10]

Thus, a navigation objective has both user and code warrant. Such an objective might be formulated as follows:

• To *navigate* a bibliographic database (that is, to find works related to a given work by generalization, association, or aggregation; to find attributes related by equivalence, association, and hierarchy).

Objectives of a Full-Featured Bibliographic System

The IFLA objectives — modified to provide model independence, continuity with tradition, and a navigation objective — would read as follows:

• To *locate* entities in a file or database as the result of a search using attributes or relationships of the entities:

1a. To find a singular entity — that is, a document (finding objective)

1b. To locate sets of entities representing

All documents belonging to the same work

All documents belonging to the same edition

All documents by a given author

All documents on a given subject

All documents defined by "other" criteria;[11]

• To *identify* an entity (that is, to confirm that the entity described in a record corresponds to the entity sought or to distinguish between two or more entities with similar characteristics);

• To *select* an entity that is appropriate to the user's needs (that is, to choose an entity that meets the user's requirements with respect to content, physical format, and so on or to reject an entity as being inappropriate to the user's needs);

• To acquire or *obtain* access to the entity described (that is, to acquire an entity through purchase, loan, and so on or to access an entity electronically through an online connection to a remote computer);

• To *navigate* a bibliographic database (that is, to find works related to a given work by generalization, association, and aggregation; to find attributes related by equivalence, association, and hierarchy).

These objectives will be referred to, respectively, as the *finding, collocating, choice, acquisition,* and *navigation objectives.* Collectively they constitute the objectives of a full-featured bibliographic system. Though care has been taken in their formulation, they are still not without problems, as the following sections show.

Operationalization of Objectives

A subsidiary purpose of the bibliographic objectives is to specify the entities, attributes, and relationships required of a bibliographic system and to serve as instruments against which to vet system features. To achieve this purpose, they need to be operational — that is, they should be formulated in such a way that their achievement (or nonachievement) can be ascertained. The finding objective meets this requirement. Whether it is attained can be measured by ascertaining through a retrieval experiment whether the attributes used to describe the documents are sufficient to differentiate them.[12] Also measurable is attainment of the acquisition objective, which requires that data about the location and availability of a document be given. Attaining the other three objectives is more problematic, either because of the nature of their measurement or because, being open-ended, measurement cannot be completed.

The Collocating Objective

The collocating objective deserves special mention because of the composite nature of its measurement. This objective states that a bibliographic system should be capable of forming certain sets of bibliographic records. An attempt to measure it was initiated in the late 1950s in the landmark Cranfield experiment mentioned earlier. Cyril Cleverdon and his colleagues at Cranfield conducted this experiment to test the retrieval effectiveness of different methods for organizing documents. To measure effectiveness they developed a means to assess the set–forming power of a retrieval system.[13] They began with a *recall measure,* defined as the number of relevant records retrieved by the system divided by the total number of relevant records in the database. It was soon readily apparent that recall by itself was not a sufficient measure of collocating power, since even if no organizing intelligence at all were applied to structuring a database, 100 percent recall could be realized simply by sequentially examining every record in the database. Implied, but not explicitly stated in the formulation of the collocating objective, is that *only* relevant records should be brought together — that is, relevant records should not be intermixed with irrelevant ones. Collocation without discrimination is meaningless. Thus, the Cranfield team developed another measure, one that would assess the degree to which a bibliographic system retrieves only relevant records. Called *precision,* it is defined as the percentage of retrieved records that are relevant. An ideal bibliographic system — one with full collocating and discriminating power — would retrieve all and only relevant documents. It would operate at 100 percent recall and 100 percent precision.

The precision and recall measures are not without problems. One problem is the difficulty in defining *relevance,* which is a key variable in their definition. Another is that the measure is a composite one and that in practice there is often a trade-off between collocation and discrimination. Each of these problems has generated a substantial body of thought and literature. Nevertheless, the measures have proved useful not only in evaluating how well a system achieves the collocation objective but also in testing system features (such as depth and breadth of indexing) in such a way as to generate lawlike statements about the impact of these on system effectiveness.

Originally applied to the evaluation of subject collocation, the precision and recall measures are useful as well to evaluate the set-forming power of other attributes, such as edition, author, and title. Until the early 1990s, there was little interest in applying them to this purpose, possibly because card catalogs were able to achieve reasonably good author and title collocation through the use of sophisticated filing rules. Online catalogs with their computer filing are a different matter, however. While they may retrieve records for all editions of a work and all works of an author, also retrieved is a horde of irrelevant records. Allyson Carlyle, who has studied how retrieval performance has deteriorated in the move from card to online catalogs, found that precision in the online display of records is very poor indeed. For popular works, such as More's *Utopia,* Joyce's *Ulysses,* and Shakespeare's *Sonnets,* it is less than 15 percent.[14]

Open-Ended Objectives

It is difficult to operationalize objectives that are open-ended. Take, for instance, the choice objective. As stated by Cutter, this objective specifies three ways in which a user should be assisted in choosing a book: by indicating its edition, its character, and its literary or topical nature. As stated in the IFLA document, the objective enjoins assistance in terms of "content, physical format, etc." The *etc.* is the rub. It could encompass hundreds of attributes of bibliographic entities and countless bibliographic relationships.

Any of these attributes or relationships might conceivably be of some use to some user at some time. (Cutter cites as a warning example someone who might be interested in books bound in human skin.)[15] Because the choice objective is capable of spawning description ad infinitum, it is economically untenable. Attempts to cope with the unwanted economic consequences of open-ended objectives surface periodically as a rethinking of a "core" set of essential metadata to be used in description.[16] Cutter, living in simpler times, was able to say that the circumstances of each local library should determine what belongs in description. This is not an option in today's global bibliographic community, where adherence to standards is prerequisite to cooperation.

Open-endedness prevents operationalization of the collocation and navigation objectives as well as the choice objective. The problems it presents are more apparent today than they were in the card-catalog era. Access to records in a card catalog was limited to the keys used for filing — author, title, and subject. Moreover, searching a card catalog must be done linearly. Access to records in an online catalog is limited only by what is not described. Any metadata element (such as publisher or illustrator) used in a bibliographic description can serve as an access point, and searching can incorporate a variety of sophisticated nonlinear moves. But the increased searching power afforded by online catalogs has a downside: it makes the collocation and navigation objectives difficult to formulate and difficult to measure. The IFLA version of the collocating objective calls for creating sets that correspond to whatever search criteria may be specified. Similarly, the navigation objective calls for creating all useful associative trails among documents. Where limits are not set, objectives cannot be measured, and if they cannot be measured, they are unrealistic. It is at the level of formulating objectives that coping with open-endedness and formulating minimal sets of data elements needs to be addressed.

Necessity of Objectives

The five objectives set out in this chapter delimit the scope of a full-featured bibliographic system. In addition to requiring that the system deal with the collocation and differentiation of documents, they require as well that it assist the user in selecting, acquiring, and navigating among documents.

Not infrequently the question of whether all these objectives are necessary is raised. Some regard the five objectives as postulates — self-evident and beyond the need of any empirical justification, while others just as categorically challenge their necessity. Neither stance is defensible across the board. But before addressing this issue directly, it is instructive, by way of providing background, to consider the degree to which the five objectives are actually implemented in practice.

Implementation of Objectives in Present Systems

The degree to which actual bibliographic systems adhere, or were designed to adhere, to the bibliographic objectives varies widely. The systems with which this book is primarily concerned are library catalogs, but even these as a class vary widely in their ability to function as full-featured bibliographic systems. All library catalogs subscribe to the traditional objectives in principle. In practice, however, many have become deranged over time, in large part due to retrospective conversion and the use of shared bibliographic records. As a result, a significant amount of organization has been lost, both in the online display of bibliographic records and in the arrangement of documents on shelves.[17] Proposals to "fix" such systems — to bring them once again in line with their original objectives — are generally dismissed as unaffordable.

Indexes are another type of bibliographic system. For the most part they are less ambitious in their objectives than library catalogs. Indexes and catalogs have existed side by side for over a century, and though it is sometimes asked why indexes cannot be more like catalogs, or vice-versa, there has been little rapprochement on either side. It's a general bibliographic truth that not all documents should be accorded the same degree of organization. Degree of bibliographic organization and degree of bibliographical control are different names for the same variable — a variable that correlates positively with cost and the perceived significance of the information to be organized. Articles in periodicals are generally perceived as requiring a lesser degree of control than books in libraries because articles consist of component parts of larger documents (they do not have an independent existence) and often their use is primarily for current awareness (they were designed for a less permanent existence than books). Thus the information they contain does not qualify them for admittance into the enduring diary of humankind, and they do not merit the bibliographic treatment reserved for documents deemed of lasting and scholarly interest, traditionally booklike objects.[18]

Indexing systems that are publicly funded are likely to confer more bibliographical control than those developed with private funds. Some systems, intentionally designed to be economical, postulate no more than a limited finding objective. No collocation is provided beyond what can be achieved by simple automatic operations applied to formal marks or character strings appearing on documents. Such systems cannot bring together a document represented as being by Mark Twain and another as being by Samuel Clemens. Bibliographic systems that rely for collocation on the automatic manipulation of character strings on documents, without attempting to interpret their meaning or to show relationships among them, are minimally featured systems. Keyword systems are of this type. While they are often useful for accessing information, they lack the retrieval power of systems in which bibliographic data are intelligently interpreted and organized through set formation and differentiation.

Most indexing systems occupy some middle ground between being minimally and fully featured. Few attempt to bring together all the editions of a work, but this is of little consequence, since the kind of documents organized by indexes tend not to be multiply manifested. Most seek to represent authors' names, as well as names of corporate bodies and places, in a uniform manner. As to subject collocation, while some rely solely on keywords, others, such as the systems created by the National Aeronautics and Space Administration (NASA) and by the National Library of Medicine and Chemical Abstracts, are very sophisticated in their set-forming capabilities — indeed, significantly more advanced than library catalogs.

In contrast to traditional indexes and catalogs are the new bibliographic systems that are being created to deal with documents on the Internet. Internet documents clearly vary in the degree of control they deserve. Many are of intellectual and lasting significance and warrant being archived for posterity, with the full bibliographic treatment this implies. Others are of an ephemeral nature, and for them the keyword access provided by low-end search engines is all that is needed. In between is a large class of documents whose bibliographical control is to be decided. This is presently the locus for innovation and experimentation.

One of the more popular systems created to deal with introducing order into the Internet is the Dublin Core. Developed at the Online Computer Library Center (OCLC) and promoted in a series of workshops, the Dublin Core provides a form of bibliographic control midway between cataloging and indexing. It differs from cataloging primarily in using many fewer metadata — thirteen as compared to several hundred. It differs also in the agents who provide bibliographic descriptions, these being not professional catalogers but frequently document authors and casual indexers. Finally, it differs in using a laxer form of vocabulary control, insofar as the use of any given metadata element, such as subject, may or may not promote collocation and differentiation depending on whether the indexer chooses to use values from a controlled vocabulary. Thus, the degree to which the Dublin Core when applied achieves the bibliographic objectives is as yet unpredictable.[19]

The rise of the Internet is affecting the actual work of organizing information by shifting it from a relatively few professional indexers and catalogers to the populace at large. In other words, this work is becoming deprofessionalized. Anyone and everyone can set up a website and organize information. The organization effected by nonprofessionals is often free and (it cannot be denied) effective. To the extent that the bibliographic universe can be organized by keyword access and beyond that by the voluntary efforts of individuals who mount information on the Web, it is self-organizing. While not consciously teleological, a self-organizing bibliographical universe nevertheless succeeds in meeting the bibliographic objectives in part, occasionally, and somewhat randomly. And for many documents and many users this is all that is needed.

An important question today is whether the bibliographic universe can be organized both intelligently (that is, to meet the traditional bibliographic objectives) and automatically. The question is important because of the ever-present danger that objectives will be sacrificed because of their cost. Can automation come to the rescue? Succeeding chapters address this question. Presently semantic barriers frustrate attempts to extend automation beyond keyword capabilities to incorporate the intellectual techniques required for collocation and differentiation. Yet the future may see the eventual creation of linguistic structures that can be used to break through these barriers, at least in part.

Implementation of Objectives in Future Systems

The question raised at the beginning of this section was whether full-featured bibliographic systems, ones that attempt to fulfill the traditional five objectives, were necessary. In an ideal world no one would question the desirability of such systems, but in the real world of economic exigency other considerations apply. In the following paragraphs, some of the traditional arguments relating to the necessity of the bibliographic objectives are presented — first those that question the necessity and then those that support it.

Of the several arguments put forward for the use of a less than full-featured system, the most frequent and the most persuasive is the cost argument. Particularly costly are the system features needed to fulfill the collocating objective. To supply these means going beyond the simple, clerical task of transcribing attributes of a document to address the not-so-simple intellectual task of ascertaining whether the document is known by more than one title or if its author has written under different names. Any task that requires an organizing intelligence to engage in research is costly. Also, as noted earlier, fulfilling the open-ended objectives is costly, requiring seemingly bottomless pockets.

Another argument favoring a less than full-featured system is user-based. A number of experimental studies have shown that often users neither need, nor are capable of exploiting, the power of a highly organized database.[20] One of the most frequently cited is a second experiment that was conducted at Cranfield, which found that an index language designed to provide only partial subject collocation satisfied users quite as well (measured in terms of precision and recall) as one that provided full collocation.[21] Similar experiments have been performed by different researchers in different environments, some with comparable and others with conflicting results.[22] Another type of experiment aiming to show that users do not require full-featured systems was performed by Alan Seal at Bath.[23] Seal attempted to assess the value of various data elements (not just subjects) used in traditional bibliographic descriptions. To this end he set up two parallel catalogs — a traditional one consisting of records with full descriptions ("full entries") and an experimental catalog consisting of short entries.[24] Observing the use of these catalogs over a two-month period, he found a failure rate for the short-entry catalog of only 8 percent, where *failure* was defined as the inability to locate a record in the short-entry catalog that could be located in the full-entry catalog. Both the Cranfield and Bath experiments used limited samples, and so their results are limitedly valid. Nevertheless, in some situations users need not be aware of the organizing power of a full-featured system.

A third argument supporting the use of less than full-featured bibliographic systems contends that such systems are not needed for every purpose. Hans Peter Luhn, the modern "inventor" of keyword searching, defended this easy and inexpensive form of accessing bibliographic information on the grounds that it served the purpose for which it was created — that is, current awareness.[25] He made it clear that keyword searching could never supplant the kind of scholarly, retrospective searching that calls into play the panoply of features mandated by the traditional bibliographic objectives. The point is well made and has been made by others as well: bibliographic systems are many and take varied forms; no single one need aspire to meet all the needs of all users.[26]

On the other side are the arguments in support of full-featured systems. These all reference the user, the bottom line being that users are shortchanged by systems that do not adhere to the traditional bibliographic objectives. One argument is that just because some users some of the time do not need the bibliographic power conferred by the objectives does not mean that other users at other times do not require such power for their research. Among the latter are scholarly users. Particularly important to these users is the collocating objective, as it mandates comprehensive retrieval. A historian needs to retrieve all documents relating to the event being studied. A mathematician needs confirmation that he is ahead of his colleagues in solving a particular problem. An inventor needs to be sure of his rights to a patent. From Panizzi's time to the present day, examples have been cited of how indispensable information could never have been found were it not for the organizing power of a full-featured bibliographic system.[27] Though such evidence is anecdotal, it is logically sufficient to refute any broad generalization inferred from the needs of indiscriminate or casual users.

Going beyond anecdote, survey research that looks at users' searching behavior also supports the need for full-featured systems. It has been shown that users have difficulty in finding appropriate search terms, in expanding a search when too little is retrieved, and in limiting a search when too much is retrieved.[28] A system for organizing information needs to address these difficulties. It must assist the user in finding correct search terms and in reaching a desired retrieval goal, even when the user is not sure exactly what this might be. It must bring to the user's attention all manifestations of a given work with sufficient precision to enable him to select the best one for his purposes. It must show him all the works of an author and all works on a given subject without these being intermixed with masses of irrelevant documents.

Empirically warranted by studies of users' needs, the five objectives can be looked on as a statement of what users have a right to expect from systems for organizing information. It is in this sense that the objectives constitute a hypostatization of users' needs. Pettee describes how these objectives have changed and been refined over time and how library catalogs have developed in response to them. [29] The first catalogs were developed for monasteries and served a simple inventory function. They were no more than registers that listed books, along with other valuable property, with no regard to arrangement. As the need arose for locating particular information, a systematic order was introduced into the lists by arranging entries by author. Catalogs, thus, began to adopt a finding objective. Then as scholarly needs for comprehensive and retrospective retrieval became sufficiently demanding — Pettee marks the date with the 1674 Bodleian catalog — catalogs adopted a collocating objective and, in so doing, assumed the character of a bibliographic tool. To Pettee's account can be added a further evolutionary step — that is, the adoption by catalogs of a navigation objective in response to the need for bibliographic relationships to guide the seeking of information. The bibliographic objectives thus can be seen as historically determined: they have emerged as the bibliographic universe has expanded and has triggered ever-increasing difficulties in the search for information and as users' needs have become more demanding.

A final argument in defense of full-featured bibliographic systems is that they are required if knowledge is to advance. Progress depends on cumulative scholarship, which in turn depends on scholars' ability to access all that has been created by the human intellect. Ensuring such access is the goal of ongoing efforts to achieve universal bibliographic control. The concept of universal bibliographical control originated in the second half of the nineteenth century. In 1853 Charles C. Jewett, librarian at the Smithsonian Institution, envisioned a universal catalog, his idea of the best means for carrying out the Smithsonian's mandate to promote "the increase and diffusion of knowledge among men."[30] Toward the end of the century universalism was the intention behind creating the general classifications, which to this day are used to organize the world of knowledge: the Dewey Decimal Classification, the Library of Congress Classification, and, most notably, the Universal Decimal Classification.[31] During the latter half of the twentieth century, the concept of universal bibliographical control was realized politically, in large part due to IFLA's endeavors to develop and gain worldwide acceptance for standards of bibliographic description.[32] Adherence to these standards by the national and research libraries that participate in the IFLA Universal Bibliographical Control program is mandatory, and, since these standards entail the traditional bibliographic objectives, it follows that adherence to them also is mandatory.

Given the need for (some) full-featured bibliographic systems, a question of some urgency is how to afford them. Attempts to cope with expenses are being met on two fronts, both of which have been mentioned. One is the research front that aims to develop automatic means to replace the intellect- and labor-intensive tasks involved in designing and maintaining full-featured systems. The other is the political front that aims through establishing standards to promote cooperative efforts and distribute costs. Remarkable advances have been made on both fronts. In fact, the history of bibliographic organization in the second half of the twentieth century could be charted in terms of landmark advances in automation and international cooperation. As intelligent information organization is a never-ceasing quest, it seems likely that its future history could likewise be charted.

3

Bibliographic Entities

Introduction: Ontology

Objects of Description

Ontology is the science or study of being. More particularly, it is "a theory regarding the entities, especially abstract entities to be admitted into a language of description."[1] Willard Quine characterizes the entities encompassed by a scientific theory as consisting of the values of its variables.[2] A bibliographic theory can be similarly characterized, its variables being the entities that populate the bibliographic universe. Examples of such entities are works, editions, authors, and subjects. These are the primary objects, abstract and concrete, admitted into a language of bibliographic description and, as such, the fundamental constructs of bibliographic theory.

In simpler times when cataloging was a local concern, the object of a bibliographic description was whatever came across a cataloger's desk. There was no need for formal definition, much less a theory regarding the abstract entities admitted into a language of description. Except for an occasional footnote in a descriptive code and observations on the nature of the work, bibliographic ontology was a nonissue. Today it has become an issue, in part as a consequence of the emergence of global cataloging, which has clogged the databases of the bibliographic utilities with multiple records for the same entity. Attempts to clean up these databases have given rise to the question of duplicates — when do two descriptions describe the same entity? — which, in turn, is rooted in the more general question: under what conditions is a new bibliographic description to be made? Thus is brought to the fore the ontological question: what are the objects of bibliographic description?

One approach to the ontological question is to build a model that delineates entities, attributes, and relationships. [3] As a means to explicate theory, model building reflects a trend wherein a database is conceptualized through a process of abstract formalization. [4] The conceptualization is subject to certain constraints, chief among which is the purpose to be served by the database to be modeled. In the case of a bibliographic database this purpose is codified in the objectives adopted by the system.

While objectives determine ontology, once an ontology is specified, alternative models can be developed. For instance, one model might characterize a given variable, such as author or subject, as an entity; another might characterize it as an attribute; and still another, as both. The choice of one among several alternative models again depends on the use to which it is put. One model might be optimal for drawing up specifications for a retrieval system, another for designing a descriptive code, and yet another for theory development. In this book, an attempt is made to keep the discussion independent of any particular model. However, at times (for instance, in the discussions of automation), reference is made to a set-theoretic model — a model that regards the bibliographic universe as consisting of documents, sets of these (formed by attributes such as work, edition, author, and subject), and relationships among them.

Conceptual and Operational Definitions

Bibliographic entities may be defined conceptually or operationally. A *conceptual definition* is one that is intentional or connotative; it characterizes what is to be defined in terms of its properties, such as intelligence is the "capacity to know or apprehend." [5] An *operational definition,* on the other hand, is constructive. It specifies rather than characterizes. What it specifies is a set of operations or steps to be followed to identify what is being defined. A chocolate cake, for instance, is identified, or operationally defined, by its recipe. Intelligence is operationally defined by a test used to measure intelligence quotients.

Operational definitions can be looked on as empirical correlates of conceptual definitions — for example, an IQ test is an empirical correlate of the "capacity to know or apprehend." These definitions may or may not be valid, according to how well they reflect or how badly they distort the concepts they define. Invalid operational definitions are the cause of much of the distrust of measurement and quantification in the social sciences. A particularly egregious definition — one actually used in research — is that of *mother-love,* defined in terms of the number of kisses a mother bestows on her child in a given time period.[6] A controversial example is the definition of *intelligence* using the standard IQ test, which is criticized for being invalid because it incorporates cultural bias.

Just because some operational definitions are invalid does not mean they all are. In fact, it can be argued that operational definitions are needed in a discipline if the discipline is to advance. Defining the fundamental concepts *usefulness of O. D.* of a discipline operationally enables generalizations to be made about relationships among them. A. S. Eddington illustrates this point in a discussion of the kind of knowledge handled by exact science.[7] He asks the reader to visualize an elephant sliding down a grassy hillside and to consider its mass. What is this mass? It could be regarded as a property of the elephant ("a condition which we vaguely describe as 'ponderosity'"), or it could be regarded as a pointer reading on a weighing scale (such as two tons). While it may be intuitively satisfactory to regard mass as a property, Eddington observes that "we shall not get much further that way; the nature of the external world is inscrutable, and we shall only plunge into a quagmire of indescribables." It is more productive to regard mass as a pointer reading (that is, as a value of a variable), for not only does this give a method for testing the proposition "the elephant weighs two tons," but it enables the two tons of the elephant to be related mathematically to other pointer readings, (that is, to values of other variables, such as velocity, coefficient of friction, and so on).

One approach to operationalizing bibliographic constructs is to define them in set-theoretic terms. Take the entity *work,* for example. Conceptually, a work is an abstract, Platonic concept. It consists of a certain amount of delimited information, some piece of intellectual or artistic content. Operationally, a work is definable in terms of the procedures to be followed to construct the set of all documents that have in common that they contain essentially the same information. The constructive definition requires specifying how members of the work can be identified — such as by having the same author and title or by being a transformation of a given ur-document that preserves identity, such as revision, update, abridgement, enlargement, or translation.

There should be no confusion in moving between conceptual and operational definitions when talking about bibliographic entities. The literature of the field warrants this ease of movement because different views of these entities are useful for different purposes. However, the relationship between the two different views frequently is subject to misunderstanding, and therefore consideration needs to be given to whether a given operational definition constitutes a valid empirical expression of its correlative conceptual definition. Much of the recent discussion about the nature of the work has addressed this consideration.

At this point a reader might wonder why a discussion of the intellectual foundations of information organization should be complicated by introducing operational definitions and set-theoretic notions. There are two reasons. First, as observed above, it is by defining fundamental constructs operationally that a discipline advances theoretically. An operational definition transforms a concept into a variable that can be used in an hypothesis; if substantiated, the hypothesis results in a generalization or a theoretical statement. The second reason for introducing operational definitions of the fundamental bibliographic entities is more practical. Using operational definitions to define bibliographic entities furthers the uniformity of perception required by cooperative cataloging and document exchange. But more than this, they provide the uniformity of perception needed to automate the operations involved in organizing information.

Entity Types

Documents

The smallest or basic entities in the bibliographic universe are *documents*. Documents, which have been defined as information-bearing messages in recorded form,[8] are individuals or singular entities. A document may assume a variety of material embodiments: a copy of a book, a video, a sound recording, text or images on the Internet, or a one-of-a-kind work such as a manuscript or a painting. Individual documents are sometimes referred to as *items* or *copies*. Use of the latter term implies the entity is one of a set of similar entities.

An individual document is a real-world object with substantive existence. However, it does not necessarily have an independent existence.[9] It can be an article in a periodical, an essay in a book, a band on a CD, or a map in an atlas — that is, it can form an integral part of a larger document.

Individual documents can be collected into *sets,* which themselves are bibliographic entities. Sets represent equivalence clusterings of documents. The individual members of a given set are equivalent with respect to the attributes they have in common. Potentially any attribute or collection of attributes can be used as a specification for set formation. Sets of potential interest to users can vary unlimitedly. Five, however, are of special interest in that they are explicitly mandated by the collocating objective:

- The set of all documents sharing essentially the same information (work),
- The set of all documents sharing the same information (edition),
- The set of all documents descended from a common origin (superwork), ??
- The set of all documents by a given author,
- The set of all documents on a given subject.

Works

Critical as it is in organizing information, the concept of *work* has never been satisfactorily defined.[10] Lubetzky dichotomized the work and the book to distinguish between the intellectual and physical aspects of a bibliographic entity, between a communication and its packaging, and between a message and the medium of its expression. He wrote that "the book . . . comes into being as a dichotomous product — as a material object or medium used to convey the *intellectual* work of an author." He lamented that the material *book* and the intellectual *work* were often confused, a serious confusion in that it implied that the objectives of the catalog were not understood.[11]

The concept of a work as an intellectual or artistic creation — a Platonic object consisting of disembodied information content — is intuitively satisfactory. However, it is less satisfactory in actual practice, where the problem to be faced[12] is how to determine what work a given document represents. In this practical context the operational definition of work becomes useful, since it allows the problem to be reformulated in terms of specifying set membership: when are two documents sufficiently alike to belong to the same work set? Once this question is answered, information organization, which is an abstraction, can be translated into a series of performable operations.

Operationally, then, a work is a set or family of documents in which each document embodies essentially the same information or shares essentially the same intellectual or artistic content.[13] The forming of work sets constitutes the prototypical act of information organization. It is the act that collects in one place all documents that contain the same information, that systematically integrates each new document into a database, and that transforms a database from a simple finding list to a sophisticated bibliographic tool.

In structuring a database, work sets are used to perform two essential functions: to organize displays and to provide nodes for linking related bibliographic entities. These functions are accomplished by assigning to each document the identifier of the work it represents. The work ID is then used as a filing key. Identifying a document as representative of a particular work is a way of ensuring that documents containing the same information collocate in display. A work ID also serves as a reference node, linking the work manifested in a document to related works.[14]

Defining a work operationally amounts to specifying what two documents must have in common to be included in the same work set. Specification is not easy. Whether two documents represent the same work cannot always be inferred from formal marks on the documents themselves. As observed earlier, two documents may manifest the same work but not appear to do so because the author's name appears on them in different guises (such as Samuel Clemens and Mark Twain) or because they bear different titles (such as Emerson's *American Scholar,* which is also known as *An Oration Delivered before the Phi Beta Kappa Society, at Cambridge, August 31, 1837*).

Various criteria have been suggested for determining work membership. Akòs Domanovsky suggests a criterion that combines the notions of interchangeability and descent from a common origin.[15] Two documents represent the same work if they are either an original text or descended from it and if they are likely to be considered interchangeable by a reasonable number of readers.[16] However, Domanovsky himself rejected this criterion as being vague and offered another: two documents represent the same work if they are linked by relationships that preserve identity.

For book and booklike documents, the relationships of revision, updating, enlargement, and translation are generally assumed to preserve identity.[17] But identity is a philosophical notion that can be confusing. Wilson questions whether the operation of translation results in a text that is equivalent to the original with respect to workhood.[18] (Can a translation of a work that is so dumbed down as to be putative be regarded as the same work?) The concept of identity is further strained when translation is made to another medium. Does a movie version of *Hamlet* share essentially the same information content as the original text of the play? The answer (generally) is no. For nonbook documents there is considerable difference of opinion regarding the transforming relationships that preserve identity — a fact that throws serious doubt on the appropriateness of the concept of work for nonbook materials. Are two aerial photographs of the same cloud formation enough like to be considered the same work? Does a sketch for a painting stand in a work relationship with the painting itself?[19] Do a sound recording and a video of a musical performance constitute the same work? The criterion of maintaining identity is vague, which means there will always be instances that are undecidable. In practice, such instances have to be resolved, with discretion, interpretation and a certain amount of arbitrariness.

For book materials (at least), a work W_i can be defined as the set of all documents that are copies of (equivalent to) a particular document a_{w_i} (an individual document chosen as emblematic of the work, normally its first instance) or related to this individual by revision, update, abridgment, enlargement, or translation. In set notation this would appear as

$W_i = \text{def } \{x: x$ is a copy of a_{w_i} or x is a revision, update, abridgment, enlargement, or translation of $a_{w_i}\}$

While this definition is formal, it is not wholly operational because it is not sufficiently constructive to identify unequivocally all documents belonging to a work set. To make such an identification, it would have to go further and specify what constitutes a revision, update, and so on, possibly in terms of character strings appearing on the documents in question. A start toward such a definition might make the simplifying assumption that all documents bearing the same author and title information represent the same work and then go on to stipulate how such information might be recognized. An approach like this would succeed for limited classes of materials — for instance, for many English language monographs. From these, author or title data can be extracted using clues, such as location on a page and type size, and then a normalizing dictionary can be applied to resolve problems of synonymy and homonymy.[20]

Superworks

Domanovsky's criterion of descent from a common origin may be used alone without the additional stipulation that identity be preserved to form an entity sometimes referred to as a *superwork*.[21] A superwork may contain any number of works as subsets, the members of which while not sharing essentially the same information content are nevertheless similar by virtue of emanating from the same ur-work. Organizing a *Hamlet* superwork would have the effect of collocating the original text, motion pictures, sound recordings of readings, analyses of the play, commentaries, playbills, derivative works like *Rosencrantz and Guildenstern Are Dead,* and so on. Though members of the same superwork, they are nevertheless not members of the same work. The concept of superwork is interesting in itself as an object of literary study[22] and in retrieval as an effective means for furthering the navigation objective.

In set-theoretic notation, superwork may be defined as

$$SW_i = \text{def } \{x: x \text{ is derived from } a_{w_i}\}$$

Editions

An *edition* is a particular manifestation of a work. The various editions of a work share essentially the same information content but differ with respect to particulars, such as size of type, illustrations, preface, footnotes, language, new chapters, and updated information. The identifying of editions serves the needs of two kinds of user: the user who comes to a search with citation in hand looking for a specific edition (such as the latest edition) of a work and the user who may know the work he wants but not the edition best suited to his purposes. Recognizing that users need edition information, Panizzi stipulated that a catalog should be full and complete; that is, it should contain "*all* that information respecting the real contents, state, and consequent usefulness of the book which may enable a reader to choose, from among many editions, or many copies, that which may best satisfy his wants, whether in a literary or scientific, or in a bibliographical point of view."[23]

In addition to serving readers, editions serve internal library functions, particularly the functions of acquisition and cataloging. Editions — or, more precisely, documents that are edition exemplars — are the objects libraries acquire and count among their inventory. Moreover, when received by libraries, editions are the objects that trigger the making of bibliographic records. As the referents of bibliographic records, they constitute the *primary* objects of bibliographic description.[24]

Like work, the concept of edition has fuzzy boundaries. The problem (again) is to identify differences and assess their degree of significance — to distinguish between sharing essentially the same content (workhood) and sharing the same content (editionhood). How this problem is solved has practical consequences. In their daily work, catalogers are often called on to decide whether two documents represent the same or different editions of a work. Since it is not (yet) economically feasible on a routine basis to compare two documents, character by character, to determine if in fact they share the same content, a basis must be designated from which the determination can be inferred.

Traditional Anglo-American cataloging rules provide two complementary bases for defining *edition*. Documents represent the same edition if they are

• "Produced from essentially the same master copy . . . and issued by the same entity";[25] or
• If they identify themselves prominently (such as on their title pages) as representing the same edition.[26]

The first definition guarantees content similarity by requiring documents to be "produced from essentially the same master copy." But since it is not always possible to tell whether documents are in fact copies, the second definition is at hand to help: they are copies if they identify themselves as such. The second definition relies on self-representation and assumes the existence of outward or formal marks on documents as reliable indices of content. For the most part, the assumption is warranted, at least for modern books published in Western cultures. For other classes of documents, however, it presumes too much. For instance, it is not always possible to tell if two versions of a film are the same based on the information given in their beginning and ending frames.[27] Particularly problematic are electronic resources. To indicate modifications these may use terms like *version*, *release, level, revision,* and *update* that are not standardized and therefore not reliable as edition indicators. Two recent bibliographic guidelines address the edition problem as it relates to electronic resources: the *International Standard Bibliographic Description for Electronic Resources (ISBD(ER))* and the *Guidelines for Electronic Text Encoding and Interchange.*[28] The former allows that a candidate document for description may represent a new edition of a work "whether *or not* (my underlining) the item bears any formal statement to this effect."[29] The latter even more boldly suggests that in the case of doubt the "simplest rule is: if you think that your file is a new edition, then call it such." Not requiring an edition to identify itself as such is a departure from traditional principles. While there may be no alternative, this opens the door to subjective judgments, which, in turn, can populate the bibliographic universe with ghosts and subvert standardization efforts.

A constructive approach to identifying editions need not rely on formal marks alone. A document may not advertise itself as being a particular edition of a work but may indicate this by other signs. In the 1940s, a study was conducted at the Library of Congress confirming the hypothesis that two different editions of the same work could be distinguished by differences in paging.[30] While the study sample was restricted to books, a similar approach has recently been successfully applied to a sample of films, wherein it was shown that two versions of a film are likely to contain essentially the same content (measured by continuity) if they are of the same length.[31]

The dual bases for the definition of *edition* require further comment. A definition of *edition* that combines criteria of *content* (produced from the same master copy) and *publication* (issued by the same entity) can cause a quandary. It can happen that two documents produced from the same master copy may be identical in content but differ with respect to publication conditions. Normally, libraries create separate records — separate bibliographic descriptions — for these, in effect labeling them as different editions. This practice can potentially mislead users who expect *edition* to be defined, as is commonly understood, in terms of content. Bibliographers, often more rigorous in their definitions than catalogers, are careful to distinguish between the two kinds of editions: those that differ intellectually and those that differ simply in their conditions of publication. They restrict the term *edition* to the former (all copies made from a given typesetting) and introduce the term *subedition* for the latter (groups of typesettings that differ from others by virtue of a publishing decision).[32]

The distinction between editions and subeditions is useful for the discrimination it provides but is not generally recognized in library cataloging. One reason for this has to do with the nature of the bibliographic record. Conceptually viewed, the referent of a bibliographic record is an edition; practically viewed, however, it is a physical object acquired and inventoried by a library. The physical object actually inventoried by a library, however, is not always an edition; it can sometimes be a subedition. The inventory function of the bibliographic record is its earliest and most enduring function. This function is essential, since if not carried out all other library functions would be jeopardized. In its inventory function, a bibliographic record stands as a surrogate for a physical object.[33] Most of the time this physical object is coincident with the conceptual object — that is, an edition defined in terms of content. If occasionally this is not the case, it does not much matter; a little fudging to suit the convenience of the cataloger does not rob a database of its integrity. The problem comes when the fudging becomes common practice.

Fudging is a foreseeable danger, given that inventorying is a library-specific function and at odds with the present trend toward the globalization of information access. Fudging is also foreseeable given the proliferation of nonbook documents. Because of these the referents of bibliographic records are becoming increasingly muddied. Whereas in simpler times lapses in the coincidence between the conceptual and physical referents of bibliographic records happened only infrequently, today they occur on a regular basis. Causing the problem are entities called *versions*. A version is an edition subset that is distinguished by physical attributes. A book and a microfilm of it represent two different versions of the same edition, as do a sound recording in CD form and a copy of it in cassette form. Do these different versions require separate bibliographic records? This is a difficult question, and attempts to answer it have given rise to what has been dubbed "the multiple versions problem."[34] Some bibliographic guidelines make it quite clear that version or carrier differences alone do not constitute a new edition,[35] the implication being that such differences do not warrant making new bibliographic records.[36] Except for documents that are obvious reproductions, however, new records are in fact made.[37] As a consequence catalogs become burgeoned with multiple records for a single intellectual expression of a work. Expense is incurred, and users expecting one record per edition become confused.

Rigor might be introduced by replacing the traditional ambiguous concept of edition with three more distinct entities: editions, subeditions, and versions. But at the same time it might introduce inconsistency into practice. Universal bibliographical control is predicated on a universal ability to recognize the object of a bibliographic record. A common perception of this object is essential. To define it idiosyncratically in terms of whatever a particular cataloger understands an edition to be or whatever a particular library inventories is clearly unacceptable. In an effort to achieve uniformity, agencies — such as the Online Computer Library Center (OCLC), the Research Libraries Information Network (RLIN), and the Library of Congress (LC) — have established input standards enumerating the conditions under which the making of a new record is warranted.[38] As yet the input standards are themselves not standardized, so that what is recognized as the object of description by one agency may not be so recognized by another.

Input standards that enumerate the conditions warranting the making of a bibliographic record are operational versions of the *AACR2R* definitions of *edition*. The enumeration of conditions contributes to standardization. However, as Socrates long ago observed, enumerative definitions fail to convey the essence of what is denoted by the word being defined. They fail to provide a conceptual grasp, to impart the understanding necessary for extrapolation, or to supply a mental algorithm for "how to go on." In the case of editions, a cataloger faced with a situation not covered by what is enumerated in the input standards is at a loss for what to do. Further, definition by enumeration makes edition an artificial construct, diverging both from the user-understood concept and the concept implicit in the bibliographic objectives. Dilemmas abound. One of the most challenging of the ontological questions is the question of the function of the bibliographic record in a multimedia online environment.[39]

From a set-theoretic point of view an edition is a subset of a work. Any document that is a member of an edition set is also a member of the work set subsuming the edition. An inheritance relationship holds between editions and works. While many, indeed most, work sets contain only one subset (since normally only one edition of the work is ever published), others, like the Bible and classical works in the humanities, may contain hundreds of subsets. Subeditions and versions are subsets of editions. These various entity types (they are themselves entities) may be defined formally as follows:

Edition E_jW_i = def {x: x is a member of W_i and x is produced from mastercopy A_k}, where E_i is a particular edition of a particular work W_i and is produced from mastercopy A_k;

Subedition S_iE_j = def {x: x is a member of E_j and x is published by publisher P_k}, where S_i is a particular subedition of a particular edition E_j and is published by a particular publisher P_k};

Version V_iE_j = def {x: x is a member of E_j and x is embodied in format F_k}, where V_i is a particular version of a particular edition Ej and is embodied in format F_k}.

Author Sets

In Western cultures and since medieval times, authorship has been the primary identifying attribute of works. Users tend to remember and search for works by the persons responsible for their creation. This is evidenced by the primacy (in Western cultures) of the author catalog, where entries are arranged so that a user will find all works of an author collocated together.

In his *Rules*, Cutter defines *author* narrowly as a "person who writes a book" and more broadly as the "cause" of the book's existence.[40] Later descriptive codes replace *cause* with *responsible for* or *immediately responsible for*. They also specify in a general way what an author should be responsible for: not merely the book's existence (a publisher could meet this condition), but the "intellectual content" of the book, literary, artistic, or musical."[41] Some codes go even further and enumerate authorial functions: writing, editing, illustrating, originating, composing, performing, and so on.

Perceptions of authorial functions have changed over time. In the golden age of cataloging, when the theory of the author catalog was being developed, authorship was broadly interpreted. Julia Pettee characterized this perception as an attempt to stretch the concept of author to bring in "lambs outside the fold."[42] Notable among the new lambs were corporate bodies and editors. In the last quarter of the twentieth century, however, the perception changed, and these lambs began to be looked on askance. Domanovsky, for instance, questioned the practice of regarding editors as authors, finding it untenable on the grounds of user expectations, logic, and tradition.[43] He and others questioned the practice with respect to corporate bodies: how can a corporate body put pen to paper?[44] Consequently, in 1974 editors were driven from the Anglo-American authorship fold, and the same fate befell corporate bodies in 1981. Oddly enough, at this later date spirits and (some) performers were allowed to sneak into the fold.

The nature of authorship has changed significantly over the last hundred years. For one thing, it has become increasingly collaborative. A scientific work reporting the results of team research may have dozens of authors, many of whom are honorary — which is to say, not directly involved in writing. But then are they authors? In the abstracting and indexing media the answer is likely to be affirmative. An editorial in the *Annals of Internal Medicine* stipulates that to be regarded as an author a person need only to "have read the entire contents of a paper and assented to its publication before it is sent to a journal"[45] — hardly authorship as the primary identifying attribute of a work!

Authorship has also become increasingly diffuse and mixed. It is diffuse when no one person is obviously responsible for a work, as is the case with conference proceedings, edited works, and works issued by corporate bodies. It is mixed when the responsibilities involved in the production of a work are performed by different persons. Mixed responsibility is normally the authorship condition characterizing the intellectual and artistic content of many nonbook works, such as films. In fact, for such works, the concept of author may be inappropriate. Some descriptive codes for nonbook materials eschew defining *author*, choosing instead to use the term *creator*; and instead of using the word *responsibility* they use *attribution* or *significance* (primary, bibliographic, or manifest).[46] The changing terminology reflects a changing view of authorial responsibility.

Deconstructuralists might ask, "What does it matter who is speaking?"[47] and for the person seeking information it often really does not matter. It has been suggested that in an online catalog where any name appearing in running text is keyword searchable, there no need to single out a particular name as belonging to an author.[48] Unlike a card catalog, which is an author, title, and subject catalog, an online catalog is an "every-attribute" catalog: searches can be conducted and displays organized by any attribute whatever. A problem with this, however, is that major responsibility would not be distinguished from minor responsibility, and this would adversely affect both precision and recall. But more seriously, to ignore authorship, where it *is* clearly ascertainable, is to ignore users' search objectives and the need for an effective device to relate, organize, and display bibliographic information.

In those cases where it is useful to identify the author of a document, a constructive (as opposed to a deconstructive) approach is to capitalize on the fact that a thing is usually what it represents itself as being. Lubetzky does this when he defines *author* as "the person or corporate body *represented* as chiefly responsible for the work, i.e., the one in whose name the work is issued and who is purportedly responsible for it . . . except when one has erroneously, fictitiously, or dubiously been represented as the author of the work."[49] This definition is open-ended in that allows the various ways in which an author may be represented to be explored. This brings definition (again) around to enumeration, with the intriguing implication that no common or essential component may exist in all instances of authorship.

Being able to enumerate the various ways in which an author may be represented is the key to automatic author identification. Both linguistic and location criteria can be used to identify authors of documents automatically. Certain character strings (such as *by*) usually identify authors, while other strings (such as *edited by*) are likely to indicate nonauthors.[50] Moreover, authors' names are likely to appear in key locations, such as in the top third of a title page. Further refinement can be achieved with the use of normalizing dictionaries to link the variant names of authors and to distinguish authors from corporate bodies. Obviously, automatic author identification is possible only in those cases where authorship is not diffuse.

The set of all works by a given author might be formalized as

$$WA_i = \text{def } \{x: x \in W_j \ \& \ A_i \text{ is the author of } W_j\},$$ where "is the author of" is indicated on representations of W_j by phrases $a_i \ldots a_n$ appearing in locations $l_i \ldots l_n$.

Subject Sets

Subject rivals author in importance in organizing documents and providing access to them. That all documents on the same subject must be displayed together is mandated by the collocation objective. Traditionally this mandate has been met through a subject card catalog, wherein the entries are arranged in classified or alphabetic order. The move from card to online catalogs has increased the ways in which subject searches can be performed.[51] As a consequence, the incidence of subject searches has risen dramatically — so much so that the increased importance of organizing information by subject has been heralded as a paradigmatic change.[52]

Quality indexing, successful retrieval and effective automatic indexing depend on being able to define *subject*. Sometimes the term is defined analytically using near synonyms, like *theme, topic, thought content,* or *overall idea*.[53] Analytic definitions, however, often lead nowhere. An exception is the definition of *subject* through the related concept of aboutness. In a classic paper, Bill Maron defined *aboutness* behavioristically, in terms of beliefs, opinions, or psychological states of mind.[54] He postulated a *subjective about* and an *objective about,* characterizing the former as a private, complex and unanalyzable perception relative to a particular person, and the latter as the set of index terms that a large number of people would agree to be useful when searching for it in a database.

The view that subject determination is wholly subjective is disturbing — like the view that a falling tree makes no sound if no one hears it. Christopher Fox and Terry Norreault challenged Maron's subjective stance, arguing that since there is a fair amount of agreement among people on how to use the word *about,* there must be common conventions governing its use.[55] Further, to assume that perceptions of aboutness are subjective does not allow for mistakes, whereas mistakes can be made: to say that *Hamlet* is a treatise on thermodynamics is to be mistaken.

As is often the case with two opposing stances, neither is wholly defensible. A common fallacy in addressing the concept of aboutness is attempting to define it in isolation and not recognizing that it is a variable. The degree to which aboutness varies — that is, the degree to which a document can be said to be about something — depends on several factors, one of the most important being the nature of the language it uses.[56] The way language affects aboutness can be illustrated using a subject analysis model based on sentence grammar.[57] The grammatical subject of a sentence denotes what the sentence is about while its predicate comments on this. The sentence "Snow is white" has as its grammatical subject *snow*. Its predicate, *is white*, comments on snow, is a condition attaching to snow, states a fact about snow, gives information about snow, and embodies a proposition about snow. By extension, a collection of sentences about snow results in a document about snow. By further extension, many documents about snow result in a literature about snow. Snow, having associated with it a literature or a systematized body of ideas,[58] achieves the status of a subject: it occupies a position in the bibliographic universe.

The *grammatical model* underlies approaches to subject analysis that view it as a process of summarization. It is implicit in Kaiser's Systematic Indexing, which recognizes as modes of existence the two categories of things and processes:[59] *things* are what a document speaks of, and *processes* what is said about them. It is implicit as well in Brian Vickery's contention that the subject of a document can be inferred from the noun phrases of its individual sentences[60] and in W. Kintsch and T. Van Dijk's explanation of text comprehension as a cognitive reduction that synthesizes the propositions of a document into macropropositions.[61]

But the grammatical model cannot fully explain how a subject is analyzed. Among its critics is Patrick Wilson, who rejects the model on the grounds that it is not possible to generalize from the aboutness of individual sentences in a document to the aboutness of the document as a whole. The difficulty he sees is not being able to determine what or how much one must know to know what a sentence is about.[62] Another critic of the grammatical model is William Hutchins, who argues that what a sentence is about is not necessarily what is stated by its grammatical subject.[63] In response to such criticisms, it might be observed that models generally simplify and, at times, oversimplify. However, because a model is invalid in some situations does not mean the model cannot be used to good effect in general explanation. In fact, an analysis of exceptions to a general explanation is itself enlightening. In particular, the exceptions to the grammatical model throw light on the factors determining aboutness.

Implicit in the example of snow given above is that the grammatical model works best when language is used referentially. A document is about snow if and only if it contains a sufficient number of propositions that refer to or state facts about snow. In its reliance on propositions, the grammatical model is positivistically oriented. One of the tenets of logical positivism is that the totality of true propositions provide a picture of what there is.[64] But — and it is an important *but* — language is not always used in a propositional mode. It is not always used to refer to what exists or to picture a state of affairs. In fiction, poetry, and films, it is often used expressively or in an emotive mode. This is obviously true also of nonverbal languages, like the languages of painting or music.[65] While painterly language and musical language can be used to refer (a seascape may represent water and pastoral music may represent the sound of a cuckoo), their chief use is to create a sentient or emotional experience. If one were to ask what the subject of a painting or a piece of music is, a controversy would likely ensue, but such would not be the case if the query were about the subject of a scientific paper. Between a scientific work and a work of art, there is a broad spectrum of language use in which sometimes referential uses dominate and sometime expressive uses. In any case, it is a mistake in attempting to define *subject* to assume that what is true of language used in one mode is true of language used in another mode — in particular, to assume that what can be said of language used referentially can also be said of language used expressively.[66] The scientific model of aboutness is limited, as indeed is subject analysis itself.

Another assumption implicit in the grammatical model is that subjects have names. Thomas Carlyle believed that knowledge consisted in being able to give the right names to things — "not only all common speech, but Science, Poetry itself is no other than a right naming."[67] That subjects must be referable to in the shorthand of names is implicit in the definitions of *subject* used by the Ranganathan school. Among its criteria for identifying a new basic subject are that it should have literary warrant and some specialization in academic circles in the form of courses or periodicals devoted to it.[68] For Cutter, as well, a topic to be raised to the status of a subject had to be given a name.[69] It has been suggested that Cutter's views on this matter derive from the nineteenth-century Scottish philosophy of common sense, which held that the cumulative acquisition of knowledge consisted in part of creating names for things.[70]

Problems :

The assumption that subjects must be nameable is positivistically oriented and, as such, represents a limited view of language. Arguably, some subjects can be referred to in discourse but not named. Such subjects can be characterized as linguistically indeterminate. It makes sense to say that *Moby Dick* is about something, but this something is more than just a whale; however it is characterized, it cannot be neatly packaged into a word or short phrase. Scientific language exhibits a great degree of linguistic determinacy, since the subjects of interest to a scientist must have names if they are to function as variables in equations. But the subjects dealt with in the belles-lettres and the arts, and not infrequently in scholarly works in the humanities and social sciences, can take pages or even volumes of words to delineate. This makes subject indexing difficult, and, in fact, often no attempt is made to do it for works that, wholly or in part, have subjects that cannot be named. Many fictional works and works in audio or visual form fall into this category.[71] Instead, such works are often described using subjectlike attributes, such as genre.[72]

Where subject determination is relatively clear cut, attempts have been made to automate it. In the early days of automatic indexing, subject determination was based on simple location and frequency data: a document was on the subject indicated by a character string if the string occurred above a certain frequency in the document and was not a stop word or if it occurred in a given location, such as the title. Algorithms based on statistical and locative data continue to be used for automatic subject determination, but they have become far more sophisticated. Use also is made of linguistic data: parsing algorithms to determine if sequences of words (word phrases) represent subjects; synonym and disambiguation dictionaries to refine inference by basing it on concepts rather than words; and linguistic frames employing "isa" hierarchies to deduce specific subjects from more general ones. Perhaps most impressive from the point of view of success, speed, and cost are the clustering algorithms that are used to make inferences of the kind: if document A is on subject X, then if document B is sufficiently similar to document A (above a certain threshold), then document B is on that subject. Defining *subject* in operational terms for use in automatic indexing is a challenge that is intriguing, both philosophically and technologically, and one that, if met, could significantly reduce the costs of information access and organization.

A simple example of a constructive set definition of subject is the following:

WS_j = def $\{x: x \in W_i \ \& \ W_i$ is about $S_j\}$, where "is about" is indicated on representations of W_i by phrases $a_i \ldots a_n$ appearing in locations $l_i \ldots l_n$.

Other Entities

The bibliographic universe is dynamic. It is, in Ranganathan's words, "a growing organism."[73] Any model of it should be extensible, in the sense of being able to represent entities that are as yet unspecified. The advantage of a set-theoretic model is that any attribute or any collection of attributes can be used to create entities through set formation. In this chapter sets formed by work, edition, author, and subject attributes have been discussed. While these are of primary bibliographic significance, they are not the only ones of interest. Others include the following:

text　　the set of all documents that match exactly with respect to character strings and symbols,[74]

impression　the set of all documents forming an edition of a work that are published by a given publisher or a set of joint publishers on a given date,

imprint　the set of all subsequent printings of a document that preserve the image of a previous printing,

archive　the set of all documents having the same provenance,

collection　a set of documents gathered on the basis of one or several attributes to be described collectively.

As noted in the beginning of this chapter a theory of description must specify its variables; it must define the entities to be described. A bibliographic theory has trouble doing this because the entities it deals with exhibit immense variety and complexity. Some of these entities cannot be accurately described using the traditional bibliographic concepts, like work, edition, author, and subject. When the attempt is made to do so, the concepts are so stretched as to lose meaning. It would seem that there is not a common (essential) ingredient in all instances of their use. To deal with this complexity, enumerative approaches to definition, based on the sharing of family resemblances rather than essential properties, can be introduced. But while these are useful, even necessary, for automation and standardization, at the same time they are likely to be counterintuitive for both catalogers and users.

In the last analysis, bibliographic description is an art and therefore will always be approximate. There will always be instances that are undecidable or where decisions must be made arbitrarily. The variables of interest in bibliographic theory will inevitably exhibit a certain amount of vagueness, ambiguity, and limited applicability. As long as practice is affected by this only sporadically, there is no reason for concern. But if the numbers of bibliographic entities that can be described in a uniform and exact manner begin to get out of hand, then it is time to question traditional concepts and theories.

4

Bibliographic Languages

Introduction

Information to be organized needs to be described. *Descriptions* need to be made of it and its physical embodiments.[1] Traditionally, descriptions are recorded on bibliographic records, which stand in for or surrogate the documents embodying information. The language used to make such descriptions is a bibliographic language, a special-purpose language that is designed and applied in accordance with a special set of rules. Its function is to communicate to users information about information. In this role, it serves as a bridge connecting the language of documents with that of the users who seek them. It is an artificial language that, purged of the anomalies of natural language, is capable of providing systematic, as opposed to chancy, access to information in recorded form.

A description is "a statement of the properties of a thing or its relations to other things serving to identify it."[2] The things described by bibliographic languages are information entities. As a first cut, bibliographic languages can be divided into those that describe information and those that describe its documentary embodiments — that is, those that describe works and those that describe their particular space-time manifestations in the form of books, videos, CDs, and so on. A *work language* describes information in terms of its attributes, such as author, title, edition, and subject. These are intellectual attributes independent of any space-time manifestation of the information. Thus, in addition to being an information-content language, a work language can be characterized as an intellectual-attributes language. By contrast, a *document language* describes attributes that are specific to particular manifestations of works — publication attributes (such as publisher, place, and date of publication), physical attributes (such as size, color, and medium), and location attributes (such as a journal, website, or library).

Bibliographic languages can be further subdivided by attribute. Thus, an author language is one whose objects of description are persons and corporate bodies[3] associated with works. A classification by attribute of work and document languages into sublanguages can be constructed as follows:[4]

Work language
  Author language
  Title language
  Edition language
  Subject language
    Classification language
    Index language
Document language
  Production language
  Carrier language
  Location language

In a work language, an author is treated as an attribute of information. In an author language, an author is treated as an entity — as an object of description in its own right. As noted in the previous chapter, how a thing is represented in a model, whether as an attribute or an entity, depends on the cataloger's point of view or purpose. Traditional bibliographic practice has regarded certain of its fundamental constructs, like authors and subjects, *both* as attributes and entities. Thus, they figure in bibliographic descriptions as metadata referencing attributes of works and as independent objects of description. (Descriptions of author entities are called *authority records,* rather than *bibliographic records.*) The chapters in the second half of this book discuss, accordingly, document, work, and subject languages. Although subject languages properly form a subclass of work languages, they are singled out for special treatment by reason of literary warrant. Since the beginning of the twentieth century, subjects of works have been treated separately from other work attributes, like author and title, and a large literature has developed around subject analysis and description.

Components of a Bibliographic Language

A language consists of a vocabulary, semantics, syntax, and pragmatics. The vocabulary of a bibliographic language consists of the simple and complex expressions used to name the values of the three variables: entities, attributes, and relationships. Its semantics consists of the relationships among these names, such as the equivalence relationships that exist between author names like Mark Twain and Samuel Clemens and subject names like Bulbous domes and Onion domes.* Its syntax consists of the ordering relationships among the component elements of complex expressions in the language. Its pragmatics consists of specifications and conditions for the application of the language, such as a specification indicating how much description should be given or the conditions under which a given descriptive term can be applied to a work.

Different bibliographic languages have developed differing degrees of sophistication in their vocabulary, semantics, syntax, and pragmatics. All use a specialized vocabulary. All work languages employ some sort of semantics. Both work and document languages employ syntax, with subject languages being the most linguistically advanced and document languages the least. Most languages are fairly underdeveloped in their pragmatics, an exception being the Dewey Decimal Classification (DDC).

Vocabulary

A vocabulary is a "list or collection of terms or codes available for use (as in an indexing system)."[5] The terms or codes of a bibliographic language are called by various names. In subject languages they are called *keywords, descriptors, index terms,* or *classification numbers.* In work languages and the languages used to describe the physical and production attributes of documents, they are referred to simply as *data elements* or *metadata.*

The rules governing the vocabulary of a bibliographic language state criteria for its use, such as the source from which vocabulary elements should be drawn and the form these should take. The purpose of source rules is to provide warrant or justification for admitting terms into the vocabulary. A term may be admitted on the basis of literary warrant, use warrant, or, in

---

* It is conventional practice when referring to the terms of a subject language to capitalize the initial letter of a term and not to use italics.

the case of classification languages, structural warrant. The purpose of form rules is to ensure the consistency in description that is required for systematic access to bibliographic information. Form rules specify how to select from among alternative vocabulary elements, such as between an author's real name and a pseudonym. They specify as well the linguistic form of the name, its abbreviation and capitalization style, and the language and script to be used. Vocabulary rules can be simple (such as a rule stating that the title of a document should be rendered in the form in which it appears on the piece) or complex (such as a rule that states the title of a work should be its original title or the title by which it is best known, except that introductory phrases and statements of responsibility that are part of the title should be omitted, at least under certain conditions).

The terms that constitute the vocabulary of a bibliographic language are of two sorts: *derived terms* and *assigned terms.* The former are taken as-is from documents, while the latter consist of normalizations of the as-is raw terms. The former describe an entity in its own terms, i.e., in the author's own language; the latter describe it in normalized terms, using a controlled vocabulary that facilitates the establishing of relationships among entities. The former are descriptive metadata elements; the latter are organizing metadata, whose raison d'être is to structure the bibliographic universe.[6]

Semantics

Semantics is the study of meaning, but in an extended sense it refers to the different meaning structures found in languages. The rules governing bibliographic semantics specify three such structures: a relational semantics, a referential semantics, and a category semantics.[7] To implement these structures requires normalizing natural language by introducing vocabulary or authority control. Vocabulary control is the chief means by which a natural language is processed to rid it of surface-structure inconsistencies that obstruct effective information retrieval.

Relational semantics treats of meaning relationships among terms. Chief among these is the relationship of synonymy, which holds between two or more terms that refer to the same thing. Without rules to control vocabulary for *synonymy,* documents containing the same information would be scattered, which would cause recall failures in retrieval. The usual, but not the only, way of dealing with the synonym problem is to establish one of the synonyms as authoritative and to refer to it from the other(s), using *See* or *Use* references — such as Samuel Clemens. *See* Mark Twain.

In addition to synonymy, bibliographic languages exhibit hierarchical and other relationships. (The "other" are often lumped together as *related-term relationships*.) Author and title languages employ a few hierarchical and related-term linkages — for instance, in relating the subordinate-superordinate and earlier-later names of a corporate body. Subject languages, by contrast, make extensive use of them. Indeed, there is virtually no limit to the kind or number of semantic linkages a subject language can exhibit. The most elaborate edifices constructed using hierarchical and related-term relationships are the universal classificatory languages that are used to map the universe of knowledge.

Referential semantics deals with the techniques used to limit the meanings or referents of terms. The rules specifying these techniques are a further means of controlling vocabulary. They do this by ensuring that each term refers to only one thing. A bibliographic language that contains multireferential terms — homonyms like Mercury, which can refer to a car, a planet, a metal, or a Greek god; or John Smith, which can refer to many different authors — causes poor precision when used in retrieval. The usual, but not the only, method of dealing with such terms is to split them up into several singly referring terms using qualifiers. Thus, the single-term Mercury becomes Mercury (car), Mercury (planet), Mercury (metal), and Mercury (Greek god), and Smith, John becomes Smith, John, 1832–1900, Smith, John, 1903–1986, and so on.

Category semantics has to do with the facets or grammatical categories into which the vocabulary is partitioned. Just as the vocabulary of a natural language is categorized by grammatical function, like subject and predicate, or by parts of speech, like noun and verb, so the vocabulary of a bibliographic language is categorized in terms of facets. Facets are the grammatical categories of a bibliographic language. Examples of facets are the topic, place, and form categories used by the Library of Congress Subject Headings (LCSH) and the type of composition, medium of performance, instrumentation, and key categories used to formulate uniform titles for musical works. There are a number of reasons for classifying or faceting a vocabulary, one of the most important being that facets can be used to formulate syntax rules.[8] A well-formed expression in a bibliographic language can be defined in terms of facets (for example, topic followed by place is a well-formed subject statement), much as a well-formed expression in a natural language can be defined in terms of grammatical or part-of-speech categories (subject followed by predicate is a well-formed sentence).

Syntax

The *syntax* rules of a language specify the order in which individual vocabulary elements of the language are concatenated to form larger expressions. In a natural language these larger expressions are phrases or sentences; in a subject-indexing language they may be called *statements, strings,* or *subject headings;* in an author or title language they are usually referred to as *identifiers* or *uniform headings.* In a natural language like English, a grammatically correct sentence is one that obeys a natural-language syntax rule. In a bibliographic language, a well-formed string or heading is one that is authorized by a bibliographic syntax rule. One of the syntax rules used by Kaiser in his *Systematic Indexing* is "concrete:process," by which is meant that a term from a concrete facet (that is, a term designating an object) can be followed by or concatenated with a term from a process facet (a term designating an action).[9] Coal:Mining is an example of an index language statement constructed using this syntax. It is grammatically correct and therefore constitutes a well-formed string in the index language.

Pragmatics

The *pragmatics* of a language deals with its use or application. An example of a rule governing the application of a bibliographic language is the cataloging rule that instructs that if an edition statement does not appear on a document being described, the cataloger is not to make one up. Another is the indexing rule that requires a cataloger to use the most specific heading appropriate in designating the subject of a work. Rules stating the conditions under which a new record can be made belong to the pragmatics of a bibliographic language, as do rules that specify the amount of detail to be included in a description or the number of subject descriptors to be assigned to documents. As remarked above, of all the bibliographic languages, the one with the best-developed pragmatics is the DDC. It uses hundreds of "class here and class elsewhere" instructions, often accompanied by extensive explanatory definitions, to guide classifiers in the application of class numbers.

Implementation

The design of a formal language of description occurs at a conceptual level and at an implementation level. At the *conceptual level* objectives and principles are formulated; also at this level entities, attributes, and relationships are specified. At the *implementation level* the rules used by the language to create descriptions are formulated. Also at this level it is determined how these descriptions should be recorded — that is, how bibliographic records should be designed. The conceptual level is the level of ideology; the implementation level, that of technology. Between the two a delicate balance obtains, a balance that is sometimes upset when technology, theoretically at the service of ideology, loses its direction and subverts it.

Rules

The *rules* for the design and application of a bibliographic language are typically contained in codes and standards.[10] There are literally hundreds of these. They include general author-title codes and their interpretations; material-specific codes for describing archival materials, cartographic materials, films, music, graphics, and so on; manuals for the interpretation and application of universal classifications; international general standards for thesaurus construction and indexing; subject-specific thesaurus and indexing standards; and formatting standards for machine encoding and bibliographic exchange. A representative sample of internationally or widely used codes and standards would include the following:

The International Standard Bibliographic Description (General)
The ISO Standard for Thesaurus Construction (ISO 2788)
The ISO Standard for Indexing (ISO 5963)
The ISO Standard for Bibliographic Exchange on Magnetic Tape (ISO 2709)
Dewey Decimal Classification and Relative Index
Library of Congress Classification Schedules
Library of Congress Subject Headings
Library of Congress Subject Cataloging Manual: Subject Headings
Anglo-American Cataloguing Rules, second edition, revised *(AACR2R)*[11]

In this text codes of rules are introduced chiefly to show how bibliographic languages are implemented. The Anglo-American Cataloging Rules are is used to illustrate work and document languages.[12] The current edition of these rules *(AACR2R)* is divided into two parts. The rules in Part 1 apply mostly to the description of documents; those in Part 2 to the description of works. To illustrate subject languages, the codes used are the Dewey Decimal Classification (DDC), the Library of Congress Subject Headings (LCSH), together with the accompanying manuals for their use, and various thesaurus standards. The rules that make up a code can be viewed as constituting a system that can be characterized and evaluated. How they are characterized and evaluated is discussed in the following sections.

Classification of Rules

The characterization of a rule system frequently takes the form of *classification,* which usually is the first step in a systematic research. The *AACR2R* rules have been classified in terms of their use, function, and the objects they describe:

- *Use* It has been shown that the AACR rules follow a Bradford-like distribution: a few rules account for most of the code's use, or, conversely, most rules are seldom used.[13] Infrequently used rules do not require high visibility in the sense of being immediately accessible. Whether a rule is core or peripheral becomes of practical significance in contexts such as learning the rules, revising them, automating them, and developing interfaces to them.[14] It is generally the case that user convenience is served by limiting the amount of information presented and suppressing information not of immediate use.

- *Function* There have been several classifications of AACR rules with respect to the functions they perform. This book classifies them by linguistic function, whether rules pertain to vocabulary, semantics, syntax, or pragmatics. Another classification using an entity-relationship approach divides them as specifying content, format, and sources of information; establishing entities, relationships, and attributes; supplying valid values of attributes; and specifying access points.[15] Still another, this one designed for use of *AACR2R* in electronic form, classifies them as to source, choice, form, and definition.[16] It is difficult to create a mutually exclusive and totally exhaustive classification of AACR rules, since the language used in the code mixes rules of different types in one expression. Besides being theoretically unsatisfactory, this is an obstacle in practical applications such as constructing interfaces and expert systems for cataloging.

- *Objects described* A recent object-oriented approach to deconstructing the bibliographic record looks at *AACR2R* rules from the point of view of the bibliographic entities they describe, whether works (texts), publications (manifestations), or items.[17]

A classification of rules, applicable not only to AACR but to rule systems in general, looks at them according to whether they are algorithmic in nature (thus amenable to automation) or intellectual in nature (thus the eminent domain of thinking beings). From the point of view of intellectual foundations, this is an especially interesting classification in that it contributes to understanding the mechanics of bibliographic description and, at the same time, points to how these mechanics might be automated.

Evaluation of Rules

The *evaluation* of a code of rules is a necessary undertaking in a practical discipline whose products are expected to be effective and efficient. A code of rules, regarded as a system designed to achieve certain objectives can be evaluated with respect to how well it achieves these objectives. Effectiveness and cost are both at issue. A code can be faulted on one or both grounds if

- Its rules are excessive in number or overly complex, creating a code Andrew Osborn labeled "legalistic" and Pettee called "an encyclopedia of pedantic distinctions."[18]
- There is overlap in the functionality of different rules, such as rules for added entries and cross-references.[19]
- Similar situations are treated differently, such as the variety of devices for indicating part-whole relationships in AACR and the former LCSH rules responsible for inconsistencies like Libraries, Catholic, but Jewish libraries; Libraries, Children's, but School libraries.
- Its rules are redundant, appearing in more than one place in a code, such as a DDC rule in the schedules that is repeated in manual notes or a general rule that is repeated for each of its special cases.[20]
- Its rules are formulated using an inconsistent, ambiguous, or complex syntax.[21]
- It fails to keep pace with changing technology.[22]
- It fails to promote reasonable uniformity in practice.[23]
- It fails to provide general guidance. No code of rules can anticipate all situations it might be expected to cover. The cataloger in such situations needs guidance in the form of objectives and principles. The omission of a statement of objectives and principles is a serious ground on which a code can be faulted, likened by Lubetzky to an attempt "to chart a map without a compass indicating the cardinal points."[24]

Bibliographic Records

History

A bibliographic record is a description of a bibliographic entity that is formatted and inscribed on a medium. Over time the forms of bibliographic records have changed, primarily in response to changes in technology. In modern times (since Panizzi), bibliographic technology has been revolutionized twice — first at the beginning of the twentieth century when card catalogs replaced book catalogs and then again in the latter third of the century when online catalogs began replacing card catalogs.

The Panizzi Era   In Panizzi's time bibliographic descriptions took the form of handwritten entries in book catalogs. Entries were displayed hierarchically.[25] Under each (main) author's name were listed alphabetically by title the works written by him. The first edition of a work held by the library was described in full. If the library held a second edition, its entry was listed under that for the first as: "———— Another edition." If needed, information that served to distinguish it from the first would be given. If the library held more than one copy of an edition, it was described as: "———— Another copy." This arrangement ensured that each document would be integrated into the catalog in the sense that it would display in the context of all the editions, translations, and adaptations of the work it manifested. For any given document, fullness of description varied according to how many of its features could be inherited by hierarchical force. Hierarchical displays not only ensured integration; they also achieved economy of expression in limiting what had to be said about an entity to only those features that could not be derived using membership and inclusion relationships.

In book catalogs, relationships of a nonhierarchical kind (that is, other than membership and inclusion) were indicated by cross-references. *See* cross-references linked related works, such as the Bible and a commentary on it. They were also used to achieve work collocation when access was sought through secondary attributes. For instance, if a document was authored by two persons, the main description (or main entry) would be made for the first author, and under the name of the secondary author a *See* reference would direct the user to the main description, which would display the document in its integrated context. The need for bibliographical references of the nonhierarchical kind to assist in navigation and collocation was well understood by Panizzi, who observed that the more numerous those references were, the more useful a catalog would be.[26]

The Card-Catalog Era   Supplementing and maintaining a book catalog was laborious. Space had to be left for new entries, and when space eventually ran out, sheets had to be interleaved in the catalog, with the overcrowding sometimes getting so out of hand that entries had to be inserted in nonalphabetical order. In the face of such difficulties, the card catalog came as a panacea. Making it even more welcome was that cards made possible the centralization, and thereby the mass production, of bibliographic descriptions. In 1901, through the agency of the Library of Congress, card-catalog copy began to be distributed to libraries throughout the United States. This was a landmark event in marking the beginning of shared cataloging — a giant step forward in the economizing of bibliographic effort, in actualizing the ideal of "once-only cataloging" and in realizing the possibility of universal bibliographical control through standardization.

The card catalog also brought with it some disadvantages. With the move from book to card catalogs, it was necessary to change the way bibliographic information was represented. Specifically, dashed entries no longer were appropriate; instead each document had to be described in full, using (normally) one card per document.[27] As a result some of the economy and structure afforded by hierarchical representation was lost, and so it became necessary to find new ways to depict inclusion and membership relationships. Elaborate filing rules were created for this purpose, so that the order of records in a card catalog mimicked the hierarchical ordering of entries in a book catalog. Each document was described in itself and also emblematically as manifesting a particular edition of a particular work. The latter was accomplished by including in the description of a document the name of the work it manifests, providing thus its bibliographic context. Added entries were introduced to indicate relationships and in part replaced cross-references. However, neither singly nor collectively could these devices restore the full relational power of book catalogs.[28]

The Electronic Era   The transition from card to online catalogs, though ongoing for over thirty years now, is still in its initial stages. This slow transition is due in part to difficulty in understanding the function of the bibliographic record in an electronic environment. Some obvious adaptations have been made. Bibliographic records have been converted from card to Machine Readable Cataloging (MARC) format and the individual metadata elements in them have been coded. But there has been a loss of bibliographic structure. The tiered structure, so neatly displayed in book catalogs and more or less preserved by strict filing rules in card catalogs, has been lost almost altogether with the inevitable move to computer filing. Also in many online catalogs the syndetic structure, the structure used to guide users from the language they know to the language used in organizing information, has not been implemented. This is not a necessary consequence of computerization but has come about due to factors concomitant with it such as high costs, difficulties in execution, and misunderstandings of catalog functions.[29] In any case, technological advance has brought with it a steady deterioration in the integrity of bibliographic structures since the time of Panizzi and, with it, an undermining of bibliographic objectives.[30]

Form and Function of the Bibliographic Record
The role of the bibliographic record in a digital environment is not yet clear. Especially unclear is what exactly a bibliographic record should describe. As observed above, a bibliographic record has served both as a surrogate for a physical document and as a description of an edition as a manifestation of a work. It has thus simultaneously (and fortuitously) served an inventory function and a conceptual or information function. But this is beginning to work less effectively. The increasing incidence of media in new formats has led to a divergence of the two functions, so that records designed for one function do not suffice for the other. It is hardly surprising that using one device to serve several functions should lead to trouble in times of technological change.

Suggestions are not lacking as to what ideally should be the objects represented by bibliographic records. Wilson argues that since the collocating of like information is the most important of all the bibliographic objectives, it follows that the entities described by bibliographic records should be works.[31] Michael Heaney concurs, arguing that the major access to information is by the abstract work, then goes even further to propose making document or publication records and copy or individual item records in addition to work records.[32]

Several suggestions as to how bibliographic records might be designed emanated from a forum convened to discuss the multiple-versions problem.[33] One was to make a composite record for an edition that would fully describe aspects common to all its versions and less fully describe (but do so to the extent necessary for disambiguation) other versions.[34] Another was to make a separate but full record for one version (a focal version) and partial records for the different versions pointing to the focal edition. A third was to make bibliographically independent records for versions and to link them. Using any of these means, hierarchical structures could be created for displaying work-level metadata followed by metadata pertaining to editions, followed by those pertaining to versions.

Complicating the question of the object of the bibliographic record is that in addition to its traditional inventory and conceptual functions, the technological revolution has imposed on it two other functions: that of communicating bibliographic information in a global environment and that of supplying data for the internal computer operations needed to create and maintain online catalogs. Having bibliographic records in a machine-readable form that is designed to be communicated globally can cause problems when these records are adapted for local library use. For instance, were a multiversion or multiedition record to be designed, it could happen that a given library would own some but not all the documents represented by it. Either the library would use the record as-is, which would confuse its users, complicate the inventorying of its holdings, and create difficulties in the exchange of bibliographic information, or it would customize it to its own holdings, which would be costly. Similar considerations apply to the bibliographic relationships represented on global bibliographic records. In adapting such a record to a local environment, should all these relationships be permitted to stand, showing the user all the bibliographic contexts in which a given document participates? Or should they be pruned and tailored to the locality, showing only those reflected in local holdings? Or should the bibliographic record show two different views, the universal and the particular?[35] These questions, caused by the incompatible demands put on the record to describe what exists in the bibliographic universe and what exists in a local library, need to be addressed in determining the record's form and function.[36]

Bibliographic records in MARC format are fairly well suited to communicating bibliographic data, at least within the parameters discussed above. However, they are not well designed for computer manipulation of this data. They have been criticized for their fixed-length, flat-file formats; for not presenting the kind of unified view of data required for efficient database design; and for being fraught with insertion, deletion, and update quirks that cause inefficiency in storing, maintaining, and performing retrieval operations on data.[37] To completely overhaul the MARC record, a standard that has been in force since the mid-1960s, is unthinkable for its economic, political, and bibliographical consequences. While MARC data can be refigured to streamline computer operations, consensus seems to be lacking on how to do this effectively and at a reasonable cost.

Given the burden put on it by the new media and the technological revolution, the traditional bibliographic record has so far remained surprisingly robust. This may yet change. Digital documents open the possibility of a radical deconstruction of the bibliographic record. Instead of gaining access to such documents indirectly through metadata on a surrogate record, access can be directly to the documents themselves, through the use of coding. Coding schemes, like the *Guidelines for Electronic Text Encoding and Interchange* and Standard Generalized Markup Language (SGML) guidelines, provide for identifying document attributes when and as they occur in the machine-readable text.[38] Where attributes essential for retrieval do not occur in the text, provision is made to supply them in document headers. The effect of this is to dispense with descriptions of documents as independent records and instead to distribute and embed the elements of description in the documents themselves.

An even more radical deconstruction is to dispense even with coding and to rely on documents to be self-describing. A system that relies on documents to be self-describing is founded on the supposition that the design of search algorithms can substitute for the crafting of individual bibliographic descriptions. The algorithms used in search engines today are still fairly primitive; many are based on keyword searching alone. As yet such systems have not been able to deal with the scatter and clog of information caused by the synonymy and homonymy of natural language, nor can they provide semantically useful displays of bibliographic data. But they have the potential to do so, transforming the theory of bibliographic description into a theory of bibliographic searching.

5

Principles of Description

Introduction

In the literature of bibliographic description the word *principle* has been used to refer to the objectives of a bibliographic system, to general rules in a bibliographic code, and to directives that guide the construction of a bibliographic language. It is the last sense that is used in this text, the sense Lubetzky used in noting that

One cannot undertake to outline a code of rules without directive principles anymore that one could undertake to chart a map without a compass indicating the cardinal points. Nor can one approach and apply intelligently a code of rules, however well constructed, without a knowledge of its underlying principles . . . without a knowledge of its cardinal direction.[1]

This is also the sense of the word *principle* used in the International Federation of Library Associations and Institutions' (IFLA) *Principles Underlying Subject Heading Languages (SHLs)*, where *principles* are defined as "general directives for determining the construction and application of subject heading languages."[2] More generally, viewed as a directive for action (designing a bibliographic language is an action), *principle* falls under the *Oxford English Dictionary*'s sense of "a general law or rule adopted or professed as a guide to action; a settled ground or basis of conduct or practice; a fundamental motive or reason of action, esp. one consciously recognized and followed."[3]

Bibliographic principles are different from bibliographic objectives and bibliographic rules. Objectives codify what a user can expect of a bibliographic system — to find a document, to find all manifestations of a work contiguously displayed, and so forth. Principles, on the other hand, are directives for the design of the bibliographic language used to create such a system. This language normally takes the form of a code of rules. However, principles themselves are not rules but rather guidelines for the design of a set of rules.

Certain general principles govern the design of all systems, bibliographic and otherwise. Two of particular relevance to the design of a bibliographic language are the principle of sufficient reason and the principle of parsimony. Originally identified by Leibniz, and called by Ranganathan the canon of impartiality,[4] the principle of sufficient reason requires that the grounds for each design decision be defensible and not arbitrary. The principle of parsimony, another of Ranganathan's canons,[5] requires that where alternative ways exist to achieve a design goal, the way that best furthers overall economy is to be preferred.

In addition to general design principles are principles specific to the design of a bibliographic language. Those that have been recognized in the Anglo-American cataloging literature and followed in practice include the following:

- *Principle of user convenience*   Decisions taken in the making of descriptions should be made with the user in mind. A subprinciple is the
Principle of common usage   Normalized vocabulary used in descriptions should accord with that of the majority of users.
- *Principle of representation*   Descriptions should be based on the way an information entity describes itself. A subprinciple is the
Principle of accuracy   Descriptions should faithfully portray the entity described.
- *Principle of sufficiency and necessity*   Descriptions should be sufficient to achieve stated objectives and should not include elements not required for this purpose. A subprinciple is the
Principle of significance   Descriptions should include only those elements that are bibliographically significant.
- *Principle of standardization*   Descriptions should be standardized, to the extent and level possible.
- *Principle of integration*   Descriptions for all types of materials should be based on a common set of rules, to the extent possible.

User Convenience

The principle of user convenience requires that bibliographic descriptions be designed with the user in mind. It requires the user to be the focus in all design decisions, no matter how minor.[6] Cutter, the user's greatest champion, elevated this principle to a categorical imperative in his often quoted dictum that "the convenience of the user must be put before the ease of the cataloger."[7] Cutter practiced what he preached. A striking example of this is his consideration for the unsophisticated user — children, the desultory user, and the man on the street who needs information quickly.[8] This consideration led him to reject the traditional European classified catalog, which was designed for scholars, and to create a whole new subject approach to information — an alphabetic approach that would allow unsophisticated users to get what they want by a name that they know, without any guesswork.[9]

It was in the context of an alphabetic-subject catalog that Cutter introduced the principle of common usage. He called usage "the supreme arbitrar,"[10] by which he meant that when things have alternative names (for instance, Cats and Felines), the choice between them should favor "the most usual name . . . , the one under which most people would be likely to look."[11] The common-usage principle was also recognized by Ranganathan, who called it the canon of the sought heading.[12] It is the cardinal principle governing the choice of terminology in all controlled vocabularies. In the current cataloging rules it is referenced by phrases like "commonly known," "predominantly identified," "most frequently identified," and "generally identified." The IFLA document on subject-heading principles calls it simply the "User Principle."[13]

Despite its preeminence as a directive, the common usage principle is both vague and unscientific.[14] Cutter himself recognized this. The problem comes with trying to ascertain what usage might be common. There is no single public, no user writ large; rather there are many users, and the way they verbalize their search requests represents many different language usages. In an operationalization of common usage, *AACR2R* interprets a "predominantly identified" form of name to mean "the form found in 80 per cent of the author's works."[15] This operationalization provides a decision rule; however, its validity can be questioned, as it represents the usage of publishers rather than that of the public. It identifies as "prominently identified" names such as Andersen, H. C. (rather than Andersen, Hans Christian) and Maugham, W. Somerset (William Somerset), rather than Maugham, Somerset.

The fact that language usage varies over place and time presents a dilemma insofar as vocabulary control has traditionally required a fixed usage. English-speaking users would expect to find Tchaikovsky's ballet listed as *Sleeping Beauty,* not under *Spîashchaîa Krasavitŝa,* which is its internationally accepted uniform title. The fact that this is a dilemma is illustrated by a request once made to the British Library that it assign two uniform titles to works: one formulated to conform to the international standard and the other formulated to be familiar to local users.[16] Relevant to this dilemma is another of Ranganathan's canons, that of local variation, which requires that the needs of local constituencies not be ignored.[17] In a digital environment, it is relatively easy to honor this canon as it applies to usage, since such an environment permits the automatic linking of various forms of names. Automatic or transparent linking allows unity to be achieved without sacrificing diversity. If all the different names by which something can be called are linked transparently, so that whichever a user chooses will make a direct match in retrieval, all usages are served, common and otherwise. Technological advance makes it possible to replace authority control with what Tillett calls "access control."[18]

During the last third of the twentieth century the principle of user convenience and its subprinciple of common usage have been the objects of research. Dozens of studies have been undertaken to determine how users search for information and what problems they encounter. While the existence of such studies underscores the importance attached to the principle of user convenience, the findings themselves are not unexpected. One finding is that users tend to use a very limited set of metadata, usually those found in bibliographic citations, such as author, title, edition number, publisher, place of publication, and date.[19] This finding could have been predicted as an instantiation of the general law that human selection from any kind of store of items tends to follow a Bradfordian distribution.[20] Another finding is that in subject searches users tend to retrieve too many or not enough citations,[21] which, again, is not unexpected insofar as it is anticipated by, and its antidote hypostasized in, the collocation objective. Another finding is that users have trouble matching their own vocabulary against that of the retrieval system they are using.[22] This is not surprising as it illustrates the above-mentioned, well-understood problem of attempting to determine a single common usage.

Representation

The principle of representation requires bibliographic descriptions to be constructed to reflect the way bibliographic entities represent themselves. This principle is used primarily to ensure accuracy of description, though it is used as well to contain costs, to prevent idiosyncratic descriptions, and to assist in the construction of operational definitions.

Accuracy

A description is inaccurate if it in any way misrepresents an entity, making it seem what it is not. In bibliographic contexts, accuracy, in the sense of honest portrayal, is equated with truth in transcription.[23] Truthfully transcribing how a document represents itself is necessary for the identification and communication of bibliographic information. The metadata in a description are truthfully transcribed, or warranted, if (1) they come from a specified source and (2) they are copied in the form in which they appear there, except for capitalization and punctuation. These two conditions ensure the likelihood that two people describing the same bibliographic entity will create identical descriptions.

Prescribing a source of information from which data elements should be derived is a way of specifying how an entity can represent itself. In simpler times, when bibliographic entities were for the most part books published in Western countries, the choice of source was obviously the title page, the "face of the book."[24] In 1884 Charles Blackburn wrote: "It is I believe one of the laws of bibliography that catalog titles should be copies of the title pages of books." [25] Lubetzky wrote regarding the title page that "the most important characteristic of a book for the purposes of cataloging is the fact that it is provided with a prominent identification tag in the form of a title page."[26] Ravilious expressed the same thought in referring to a title page as "a magnet at which bibliographic minutiae collect like iron filings."[27] Cutter spoke of "the cult of the title page" and how "its slightest peculiarities are noted; it is followed religiously, with dots for omissions, brackets for insertions and uprights to mark the ends of lines; it is even imitated by the facsimile type or photographic copying."[28]

The title page of a book is a reliable source, since it, together with its verso, usually contains all bibliographically significant data. Most nonbook materials, however, lack a convenient identification tag in the form of a title page. This difficulty has been met by specifying for each of the different kinds of nonbook materials title-page analogs — that is, the chief source from which data can be taken. Though the sources vary, depending on material type, an attempt at uniformity was made by specifying common criteria for the selection of sources. In 1975 C. P. Ravilious identified three such criteria as a result of surveying codes specifically geared to the description of nonbook materials.[29] These criteria, along with some of the problems attending them, are

• *Comprehensiveness*   Given a choice of several sources, data are to be taken from the source that gives the fullest, clearest, and most authoritative information — that is, from the source that most adequately identifies the item. A problem with this criterion is that sources do not always behave in such a manner that it is possible to identify one that is most comprehensive.

• *Proximity*   Given a choice of several sources, data are to be taken from the source that is nearest the item's content, such as an internal source. There are at least three reasons why this criterion is an uncertain guide: (1) the data on the item itself may not be complete, (2) the data may not be authoritative, and (3) it may be difficult or time consuming to get to the data (for example, when the source is unreadable without processing, as is the case with compressed or printer-formatted data in an electronic resource).

• *Persistence*   Given a choice of several sources, data are to be taken from the source that is most enduring (for example, from the item itself) rather than its packaging. Taken literally, this criterion would require taking data from a sound recording rather than the label affixed to it and from the title and end frames of a video or from the internal screens of an electronic resource, rather than from containers for these items, labels on the items, or accompanying documentation. This makes the criterion subject to the same problems as those afflicting the proximity criterion.

With modification, Ravilious's criteria were used for the various nonbook International Standard Bibliographic Descriptions (ISBDs) to develop a preference ranking of sources for bibliographic data. But ranking does not address the major problem, which is that often no single source is comprehensive. Data from a chosen source can always be supplemented with data from other sources, bracketed to signify their nonstandard origin. There is a danger, however, of too often gravitating toward the default position, where data are taken from anywhere in an item — in effect, treating several sources as a unitary source. This could imperil accuracy (the reason for prescribing a source in the first place), since a given datum, such as a title, can appear in different forms in different places on a document. The only way accuracy could be ensured would be to accompany each datum with a location-where-found annotation. Truth in transcription was once relatively easily ensured by faithfully copied title pages, but with the influx of nonbook materials it has become troublesome and has raised to a theoretical level questions about the limits and purpose of accuracy and the conditions required to ensure it.

In some cases data may be accurately transcribed from a document, and yet the resulting description is not truthful. For instance, a document may announce itself as a second edition, whereas in reality it is only a reprinting of a first edition; or it may purport to be by a given author, whereas in reality it is the work of a ghost writer; or it may be attributed to a corporate body and yet be written by a person. What is to be done is such cases? Lubetzky suggests that one can be guided by the principle of representation:

It must be recognized that it is really not "the writer of a book" or the creator of a work who will generally be regarded as the author or the one "chiefly responsible" for it, but the one who lent his name and authority to it — the one *represented* as the writer of the book or as the creator of the work, who presumably formally assumed responsibility for it.[30]

When bibliographic reality conflicts with existential reality, the former has the stronger claim. The reason for this is primarily economic. In-depth bibliographic research of the sort that pursues questions of attribution is a luxury affordable only in special situations, such as in the description of art works or rare books, not in the day-to-day work of introducing order into the bibliographic universe. Some small indulgences are permitted. When ambiguous, unintelligible, or obviously inaccurate statements appear on documents, these may be explained or corrected, within brackets and to a reasonable extent.[31] Nevertheless limitations must be set, and here the principle of representation becomes an injunction to eschew brooding over the true nature of a bibliographic entity — and, not incidentally, to eschew the temptation to make idiosyncratic descriptions.

Definitional Role of the Principle of Representation

In chapter 2 it was seen that difficulties in defining terms such as *edition* and *author* can sometimes be resolved by enumerating character strings on documents that are indicative of editionhood or authorship. A given document is a second edition if it says it is. A person is an author if that person is represented as such. The principle of representation thus has a role to play in resolving definitional ambiguities. In those cases where it is not clear how an entity (x) represents itself, conditions can be enumerated under which x is represented as y. For instance, in the classic case of a report prepared by a personal author and issued in the name of a corporate body, conditions are stated under which the report can be said to emanate from the body — for example, the report is of an administrative nature or records the collective thought of the body. A fully operational definition would go a step further to specify just which character strings on the report are indicative of "being of an administrative nature" or "representing collective thought." Presently there is considerable interest in how bibliographic information is represented on documents, and this may be expected to continue. Both standardization and automation assume that a document is what it represents itself to be and that clues in and on them can be used to infer in a mechanical or semimechanical way what a document's title is, who its authors and publishers are, and even what it is about.

Limitations of the Principle of Representation

The principle of representation if carried too far would result in bibliographic descriptions that individually are correct but when taken collectively are inconsistent. It would go against the principle of user convenience if bibliographic records — say, for books — were literal copies of their title pages. Title pages vary considerably. They contain differing amounts of information, not all of it of interest; the order in which the information is presented varies, with the author appearing either before or after the title; different conventions are used for punctuation, abbreviation, and capitalization; and so on. If bibliographic descriptions mirrored title pages, the information they impart would be difficult to grasp quickly; the eye would never know where to find a given kind of datum, such as an author or title. To facilitate scanning, certain aspects of descriptions need to be made uniform. These include the selection of data elements, the order in which they are displayed, and their punctuation, capitalization, and abbreviation. Thus, the principle of representation is curtailed by the need for consistently formatted bibliographic records.

Accuracy in description does not by itself ensure effective retrieval. Thus, the principle of representation is of limited scope in that it deals only with those aspects of description based on derived vocabulary. Descriptions cannot consist of derived data alone because the language in which a document represents itself is not necessarily the one a user would use to look for the document. A user cannot be expected to guess the name or form of name by which an author is represented on a document. To gear the language of users to the language of documents, a normalized vocabulary must be introduced to supplement vocabulary derived from documents. The principle of representation is useful in developing means to achieve the finding and identification objectives, but here its usefulness stops.

Sufficiency and Necessity

Since Aristotle's time, philosophers have debated the nature of description, attempting to distinguish the attributes of things that are essential from those that are accidental. In the context of bibliographic description, the endeavor is the same; the attempt here is to distinguish attributes that are bibliographically significant from those that are not. The directive that guides determinations of bibliographic significance is the principle of sufficiency and necessity. This principle requires a bibliographic description to be full enough to meet the objectives of a system for organizing information and, at the same time, contain no data elements extraneous to these objectives.

Panizzi implicitly tied considerations of sufficiency and necessity to the bibliographic objectives when he argued that descriptions must be full enough to distinguish one edition of a work from another and to enable a choice to be made from among similar editions.[32] Lubetzky made the connection explicit. Up until the 1940s it was generally assumed that the description of a book should faithfully reproduce all data elements on its title page. Lubetzky objected to this, arguing that objectives, not title pages, should determine what was and what was not essential in a description. If data elements on a title page did not further a bibliographic objective, they were to be excluded; if data elements were not on a title page and yet were necessary to meet one of the objectives, they were to be introduced.[33] Relying on objectives rather than on an unthinking adherence to the principle of representation was a revolutionary concept at the time (1946) and was opposed on the ground that omitting title-page elements in a bibliographic description would make it impossible to distinguish various editions of a work. This argument proved to be not valid.[34]

Nevertheless, a problem arises in referencing bibliographic objectives to determine essential data elements, at least as the objectives are currently formulated. The problem is caused by the open-ended objectives. The choice objective in encouraging the inclusion of any data element that might be useful in the selection of a document can lead to the proliferation of expensive detail. The same is true of the navigation objective and even the collocation objective. As was earlier observed, containing bibliographic detail needs to be addressed at the level of objectives — in particular, the open-ended objectives. Only when this is done can the objectives be used to settle questions of necessity and sufficiency.

Cutter was one of the first to face the problem of necessary versus unnecessary data elements. He viewed appropriate fullness of description as a variable, depending on local needs and circumstances, such as library size. Accordingly, he distinguished three kinds of catalogs — short, medium, and full. This distinction continues to be carried in cataloging codes to the present day, but it is becoming less useful as global cataloging renders distinctions based on library size irrelevant. The goal of reducing bibliographic effort so that one item need be described only once worldwide necessarily assumes adherence to a uniform level of description, one deemed adequate for national libraries.

Occam's Razor

The principle of sufficiency and necessity at times acts like the principle of parsimony, a brake limiting the metadata admissible in description. It is generally, though not quite accurately, assumed that the cost of making descriptions increases in proportion to the number of data elements they contain.[35] This leads to the conclusion that data should not be multiplied unnecessarily, which in turn leads to taking up Occam's razor and slashing elements deemed bibliographically insignificant. Decisions as to which these are have been justified on various grounds, among them reason, empirical warrant, and expert opinion.

The most celebrated wielding of Occam's razor followed on Lubetzky's "Is this rule necessary?" campaign of 1953.[36] Having achieved earlier success in eliminating title-page data not required by the bibliographic objectives, Lubetzky, as a further step in his reform to simplify cataloging, set about eliminating redundancy in the rules for providing identifiers for bibliographic entities. Observing that many of these rules were designed to fit specific cases rather than general conditions,[37] he subjected them one by one to stringent review. Was a given rule part of a larger rule already included in the code? If so, it was redundant and had to be eliminated. Was it consistent with other rules? If not, it had to be revised. A tour de force of rational argument, Lubetzky's campaign was successful, and the consequent simplification of the rules for identifying bibliographic entities was heralded as a return to principle.

The problem how to simplify bibliographic description by eliminating unnecessary metadata has been approached through empirical research. Following Lubetzky's call to eliminate unnecessary title-page data elements, a study was conducted at the Library of Congress to assess the effectiveness of page count in distinguishing one edition of a book from another.[38] (The study was needed to refute the argument that full title-page transcription was necessary to identify a document.) Though the sample was small, page count, along with author and title data, did in fact prove a reliable indicator of bibliographic uniqueness. Half a century later, in a bibliographic world significantly more complex, Ed O'Neill and others conducted a similar study at the Online Computer Library Center (OCLC).[39] For the purpose of weeding out duplicate records on the OCLC database, they developed a duplicate detection algorithm based on thirteen weighted data elements, which they then tested for efficacy. These data elements proved to be sufficient for meeting the identifying objective for a bibliographic database of over 36 million records.

Empirical research has also been used to explore the necessity and sufficiency of bibliographic data elements from a users' point of view. The Seal study mentioned earlier, which surveyed catalog use in a polytechnic library of 320,000 books and 160 nonbook materials, pitted an experimental catalog containing only brief bibliographic records against a normal catalog containing full records.[40] Participants in the experiment were asked first to search in the experimental catalog and then, only if they could not find what they wanted, to use the normal catalog. It was found that in 92 percent of the searches there was no need to resort to full records.

Several observations can be made about this and other such studies. First, as already has been observed, the results are to be expected in that the frequent use of a few data elements obeys the Bradfordian law of selection. Second, because of their limited scope and the simplifying assumption that only user-identified data elements need be included in descriptions, the studies lack external validity. In a global bibliographic environment, the act of uniquely distinguishing one information entity from another is no longer a local matter. The few metadata elements needed to distinguish 480,000 documents hardly suffice to distinguish a hundred times that many. Third, such studies, in their intent to understand the user, as represented by J. Q. Public, overlook the often more complicated needs of another class of users — those involved in database construction and maintenance. J. Q. Public may seldom need to distinguish nearly identical documents, but acquisition librarians need to do so on a daily basis. Moreover, even a sophisticated J. Q. Public may have only a limited understanding of his needs, unaware of the guidance that is given by full rather than abbreviated bibliographic records.

The most usual approach to data element elimination has been to rely on expert opinion. An example is the expert opinion lodged at the Library of Congress and promulgated in its rule interpretations. Many of the Library of Congress rule interpretations (LCRIs) are indeed interpretations in the sense of clarifying ambiguity, but some have the sole purpose of cost-cutting. LCRI 1.1F1 limits statements of responsibility by ruling on the bibliographic significance of persons whose names appear on a document (book-jacket designers are out). LCRI 2.5C1 and 2.5C2 override the *AACR2R* rule suggesting that various types of illustration be named (such as coats of arms, facsimiles, forms, genealogical tables, maps, music, plans, and portraits), recommending instead that all illustrative matter regardless of type be indicated by *ill.*[41]

Because of the need to standardize bibliographic descriptions, the expert opinion relied on for decisions of sufficiency and necessity frequently is lodged in political bodies like task forces working under the aegis of national and international associations. Through cooperative efforts such bodies work toward a consensus on minimal data-element sets. An example is the Program for Cooperative Cataloging's core-level record standard for books.[42] Others are the Cooperative Online Serials Program (CONSER) standard for serials[43] and the data-element set produced through an exercise in bibliographic modeling by the IFLA Study Group on Functional Requirements for Bibliographic Records.[44]

The principle of sufficiency and necessity can be used to justify either expanding the number of data elements in a description, as was done by Panizzi, or reducing them, as was done in the polytechnic experiment. Decisions relating to bibliographic significance are difficult but are not entirely a matter of the opinion of users or experts. An objective determination can be made of the data elements needed to identify a bibliographic entity and distinguish it from other like entities.[45] It is where the objectives are open-ended that decisions must be left to those who are able to balance user needs and bottom lines.[46]

Standardization

It has been observed that "the entire history of bibliographic control is that of the establishment of standards and their subsequent modification."[47] In the mid-nineteenth century Charles C. Jewett saw standardization as a necessary condition for the union catalog he was advocating to be housed at the Smithsonian Institution. He envisioned this catalog as containing records for the holdings of all public libraries in the United States. Such a catalog would be an instrument for national bibliographical control, facilitate the exchange of bibliographic information, and reduce duplication of effort through cooperation. For such a catalog to be made actual, bibliographic records would have to be constructed according to a uniform style. Accordingly, he wrote: "The rules for cataloguing must be stringent, and should meet, as far as possible all difficulties of detail. Nothing, so far as can be avoided should be left to the individual taste or judgment of the cataloger."[48]

Jewett did not live to see a union catalog realized. The requisite technology to mass produce and distribute bibliographic records did not exist until card catalogs began replacing book catalogs. The year the Library of Congress began its card-distribution program, 1901, marks a technological advance and the beginning of union catalog building in the United States. During periods of technological advance, cooperative fervor and activity tend to accelerate, and the drive toward standardization is strong.

The beginning and end of the twentieth century were two such periods —
first when card catalogs were introduced to replace book catalogs, and then
again when online catalogs superseded card catalogs.

To *standardize* means to bring into conformity with "something established by authority, custom or general consent."[49] A natural language is only
partially standardized through the force of custom; a bibliographic language, on the other hand, is strictly standardized through the general consent of those involved in building international codes. The development of
a standardized lingua franca for bibliographic description is a twentieth-
century achievement, due in large part to IFLA's ability to provide the infrastructure by which representatives from countries worldwide could meet
and hammer out consensual accords.[50] A milestone in IFLA's standardization activities was the 1961 International Conference on Cataloging Principles. At this conference fifty-three countries and twelve international
organizations met to agree on principles for the selection and normalization of metadata for accessing bibliographic information. Eight years later,
another important conference, the International Meeting of Cataloging
Experts (IMCE), led to the establishment of international standards for bibliographic description. Eleven years after this still another historic international meeting was convened, this time to develop a universal Machine
Readable Cataloging (MARC) format (UNIMARC).

Standardization admits of degree. Some, such as Jewett and the IMCE
experts, would argue that the international exchange of bibliographic information requires maximum standardization of bibliographic descriptions,[51]
but others are concerned that standardization can be carried to excess. One
danger of excessive standardization is conflict with the principle of user
convenience. Cutter wrote that

> strict consistency in a rule and uniformity in its application sometimes lead to prac-
> tices which clash with the public's habitual way of looking at things. When these
> habits are general and deeply rooted, it is unwise for the cataloger to ignore them,
> even if they demand a sacrifice of system and simplicity.[52]

Prophetically he observed that "no code of cataloging can be adopted in all
points by everyone,"[53] an observation echoed fifty years later by J. C. M.
Hanson: "Should an international code ever become a reality, many librarians would refuse to subscribe to it in its entirety."[54]

A second danger of standardization carried too far is that the reasons
and principles underlying a bibliographic code become obscured. Andrew

D. Osborn argued this point, using the term *legalistic* to damn a code that attempts to include rules and definitions to govern every point that arises.[55] Lubetzky did as well, finding himself unable to "view with equanimity the continuous proliferation of the rules, their growing complexity, and the obscurement of the objectives and design of the code as a whole." This led him to ask his riveting question: "Are all these rules necessary? are all the complexities inevitable? is there an underlying design which gives our code unity and purpose?"[56] To which his answer was that cataloging should be done by principle rather than by a slavish following of rules. Paul Dunkin in his *Cataloging U.S.A.*, a history of Anglo-American cataloging, relates how over the years the pendulum has swung between the opposing forces of legalism (the law, as represented by Jewett) and romanticism (the prophets, as represented by Cutter, Osborn, and Lubetzky).[57]

A third danger of overstandardization is its tendency to inhibit change. Bibliographic change is necessarily conservative. Where technological, political, and economic forces make change seem desirable, expense of money, spirit, and effort is often sufficient to counter it. For example, while it might be desirable to modify the present MARC format to make it more suitable for communicating bibliographic information and for database design, so entrenched is this standard, so hard-won through years of cooperative effort, that to set in motion the elaborate and time-consuming political mechanisms needed to effect a major change is hardly an option. Where changes to bibliographic codes and formats are introduced, they are normally minimal and incremental, which sometimes leads to sacrificing conceptual consistency for a quick Band-Aid fix.[58]

Given that standardization in bibliographic description can be excessive, the question arises of how to limit it — how to determine just which aspects of description need to be standardized. Ron Hagler suggests limiting standardization to only those aspects that are essential for the identification of works and documents. While the rules governing these should be prescriptive, those governing other aspects of description could well be discretionary.[59] The suggestion has merit, not the least because it can be acted on, since it is in fact possible to ascertain those data elements essential for identification.[60]

One aspect of bibliographic description that does not require standardization in the traditional sense has already been mentioned. This is the standardization achieved by normalizing of names for works, authors, and subjects. Whereas in a card-catalog environment, normalization required the choice of one authoritative name, in an digital environment, transparent linking allows authorized names to be replaced by compatible names.[61] This does not mean that rules for normalizing can be dispensed with entirely but only that different rules are needed to ensure a uniform practice. In any case, the principles of standardization and common usage need no longer conflict. Insofar as universalism in any endeavor is furthered by the preservation of diversity, standardization that does not abrogate the need for local variation is a giant step forward in universal bibliographic control.

Integration

The principle of integration is a directive to use a common set of rules for all media, with exceptions being made only for material-specific attributes. Both the principle of standardization and the principle of integration mandate uniformity in description — the former across space and time and the latter across material type. Uniformity in describing bibliographic entities, irrespective of the medium in which they are embodied, is desirable for several reasons: it serves the objectives of the catalog, particularly the collocating objective; it serves user convenience in providing a common interface to bibliographic information; and it serves the principle of parsimony in achieving economy of expression.

Since Panizzi's time, descriptive codes have had to deal with documents in some way out of the ordinary — for example, those using typography other than alphanumeric characters, such as musical notation, or those not packaged in book form, like a single map. For documents such as these, special rules had to be developed. Panizzi and Cutter both sought the help of experts to develop rules for music materials. In the 1940s and 1950s, the Library of Congress also turned to specialists to draft rules for its growing collections of motion pictures, sound recordings, and pictures. The Library of Congress rules proved difficult to use and, as a result, were rejected by most school and public libraries. This led to a proliferation of locally developed manuals to describe nonbook materials, simultaneously abrogating the standardization principle and that of integration.

Early in the 1970s reaction set in, and a swing began away from specialization and toward integration. Committees first in Canada and then in

England and the United States began to formulate rules for nonbook materials that would be compatible with those used for books. As might be expected, some opposition to this was voiced, with one critic complaining that "what was good for monographs and serials suddenly seemed equally desirable for cartographic materials, old or rare books, music and nonbook materials in general."[62] Particularly strong opposition came from the Association for Educational and Communications Technology, which, though it has since come round somewhat, still today favors an anti-integration stance.[63] Despite the opposition, the drive toward integration gathered steam, culminating in the early 1980s with the publication of *AACR2*, which was hailed as "a major breakthrough" in integration.[64] Belief that integration was a good thing elevated it to a principle.

The attempt to extend a bibliographic language originally designed to describe documents in one medium to encompass all media tests the theoretical soundness of the language. The language becomes strained as problems are encountered and its flexibility is challenged. Some problems are relatively easy to solve. The fact that nonbook entities lack authoritative sources of information such as title pages is a problem; but (as has been seen) means for designating title-page substitutes can be devised. The fact that many nonbook entities lack titles is a problem;[65] but this can be dealt with by generalizing already existing rules devised for books that lack titles. The fact that many nonbook entities require special equipment to be experienced is a problem; but it can be handled by requiring technical specifications and summaries in bibliographic descriptions.

Problems not easy to handle in generalizing a book-oriented language are definitional in nature. The definitions of *publication* and *publisher* are examples of this. The concept of *publication* may be extended beyond its traditional connotation of formal publication to its broader etymological meaning of "to make public" and that of *publisher* to "any release agent." However, doing so results in the loss of useful distinctions, spawns difficult-to-decide cases, and causes inconsistencies. Take the case of electronic documents. The *International Standard Bibliographic Description for Electronic Resources (ISBD(ER))* considers these to be published.[66] But it is a question whether they are any more "made public" than manuscripts and original works of art, which, though they may be viewed by many people, are not technically published.

As for the concept of publisher, when defined broadly it assumes a chameleon quality. For instance, if an electronic document is not identified as having a formal publisher (in a traditional sense), the author, regarded as "release agent," might be taken as publisher; if the same document happens to bear not only the author's name but also that of a distributor, then the distributor might be taken as publisher; if the same document bears the name of the author, distributor, and also that of a publisher — well, of course, the publisher is the publisher. But when the concept of publisher varies with what happens to be written on the document, it begins then to lack intrinsic meaning.[67]

Even more serious are the definitional problems attaching to the concepts of work and edition. The difficulty of interpreting these concepts for nonbook materials (discussed in chapter 3) is the kind that strikes at ontological commitment and shakes theoretical foundations. If it is not clear how these concepts are to be defined, then it follows that it is not clear what is meant by the bibliographic objective that calls for bringing together the various editions of a work. In other words, it is not clear what it is that is supposed to be organized.

The concept of author is also problematic in translating a book language to a multimedia language. For the century and a half since Panizzi, it has been assumed that users search for information by author. However, this assumption is not valid for many nonbook materials, particularly those of mixed authorship that involve numerous people performing different kinds of functions. In the creation of moving-image materials, for instance, many people are engaged in a variety of artistic and intellectual roles, no one of whom is an author in the commonly understood sense. For these and other nonbook materials, the concept of author wobbles, and when this happens, so too does the objective that requires collocation by author. When in a theory something as high-level as an objective begins to lose some of its universality, then the foundation of that theory begins to crack.

It is possible that the definitional problems raised by nonbook materials are serious enough to tilt the integration-nonintegration balance back toward nonintegration. An indication that this may be happening is another acceleration in the publication of manuals for nonbook materials. While these purport to be interpretations of the *Anglo-American Catalog Rules*, second edition, revised *(AACR2R)*, they clearly extend its reach. It remains to be seen whether this phenomenon is significant enough to represent a move away from a common bibliographic language that integrates rules for documents in all media, to a family of loosely related, medium-specific languages.

The principle of integration, like the principles of user convenience, representation, sufficiency and necessity, and standardization, functions as a directive guiding the construction of bibliographic languages. Principles direct in the sense of providing a rationale for design decisions. Other things being equal, where there are design alternatives, one that references a principle is to be preferred to one that does not. But this is obvious — a textbook maxim. Frequently other things, notably costs, are not equal, and frequently one principle vies with another in decision making. The following chapters on the design of specific languages illustrate conflicts of this sort and provide additional examples of how principles function — their usefulness, viability, and internal conflict — in bibliographic description.

6

Work Languages

Introduction

The first part of this book has dealt with generalities relating to the intellectual foundation of information organization: the entities that are organized, the principles and objectives of the organization, and the bibliographic languages used to effect it. The second part looks at how traditional bibliographic languages build on this foundation. The present chapter deals with work languages, which are used to identify and structure information. Chapter 7 deals with document languages, which are used to describe particular space-time embodiments of information. Chapters 8 through 10 deal with the subject languages used to characterize the content of information.

Attributes

Chief Attributes of Information
Work languages describe information entities, their intellectual (as opposed to physical) attributes, and relationships among them. Consider first attributes: These include their subjects, their titles, the persons or corporate bodies responsible for their creation, the date and context of their intended audience, the symbolisms they use to communicate information (such as lexical, musical, or graphic), and the senses required to receive the information (visual, aural, tactile, or a combination). Aside from the subject attribute, which is discussed in later chapters, the most salient of these from the point of view of identifying and structuring information are nominal attributes — those that name works and their creators, whether authors or corporate bodies.[1]

Controlled versus Uncontrolled Vocabulary

Traditional work languages use two types of expressions to name attributes: (1) those that are derived as-is from documents containing information and (2) those that are assigned. The former use *uncontrolled vocabulary*; the latter use *controlled vocabulary*. The former by using the natural language of documents ensure that bibliographic descriptions accurately represent the documents they purport to describe. The latter are constructs in an artificial language; their purpose is to map users' vocabulary to a standardized vocabulary and to bring like information together. This standardized or controlled vocabulary consists of normalized expressions used as access points in bibliographic searching, such as names of persons and corporate bodies and titles.[2]

The effect of using two kinds of vocabulary, controlled and uncontrolled, is that a given attribute, such as an author's name, may be represented in a description in two forms: in a normalized form and in the form in which it appears on a document. Frequently these forms are the same, but when they differ, they are differently fielded in bibliographic records formatted using the International Standard Bibliographic Description (ISBD) or Machine Readable Cataloging (MARC) formats, uncontrolled name forms are put into descriptive fields and tagged as descriptive data elements, while controlled name forms (called *entries* or *access points*) are put into organizing fields and tagged as organizing data elements. While this may seem redundant, the dual representation serves to facilitate two different approaches to information: a keyword approach useful for identification and finding and a controlled-vocabulary approach required for collocation.

The collocation objective requires vocabulary be controlled. If names are not normalized, there will be precision and recall failures in retrieval. A precision failure is caused by a name that is not distinctive — for example, a search on John Smith will retrieve citations by many different authors. A recall failure occurs when an author writes under more than one name — for example, a search on Mark Twain will not retrieve documents in which the author is represented as Samuel Clemens. Vocabulary control involves both rendering names like John Smith distinctive and linking related names like Mark Twain and Samuel Clemens.

Vocabulary control is the *sine qua non* of information organization. Information is not organized if it is scattered or if its collocation is cluttered. A natural language cannot be used to organize information effectively because its synonymy and homonymy would cause scatter and clutter. Vocabulary control controls for synonymy and homonymy by normalizing names of attributes and entities. It is the means by which a one-to-one correspondence is established between terms and their referents. The imposition of vocabulary control creates an artificial language out of a natural language. Traditionally, the work of imposing vocabulary control is done in three steps: the first step is to choose an authoritative form of name; the second is to disambiguate the name — that is, to render it distinctive, if it is not already; and the third is to map the authoritative name to other variant names for the same entity.[3]

Choice of Names: Common Usage

Personal Names

The choice of a normalized name for a person (called also an *authoritative* name or a *uniform heading*) is guided by the principle of common usage. The Anglo-American Cataloging Rules (AACR) rule is to choose the name that is commonly known.[4] Subrules address the question of what is meant by *commonly known*. If possible, the commonly known name of a person or body is to be determined from publications of the works of that person or body.[5] Where this cannot be ascertained — for example, when the medium of the work is an art form — the commonly known name is the one that is used in reference sources. If this approach should also fail — for example, when more than one name is used in a reference source or the person is not represented in a reference source — then the latest name is chosen. As the principle of parsimony favors this last approach, it is sometimes taken without first consulting reference sources.

Names of Corporate Bodies

For a corporate body, the choice of an authoritative name form is governed by the principle of common usage, and again the common usage name is interpreted to be the name appearing on publications issued by the body in its language and, when this fails, the name found in reference sources. Often publications of a corporate body refer to the body by variant forms of a name or by variant names. When this happens, special rules must be formulated to establish a common usage. These can be quite elaborate, as in the case of naming a local church, where the first choice of a name is that "of the person(s), object(s), place(s), or event(s) to which the local church . . . is dedicated or after which it is named."[6] The second choice is "a name beginning with a word or phrase descriptive of a type of local church."[7] The third choice is "a name beginning with the name of the place in which the local church . . . is situated."[8]

Titles

Though theoretically required, variant titles of a work are not always normalized. An example is a revision or updating of an edition in the same language as the original but bearing a different title. *Scandinavia* and its updated revision *The United States and Scandinavia* are not related by vocabulary control using a uniform heading. Another example is a print and an electronic version of a periodical, such as *The Engineering Index* and its online version known as *Compendex*. Cases like these are already now too numerous to be regarded as anomalies. They present obstacles to information organization, which requires the use of work identifiers to collocate entities with the same information content.[9]

When titles are normalized, common usage is again the arbiter. Here common usage is interpreted as the original-language title by which the work has become known through publication or in reference sources. A problem with this in that such a title most probably would not be known to someone searching for the work in a language other than the original — for instance, the English speaker confronting the editions of Tchaikovsky's *Sleeping Beauty* collocated under *Spîashchaîa Krasavitsa*. The use of an original-language title as the uniform title is a result of an international compromise agreed to in the interest of furthering standardization on a global level. However, as earlier noted, while the principles of common usage and standardization conflict in a card-catalog environment, this need not occur in a digital environment where transparent mappings and custom tailored displays are possible.

Disambiguation of Names: Added Elements, Context, and Syntax

Personal Names

Choosing one name as authoritative and mapping alternate names to it frequently is all that is needed for vocabulary control. However, where the chosen name is not distinctive, further action needs to be taken. The way that a work language disambiguates such names is to add elements to them to make them distinctive. The rules used to do this include vocabulary-selection rules to select qualifying elements and syntax rules to specify the order in which the elements are to be added. The AACR disambiguation rules run a gamut of complexity. The most frequently used is the simplest. It prescribes the use of birth and death dates following the name. Thus, Smith, John, 1837–1896 is a well-formed expression in the AACR language.[10]

Qualification by birth and death dates usually, but not always, suffices to render personal names distinctive. For instance, in the Harvard Library catalog of 1995, there are 806 records describing works by Smith, John.[11] For names like this, fairly elaborate disambiguation rules are needed. AACR suggests adding to the name qualifiers such as occupation, term of address, title of position or office, initials of an academic degree, or initials denoting membership in an organization. But other qualifiers might be used as well. In an interesting case of automation, the various instances of Smith, John in the Harvard catalog were distinguished by an algorithmic syntax using as qualifying elements title of work, date, language, and country of publication.[12]

Names of Corporate Bodies

To render the name of a corporate body distinctive, it must first be perceived as being nondistinctive. AACR aids this perception by enumerating types of names considered to be nondistinctive, such as a name that begins with the word *Department*. Nondistinctive names of corporate bodies may be disambiguated by either of two methods: by adding elements to them as qualifiers or by embedding them in a distinguishing context. With the first method, the usual qualifying element is place, such as Esso Refinery (Fawley, England). However, other types of qualifying elements are appended as well, even "what it is" — such as Bounty (Ship). When several elements are added, syntax rules come into play to create faceted headings — such as International Conference on the Biology of Whales (1971 : Shenandoah National

Park). With the second method of disambiguation, that of context embedding, the context used is the name of the higher body to which the nondistinctively named body is subordinate — such as United Kingdom. Royal Navy.

Disambiguation is performed only when the common form of a personal or corporate name lacks discriminating power. It can happen that a common name is an abbreviation of a fuller form, such as Eliot, T. S. In a large database, Eliot, T. S. may not be distinctive, but Eliot, Thomas Stearns likely would be. This raises the question whether in a digital environment, where keyword and truncated searching are the norm, use of a full name as the normalized form might not serve the common usage principle with less effort and to better effect.[13]

Titles

Many works may have identical titles, such as *Introduction to Biology,* and no formal measures are taken to disambiguate them. To do so would be expensive, and it can generally be assumed that these titles, when postcoordinated at the time of retrieval with the normalized names of their associated authors, will satisfy the precision requirement of collocation. But not all titles can be disambiguated by this natural default method. The problems come with works that have nondistinctive titles and also no obvious authors. Here formal measures are required. Three situations where AACR disambiguates titles on a regular basis are for serials, music materials, and the Bible.[14] For serials, the process is relatively simple, because it is usually sufficient to qualify by place — Time (Chicago, Ill.). For musical works, many of which have common titles, such as *Sonata* or *Trio,* qualification is so complex as to require several pages of vocabulary selection and of syntax rules. The vocabulary elements may include some or all of type of composition, instrumentation, medium of performance, key, serial and opus numbers, year of composition, and year of original publication. For instance, a Mendelssohn trio might be identified as Trio, piano, strings, no. 2, op 66, C minor. Equally complex is the disambiguation of titles of books of the Bible. Here qualification is achieved through context-setting elements, such as Bible. N.T. Corinthians. English. Authorized.

The addition of distinguishing elements to titles, particularly as this becomes increasingly formulaic, may sometime go beyond what is needed to render them unique. The additional elements are introduced to serve other functions, such as naming editions and ordering them in work displays. With the supplanting of intelligent filing of bibliographic records by machine filing, it is painfully evident that a new device must be found to order editions in display. Formulaic titles, which can fool computers into filing sensibly, may be the answer. However, the use of one device to serve multiple functions (to disambiguate and to order), while favored by the principle of parsimony, nevertheless introduces a lack of flexibility that can become an obstacle as technology changes.[15]

Mapping of Names: Semantics

Mapping Personal Names

The third step in vocabulary control is to *map* the variant names, which users might use as search terms, to authorized names. Variant and authorized names have the same referent; they are semantically related in the sense of being equivalent in meaning. The setting up of equivalence relationships between variant and authorized names of an author is one of the basic mechanics of information organization. It is the means by which the language of the user and that of a retrieval system are brought into sync and the means by which everything written by that author is brought together. Traditionally, equivalence relationships have taken the form of *See* references pointing from variant to authorized names, such as Clemens, Samuel *See* Twain, Mark. The use of a *See* reference obliges the user who searches for information using a variant name to formulate a second search using the authorized name. The inconvenience has been seen as justifiable, a price exacted for organizing information by author — at least in a nonautomated environment.

Identity problems can arise when trying to establish equivalence relationships between variant and authorized names. Mark Twain is the same person as Samuel Clemens; but what about Lewis Carroll, the author of *Alice in Wonderland,* and Charles L. Dodgson, the author of books on mathematics? In reality these refer to the same person, but are they identical from a bibliographical point of view? For more than a century the answer to this question was yes, but this changed with the publication of the *Anglo-American Cataloging Rules,* second edition, revised *(AACR2R)* in

1988. Now the two names are construed as referring to separate bibliographic identities. While this serves user convenience in obviating two-step access, it separates the works of Carroll-Dodgson in display. The two names, Carroll and Dodgson, formerly linked by a *See* reference under the old policy are now linked by a *See also* reference. The *See also* reference, like the *See* reference, is a semantic relationship, but rather than linking names equivalent in meaning, the two references link names that are associated in the sense that they name a single person's different bibliographic identities.[16]

Mapping of Corporate Body Names

The concept of a corporate body simultaneously having two names, let alone two or more separate bibliographic identities, has never been entertained. The use of a different name by a corporate body, other than a form, foreign language, or abbreviation variant, has always triggered a change of identity. Thus, while corporate bodies cannot simultaneously have different identities, they can have former and later identities. These have to be linked. The linking semantics used is like that used for names of persons: *See also* references link former and later names, while *See* references link variant forms of name. The latter can become complicated, especially where a corporate body is hierarchical in nature (such as a division of a department of an agency of a government) and has a variant name form at each hierarchical level.[17]

Mapping Titles

When a work is assigned a uniform title, how the mapping of variants to this uniform title is done depends on whether the work has an obvious author. Where there is no obvious author, the linkage is indicated simply by including the uniform title as an organizing element (added entry) in the description of the document that bears a variant title. Its presence is enough to establish the link. Where the work has an obvious author, the linkage of variant titles is indirect. It is done using what are traditionally called *name-title* references: a *See* reference links the variant title coupled with the author's name to the uniform title coupled with the author's name. In other words, instead of linking variant and authorized titles, variant and authorized names of works are linked. (Names of works are discussed in the next section.)

Entities

Like attributes, the *entities* referenced by a bibliographic language must be given unique and unambiguous names. In database modeling the normalized names of entities are called *identifiers*. A bibliographic language assigns identifiers to those information entities that are defined in terms of intellectual content: superworks, works, and editions. These further the objectives of information organization. Identifiers are designed

- To bring together all members of a superwork, work, or edition set;
- To serve as sort keys in creating displays of bibliographic descriptions;
- To serve as nodes to relate superworks, works, and editions;
- To serve as primary access points in retrieval.

Work Identifiers (Work IDs)

From the point of view of collocation the most important metadata used in bibliographic description are work identifiers. How to construct work IDs is a problem that has claimed the attention of some of the best minds in cataloging and one that has been misunderstood by many. Normally, the AACR author-title language identifies authored works using expressions consisting of the normalized name of the author followed by the normalized title of the work. Where a work has no obvious author, its ID is its normalized title.[18]

Work identifiers were introduced in the nineteenth century in the form of *main entries*. The definition of *main entry* is surrounded by confusion and controversy.[19] Defined in terms of what it refers to, it can denote

- A description of a document, in particular its full description (a meaning that is now obsolete);
- The attribute of a document by which it is most often accessed, its so-called *main access* point, such as a person, corporate body, or title.
- A work, which is designated either by a normalized name title or by a normalized title.

It is in this last use that the main entry serves as a work ID.

There are a number of reasons that work IDs should be constructed as they are — why, for instance, they sometimes consist of a composite attribute and sometimes of a simple attribute and why if they are a composite attribute, the lead element is an author's name. A composite attribute is used because often no single attribute suffices to identify a work uniquely. Authors write numerous works, and titles are often not distinctive. The author-title combination, once these elements are normalized, has proven to be effective as an identifier in databases numbering millions of records.

The reason that a composite main entry should be constructed with the lead element being an author's name relates to what a main entry should be and do. According to A. H. Chaplin and A. Domanovsky, the main entry should honor tradition, respond to users' expectations, and promote catalog consistency.[20] The use of the author as the lead element meets the first two of these conditions. The concept of authorship has occupied a position of centrality in the Anglo-American cataloging tradition. Moreover, empirical evidence supports the belief that users search for known items — that is, items for which they have citations — by author.[21] A further reason for using an author's name as the lead element in work IDs is the efficiency achieved by an identifier that can do double duty toward achieving catalog objectives by bringing together not only all editions of a work by an author but also all of that author's works.

The composite author-title work ID has not gone unchallenged. Many works have no obvious authors, many authors, or authors of a mixed or diffuse nature. Such works are given title IDs. The challengers ask, Why should there be two ways of doing something: author-title IDs for some and title IDs for others? Would it not simplify normalization rules, especially those relating to authorship determination, to use title IDs for all works, and would this not also promote greater catalog consistency (the third of Chaplin's and Domanovsky's specifications)? Also the assumption that users expect to find works by their authors is challenged. One argument is that the evidence amassed to support this belief is biased toward Western users.[22] Another is that with the emergence in the second half of the twentieth century of increasing numbers of publications by corporate bodies and in nonbook formats, authorship conditions have become so complex that increasingly works are identified and searched for by their titles. The challenges, however, have not been sufficient to overturn the composite author-title ID, one reason being that title IDs are not an acceptable alternative. Not only would the uniform use of title IDs flout user expectations where works do have clearly identifiable authors, but it would ignore the collocation objective that mandates that all works by a given author be displayed together. Also, and not inconsequentially, it would entail making untold numbers of title disambiguation rules that would equal in complexity those presently used to determine main entry.

Work IDs are intended to serve as the chief access points by which works are sought. However, works may be sought under different access points as well, such as secondary authors or variant titles. As with names of persons and corporate bodies the alternative points of access need to be controlled. Again, the method of doing this is through *See* references. Where a work ID is a title, a *See* reference maps variant titles to it. Where a work ID is a composite author-title attribute, *See* references map to it expressions consisting of the author's name coupled with variant titles of the work.[23]

Edition Identifiers

Theoretically, each subclass of a work set formed by intellectual attributes (here called *editions*) should be given a unique ID. However, because they are costly to create, edition IDs are supplied only where there is an explicit need

? cost

- To present in display an orderly sequence of the editions of a work,
- To bring together in display all manifestations of an edition, or
- To relate an edition of a work to another bibliographic entity.

For many editions, such a need does not arise or at least is assumed not to arise.[24] It tends to arise for works that are translated, such as *The Iliad,* and for editions of works with multiple manifestations, such as editions of the Bible. In cases like these, edition IDs are created by attaching elements to the uniform titles for the works. For example, the work identifier for *The Iliad* is Homer. Iliad. Identifiers for different language editions are Homer. Iliad. English; Homer. Iliad. French; Homer. Iliad. German; and so on. For a book of the Bible, the add-ons used to create edition IDs are first a language qualifier, such as English, and then a version identifier, such as Revised Standard.[25]

The uniform title is a conveniently ambiguous device. For the most part, it serves as a normalized work title. When a normalized work title is supplemented by an add-on it may be used to identify editions or even publications.[26] Functioning in an altogether different role, a uniform title is used to bring together the collected works of an author, such as Works, Selections, Chamber music. As observed earlier, the use of a single device to

perform multiple functions can make for difficulties in times of technological change, when a new way is found to perform one of the functions but
not the others.

Frequently, an edition of a work is represented by only one publication
— that is, a subclass of a work defined in terms of intellectual conditions
coincides with a subclass defined in terms of publication conditions.
Normally, publishers and cataloging agencies assign ID numbers to publications in the form of international standard numbers, such as International
Standard Book Numbers (ISBNs), International Standard Serial Numbers
(ISSNs), and International Standard Music Numbers (ISMNs). When editions and publications coincide, such numbers could serve a dual function
as both edition and publication IDs. However, the coincidences are unpredictable; moreover, the assignment of standard numbers, particularly by
publishers, is often too casual to permit their being used to organize information effectively.

Superwork Identifiers

A *superwork* is defined as the set of all documents deriving from an ur-
work.[27] Identifiers are needed to construct derivative relationships and to
collocate the subsets of a superwork. However, there is no need to create
special identifiers for superworks; the work identifiers, which they already
possess, suffice for the purpose of structuring bibliographic relationships.

Relationships

While the relationships that hold between vocabulary elements in a bibliographic language are semantic in nature, those that hold between bibliographic entities, such as works, editions, and superworks, hold by virtue of
having related information content. AACR functioning as an author-title
language depicts these relationships through different types of description
and by different devices.[28] First the devices:

• *Work IDs*   When describing a document *a* a citation is made to the ID
of the work it manifests *A,* a relationship is established between the document and the work: *a* is a member of *A*. An identifier is "cited" when it is
used as an organizing element in a description. In card-catalog descriptions
it is cited by being placed at the top of the description as a heading, either
a main entry or an added entry heading. In MARC-formatted descriptions

it is cited by being tagged as an access point in an organizing field. By pointing to the ID for a work *B* in the description of a document *a* manifesting *A*, a relationship (R) is established between *A* and *B*. The ID for *B* is placed in an organizing field. When the nature of the relationship (R) is not indicated by the pointer, it is shown in a note.

• *Notes*   A note in the description of a document may be used to show work-work or edition-edition relationships. A note may be formal — as in a schematic contents note, a series note, or a note showing the relationship among serial titles — or it may be informal. A note indicating relationships may be used alone or in tandem with related work IDs. In its latter use it serves to explain why a related work ID is included as an organizing element (such as an added entry) in a given bibliographic description.

• *Formal linkages (called* linking entries)   A formal statement may be included in the description of a document *a* to show the relationship that the work it manifests *A* bears to another work *B*. Brief, coded descriptions are given of the members of the relationship — that is, *A* and *B* — and of the type of relationship (R) that holds between them.

• See also *references*   A *See also* reference is used to point from a given work to a related work. When this is done, usual practice is to create descriptions in the form of work (authority) records for the pointing and target works.

• *Codes*   Coded information in a bibliographic description may be used to state a relationship (such as a reprint code) or the nature of a relationship (for example, that a sequential relationship is one of continuation).[29]

In addition to the above devices, AACR employs different types of description to show bibliographic relationships:

• *Emblematic description*   Emblematic description is the description of an individual item as standing in for or representing a set of equivalent items. For instance, the title appearing on the book in hand used as the basis of description is at the same time the title of all copies of this book, that is, a publication. Descriptions may be emblematic not only of publications but also of larger inclusive sets, such as editions and works. That is, they may reference (in addition to publication-specific data) elements that identify editions and works as well. By thus referencing entities other than the item in hand, bibliographic descriptions indirectly exhibit the hierarchical relationships that link publications, editions, and works.[30]

• *Hierarchical or multilevel description*   Certain relationships may be indicated by multilevel descriptions, wherein the highest-level entity is described in full and the items dependent on it are described only insofar as they are different. A classic case is the relationship between an original and a reproduction, such as between a book and a microfilm of it. Hierarchical or multilevel description may also be used to show part-whole and inclusion relationships, such as that between a set of maps and its individual members.

• *Analytic description*   Certain relationships, such as that between a part of a work and the whole, may be indicated by including in the description for the part a brief description of the whole subsuming it.

Relationships among bibliographic entities have been the object of considerable study since the publication of Tillett's dissertation in 1987.[31] They can be classified in a number of different ways. In this book, which takes a set-theoretic view of entities and relationships, they are classified as membership, inclusion, equivalence, aggregation, sequence, and commentary.

Membership

The *membership relationship* holds between an individual information entity and the sets to which it belongs: document set, edition set, work set, and superwork set. The inverse relationship that holds between a set and the items belonging to it is the *instantiation relationship*. Characterized in terms of its properties, the inclusion relationship is irreflexive, antisymmetrical, and intransitive.

The chief means by which membership is shown is by *emblematic description* — that is, the item is described as representative of the sets to which it belongs. In its description, the edition to which it belongs is indicated by an edition statement and the work to which it belongs by a work ID. The use of emblematic description obviates the need to construct explicit membership relationships of the form *a* is a member of *A*.

Inclusion

The *inclusion relationship* holds between a subset of an entity and the entity itself — for example, between an edition and a work and between a work and a superwork.[32] The relationship has the properties of transitivity, reflexivity, and antisymmetry. Its inverse, the relationship between a set and its subsets, is an *inheritance relationship,* which, when existing between a superwork and a work, is usually referred to as a *derivative relationship.*

The prototypical inclusion relationship — the one that forms the backbone of bibliographic hierarchy — is one that holds between an edition and the work it manifests. As noted above, AACR depicts this relationship by emblematic description: an item is described as representing a document, an edition, and a work. The inclusion in an item description of an edition statement and a work identifier suffices to establish an edition-work relationship. An edition is related to a work by the work-preserving relationships of revision, translation, or augmentation.[33] Which of these relationships holds in a particular case is explained in a note.

An alternative method for establishing edition-work relationships is through multilevel or hierarchical description. Using this method, top-level description is accorded to work attributes, and the succeeding levels to edition-specific and, if needed, document-specific attributes. Panizzi used such an approach in his catalog; Wilson argued for it as a means of prioritizing the objectives so that the collocating objective places first.[34]

Another of the backbone relationships that structure the bibliographic universe is the one that holds between a work and a superwork. A work is related to a superwork by relationships, such as being based on, being an arrangement of, being an adaptation of, or being a version of. Again, the usual means to indicate the relationship is emblematically, by including a superwork ID as an organizing element in the description of the item manifesting the work. For example, a description of *West Side Story* would include both a work ID for the musical and another for Shakespeare's *Romeo and Juliet*. The relationship that holds in a particular instance would be clarified in a prose note, such as a "based on" note.

Equivalence

An *equivalence relationship* holds between any two members of the same set. This relationship is reflexive, symmetric, and transitive. It is always defined with respect to set attributes. Thus, two items that manifest the same work are equivalent with respect to workhood or intellectual content, which is to say each is related to the same ur-work by a work-preserving relationship, such as identity, revision, or augmentation. Two items that manifest the same superwork are equivalent in the sense that each derives from the same ur-work by a superwork preserving relationship such as being based on, being an arrangement of, being an adaptation of, being a version of, and so on. Strictly, equivalence relationships hold between items; however, by extension they are regarded as holding between the sets to which they belong. Thus, it is said that two different editions are equivalent with respect to workhood when the members of each are members of the same work.

Normally, there is no need to indicate equivalence relations directly. These are apparent in bibliographic displays, engineered by work IDs, that bring together all editions of a work and all works of a superwork. There are situations, however, where this engineering is not applied and other devices are used to show equivalence. One such situation is the relationship between two same-language editions of a work, one of which is an updating of another. Here the relationship is shown in one by a note citing the other and explaining the type of relationship involved, such as *revised edition*. The notes act as pointers. Relating the successive editions of a work directly using pointers is an alternative to relating them indirectly by giving them the same work ID. This approach is similar to the AACR practice for linking serials that undergo name changes and to that used in the *Guidelines for Electronic Text Encoding and Interchange (TEI Guidelines)* language to link successive editions of a work.[35] While such an approach would complicate unduly the collocation of editions in a nonautomated environment, this would not be the case in a digital environment where, in fact, the usual means of showing relationships is through the use of pointers.

Aggregation

The *aggregation relationship* is the part-whole relationship. Again, in a strict sense, it holds between individual items but by extension is regarded as holding between the entities of which they are parts. Thus, "The Knight's Tale" in an individual copy of the 1958 Everyman's Library edition of *The Canterbury Tales* exists as a part occupying pages 26 to 82. Pages 26 to 82 in each copy of this edition can be regarded as a distributed part of the abstract edition entity. Aggregation relationships can be defined in terms of information content or in terms of physical description. The latter pertain to document, rather than work, languages and are discussed in the following chapter.[36] Defined in terms of information content, aggregation relationships normally hold between works, where one work is part of another. But they may hold as well between component parts of editions and the editions as a whole, such as a newspaper story published in one edition of a newspaper but not in another or a set of illustrations published in one edition of *David Copperfield* and not in another.[37] The inverse of the aggregation relationship is the component part relationship. The aggregation relationship is transitive; assuming an entity is not part of itself, it is asymmetric and irreflexive.

Of all bibliographic relationships, the aggregation relationship is the one most variously represented. How it is represented depends on a variety of factors, the most usual being the amount of money available and whether the basic bibliographic description is made of the aggregate or of the part or of both and whether the parts are integral or separate.

Description of the Aggregate

When the basic description is of an aggregate consisting of nonintegral parts that are separately authored and titled, such as a collection of short stories or musical compositions, the usual practice is to identify the parts informally in a note. When economically feasible, related work IDs are cited in the description of the basic item.[38]

When the basic description is of the aggregate and the parts are integral, such as a libretto for an opera or the illustrations for a children's book, the usual practice is to mention whatever needs to be said about the parts in the body of the basic description or in a note (*illustrations by* or *words by*) and, if economically feasible, to cite formally (by using normalized IDs) those responsible for the parts.

When a basic description is of the whole and the parts are separate with titles dependent on the title of the whole, as in the case of a kit or a computer program and a manual, the separate parts are simply mentioned in the basic description. Normally, these are not formally cited, and no provision is made for accessing them independently of the aggregates of which they are parts.

Description of the Part

When a basic description is of a part, such as a part of a monographic series or a multipart item, the usual practice is to include in the basic description a related work ID for the aggregate. There are two alternative practices. One, authorized by the MARC format but not in AACR, is to use formal linkages (linking entries) that point to the related work and specify the nature of the relationship.[39] The other is to make an analytic description consisting of data sufficient to identify the part and the aggregate — that is, the host work.[40]

Sometimes part-aggregate relationships are indicated by the use of *See* references made from the part to the whole. For instance, such a reference might point from an unused but potentially sought point of access — Tolkien, J. R. R. Lord of the Rings, 2, Two Towers — to the work ID for the comprehensive work — Tolkien, J. R. R. Lord of the Rings.[41]

Description of the Aggregate and Its Parts

When comprehensive descriptions are needed for both the aggregate and its parts, as is the case for some national bibliographies, hierarchical description may be used to show part-aggregate relationships.

Sequence

The *sequential* or *chronological relationship* is one that holds between some (but not all) entities loosely related in content but separated in time. Examples are a sequel to a novel, a supplement to a monograph, or a serial that is a continuation of another. The relationship is transitive, irreflexive, and asymmetric. It may be shown informally in a note or formally by citing the ID of the related work. In the case of serials, a practice of successive entry calls for showing the sequential relationship pointing in both directions. This involves using related-work IDs together with a note, in coded or natural language form, explaining the nature of the relationship, such as *continues* or *supersedes,* or *continued by* or *superseded by.*

The sequential relationship is also complex in the way it has been traditionally depicted. To begin with, it does not hold between all entities related in content but separated in time. Two different language editions of the same work, though one is created later than the other, are not viewed as related sequentially but as standing in an equivalence relationship with respect to workhood. Second, sequential relationships are sometimes indicated by stepwise pointing, as indicated above, and sometimes by collocation using entity IDs — for example, when two works in a series are related by citing a series ID. Here again similar relationships are constructed using different devices. The use of different devices to indicate a similar relationships is a potential problem in conceptualizing database design in an electronic environment.

Commentary[42]

The *commentary relationship* holds between a bibliographic entity and one or more other such entities. Examples are where one work is a manual for the use of, a preface to, a commentary on, a review of, an exegesis of, or a photograph of another. The commentary relationship is a type of subject or aboutness relationship. A scholarly work may comment on a particular work of an author or on his full opus. The entity commented upon need not be another work. It can be a particular edition of a work, such as a cataloging manual for the second edition of the *Anglo-American Cataloging Rules* or a review of a particular performance of *Tristan and Isolde*. The relationship is irreflexive, intransitive, and asymmetric.[43] It is shown either formally by citing a related-work identifier or informally in a note.

Relationships like attributes are inherited. If a commentary relationship holds between two works, by hierarchical force it holds between the respective editions of those works. A treatise on Beethoven's Fifth Symphony is related to the Fifth Symphony itself and also to the edition subsets of that work. However, a commentary on the third edition of *Fowler's Modern English Usage*, edited by R. W. Burchfield, is particularized to this edition, and what is said of it does not pertain to the first and second editions, even though these may be mentioned in the commentary.

Observation

To someone first looking at AACR as a work language, the manner in which it depicts bibliographic relationships must seem bizarre — so many ways of doing things, such inconsistencies, so many gaps. In part these faults may be attributed to the principle of parsimony. The construction of bibliographic relationships depends on an organizing intelligence to discover and set up relationships, and this is costly since it requires assigning formal IDs to the entities to be related. Another reason for AACR's lack of elegance in depicting relationships is tradition, with its ways of doing things dragged from book to card to online catalogs and accumulating, thus, a mixed bag of devices and techniques.

Bibliographic relationships already complex are likely to become more so in the digital future.[44] It is necessary to move with the times and to take advantage of new technologies in depicting relationships, but to do this without cleaning house and attempting to integrate new ways with the old can result in important relationships being overlooked or multiple ways of formulating a given relationship. The move from a book to a card technology introduced confusion into the relative roles of *See* references and added entries in depicting relationships.[45] It also undermined hierarchical structure by using emblematic description rather than filing rules to show edition-work relationships. The subsequent move from card to online catalogs weakened this structure even more severely by replacing intellectually designed filing rules with mechanical ones.[46]

However, despite its lack of system and method, traditional work languages, like the AACR, have achieved a certain ingenious economy of expression in depicting relationships in a nonautomated environment. In a digital environment, which favors uniform, formalized, and regular mechanisms, it succeeds less well. It could prove useful in the future to use the AACR language in conjunction with SGML-derived languages like the TEI language.[47] If compatibility of this sort is to be realized, however, steps need to be taken to regularize the means AACR uses to achieve its objectives, to ply apart multifunctioned means, and to eliminate those that are redundant. To do this would require formalizing the language to a greater degree than has been done heretofore, based on a rigorous analysis of its vocabulary, syntax, and semantics.

7

Document Languages

Introduction

The technological revolution has provided new means to achieve the objectives of information organization. It has forced a reconsideration of the form and function of bibliographic records. No less momentous is the impact it has had on the design of document languages, the languages used to describe information carriers. This chapter looks at these languages from the perspective of their purposes, the principles guiding their design, and the problems involved in their construction. Its bulk consists of a consideration of problems presented by the new media, particularly electronic documents.

A *document* is a particular space-time embodiment of information. Reviewing briefly: a *document language* describes and provides access to this embodiment. It is distinguished from a *work language,* which provides access to information in documents. Correlative to the document-work distinction are the distinctions between thought and its manifestation and between content and its carrier.[1] Thus, a document language can also be viewed as the language that describes and provides access to manifestations of works or carriers of information content.

Objectives and Principles
What makes a good document language? The answer to this question is ultimately referable to the objectives and principles of information organization as they pertain to documents, in contradistinction to works. These are

- To assist in finding a document,
- To assist in identifying a document,

- To assist in selecting a document,
- To assist in the acquiring of a document, and
- To assist in navigating among documents.

The foremost principle guiding the design of document languages is that of *integration* — that all documents, regardless of their material embodiments, be described in a uniform manner. Exceptions, however, must be made for material-specific attributes that pertain to the physicality of carriers. Clearly a CD-ROM does not have the same physical attributes as a book. However, a certain uniformity of conception can be achieved at the level of attribute types — all carriers can be described in terms of their size or extent, for example.

Another principle that guides the design of document languages is that of *sufficiency and necessity*. Descriptions should contain all and only those elements needed to meet the objectives for document description. Ideally, documents should be described so fully that users can select from among them without having to examine the documents physically. At the same time they should be parsimonious and contain only elements that are significant. An example of an insignificant datum is the width of a book, since given its height, its width is usually predictable. When it is not, such as when the width is greater than the height, then the datum becomes significant and is recorded. Attributes that can be assumed are not needed in retrieval and therefore do not belong in bibliographic descriptions.

Primacy of the Document

In the Anglo-American cataloging tradition, it is a cardinal rule that the starting point for bibliographic description should be the physical form of the item in hand.[2] Applying this rule sets up a one-to-one relationship between documents and the descriptions that are their surrogates.

Some argue that it is putting the cart before the horse to make the starting point for description the carrier of information rather than the information itself. Wilson, for instance, argues that because bringing like information together is the primary goal of bibliographic organization, description should begin with information and not with its documentary embodiment.[3] While the argument is persuasive and theoretically sound, it overlooks an important aspect of bibliographic practice. Libraries must account for *inventory*. The very earliest catalogs were inventory tools designed to keep track of valuable property housed in private libraries. Though today's catalogs have assumed the more elevated purpose of being bibliographic tools designed to meet user-oriented objectives, they have not shed entirely their original bookkeeping function. Books as well as other bibliographic entities continue to be valuable property, and some form of inventory control continues to be needed. It does not follow, however, that inventorying still requires a one-to-one relationship between items and their surrogates.

The inventory argument loses credibility when the objects to be described are electronic and available only by remote access. Yet even here the document continues to be the springboard for description. More than just the momentum of tradition accounts for this; there simply is no alternative. Disembodied information, like the grin of the Cheshire cat, cannot be grasped or retrieved. Only when it is delimited, in the sense of being packaged into a document, electronic or otherwise, does it become accessible, and only then is it a candidate for bibliographic description.

Attribute Types

The vocabulary elements used in a document language fall mainly into three categories — those that designate *physical or carrier attributes, publication attributes,* and *access attributes.* The first category includes medium and other physical attributes. The second comprises attributes associated with publication (such as publisher, place, and date) and also those associated with production and manufacture; for rare documents, it includes attributes associated with their ownership, release, or exhibition. The third category is different from the first two in comprising external access attributes rather than internal property attributes. Chief among these is location; included as well are attributes that condition access, such as use restrictions and hardware and software requirements.

Warrant and Normalization

The principle of accuracy requires that descriptions faithfully portray the entities they describe. In a work language this principle is served chiefly through *source warrant.* However, in a document language source warrant is only of limited use. This is because many relevant descriptive attributes, such as material characteristics and means of access, are supplied rather than derived; and so, while they need to be accurate, source warrant cannot be their guarantor. Important exceptions are attributes associated with publication or production, such as publisher and place and date of publication. As these data can be found in different places on a document and in different forms, consistency of description requires prescribing exactly where they can be taken from. For instance, for electronic resources, the prescribed source is a source internal to the resource as formally presented in a title screen, main menu, program statements, first display of information, the header to the file, a label, a home page, or other prominent place.

The vocabulary of document languages is normalized to the extent that it uses standardized expressions. Standard expressions are used by the Anglo-American Cataloging Rules (AACR) (viewed as a document language) for supplied data. The abbreviation *ill.*, for example, is used to indicate that a book contains illustrations. Standardized expressions, in the form of entity IDs, are used for most access addresses.[4] Formulaic, but not completely standardized, expressions are used to indicate access restrictions as well as hardware and software requirements.

Normalization in document languages does not, however, extend to constructing equivalence relationships among alternative ways of referring to an attribute, as it does in work languages. Full normalization is needed in the languages used to access information but not in those used to describe and access documents. The reason that document languages are normalized at all is for user convenience — bibliographic descriptions need to be easy to scan and their contents quickly intelligible — and for providing unique document addresses.

Physical and Material Attributes

Importance

Other things being equal, the way information is packaged determines its usefulness. A user looking for Dickens's *A Christmas Carol* will have a preference if offered a choice of a book, a sound recording, or an electronic document. In a recent study, A. Carlyle showed that physical format was the attribute first selected when users were asked to group documents by characteristics that would be useful for retrieval purposes.[5] Because of its importance in fulfilling the choice objective, AACR requires a general material designator to be placed in the beginning of a bibliographic description, immediately after the title proper. In this place of prominence, it serves the user as an early warning signal.

A document's material type also determines how it is handled in libraries. It affects its storage and the treatment given to it: a film that is nitrate-based, for example, must be housed in a special container and periodically refreshed. It also determines how a document is described, insofar as this requires the use of medium-specific rules: a book is measured by its length, and a sound recording by the diameter of its carrier and its duration. The need for special rules for special materials has been a significant determinant in the development of bibliographic languages in the second half of the twentieth century. The chapters in *AACR2R* that pertain to document languages are organized by medium, with each different format having its own chapter. Supplementing *AACR2R* are medium-specific manuals that deal with aspects of description peculiar to a single material type. The original MARC formats for encoding bibliographic descriptions were developed in disjoint and segregated fashion, a different manual being created for each format type. Thus, not only in the retrieval of information but also in the mechanics of its organization, material embodiment has an important role to play.

Classification by Medium
Given the role played by media in the organization of information, much depends on how they are classified. Several classifications exist and are being used concurrently. The AACR document language uses both a general and a specific classification of material types, which here are respectively referred to as a *format classification* and a *document-type classification.* The format classification uses twelve broad media categories: books, pamphlets, and printed sheets; cartographic materials; manuscripts (including manuscript collections); music; sound recordings; motion pictures and viderecordings; graphic materials; computer files; three-dimensional artifacts and realia; microform; serials; analysis (i.e., component parts). The document-type classification includes classes of specific materials, such as broadsides, portfolios, condensed scores, vocal scores, sound discs, sound track film, film loops, videodiscs, posters, slides, flipcharts, computer reels, and jigsaw puzzles. The *AACR2R* list of document types is somewhat skimpy

when compared to other lists. For example, the *Thesaurus for Graphic Materials* includes over fifty pages of terms denoting document types within the broad format of graphic materials.[6]

The AACR format classification breaks the rule that the categories created by a classification should be mutually exclusive. When this rule is broken, the result is a cross-classification which allows a given document to be classified in more than one category. An example of a document that would be cross-classified by the AACR scheme is an electronic document in serial form. Cross-classification causes problems. In the context of code design, the problem is having two sets of rules equally applicable to the description of a given document and not knowing which to use, such as the rules for electronic documents and those for serials.

In the late 1980s an effort was mounted to redress the faults caused by cross-classification in the MARC formats. Called *format integration*, it aimed to eliminate restrictions that made a given data element valid for only one type of material. A secondary aim was to eliminate ambiguities, redundancies, and inconsistencies in the treatment of different forms of material. The results of the integration effort consisted of little more than applying a few quick fixes. To determine which attributes to use in description, the integrated rules require first determining whether a document is basically textual or not. This is a hard call and skirts cross-classification somewhat arbitrarily — for example, a computer file is classified as "basically" nontextual. Also, in combining in additive fashion special rules for special media, the integrated rules introduce redundancy by requiring the same data element to be repeated in different fields. In other words, when two different sets of rules apply, both are applied.

Nevertheless, the format-integration solution may be as good as can be got. No attempt to impose system and method on what is by nature cross-classified can succeed wholly and still be practical. In theory a rigorous classification of media is possible. An example is a classification proposed by John Helmer, wherein media formats are classified first by the senses used for experiencing them, then by their dimensionality, and then according to whether they are dynamic or static.[7] Thus, a motion picture would fall into the category of documents that are visual, aural, two-dimensional, and dynamic. In addition to its rigor, a classification like this has the further virtue of being impervious to changing technology, which is to say it is able to accommodate whatever new medium might be invented and thus can never be outdated. But such a classification would be unsatisfactory on the grounds of nomenclature. It would result in categories with artificial names, which would abrogate the principle that a user should get what he wants by a name he knows. The names of formats as evolved by natural language reference different and sometimes multiple characteristics, such as terms indicative of

- The process or technique used in production (such as videorecordings),
- Publication type (serials),
- Type of control (archival collections),
- What is represented (cartographic materials), and
- What is seen and heard (moving images) or a type of graphic (musical scores).

Usage, Cutter observed, is the supreme arbiter,[8] and in the case of media classification it arbitrates against system and method. Because natural language resists being straitjacketed, it is not possible to create a nomenclature that is both rigorous in consisting of mutually exclusive categories and at the same practical in being user friendly.

Document types (indicted on bibliographic records by specific material designators) are subject to the same nomenclature and classification difficulties as those affecting formats. The names applied to specific document types often do not reflect physical or material characteristics but rather those of genre or function. This is exemplified in the *International Standard Bibliographic Description for Electronic Resources (ISBD(ER))* classification of electronic documents first into data, programs, or a combination of the two and then into types such as electronic games, electronic journals, and so on. Sometimes physical characteristics are inextricably mixed with genre characteristics in one name, such as broadsides.[9] For document types, as for general-format types, it is not possible to construct a classification that is both natural and whose categories are mutually exclusive. But it matters less, since it is seldom necessary to treat a document type in a unique fashion — for example, to describe it by one set of rules, to file it in a single location, or to assign it only one document-type descriptor.

Multiple Versions

The same information can be embodied in different carriers. In organizing information this fact needs to be brought to the attention of users. Present practice does this, approximately and derivatively, through the collocation of editions and works. Some catalogs in their displays present an orderly sequence of the different physical versions of a given work. (This is done by filing under terms indicative of format.) Most, however, leave it to the user to ferret out version information by searching sequentially through all manifestations of the work. Another method used to alert users to the existence of alternative carriers is to reference them in notes on bibliographic records. This method can be cumbersome, especially when separate records are made for each different carrier manifestation.

The present practice of conveying carrier information to users is not satisfactory in part because it employs different means to a single end but more seriously because it has given rise to the multiple-versions problem mentioned earlier. Simplifying somewhat, this is the problem of how to construct bibliographic records when the same information is manifested in different carriers. According to the cardinal rule that requires the starting point for description to be the item in hand, each different carrier or version of a work warrants a separate bibliographic record. Following this rule to the letter would require a new bibliographic record to be made every time a document is microfilmed, which, besides being expensive, would confuse the user by burgeoning catalogs with clusters of records so similar as to be difficult to distinguish.

A multiple-versions conference was convened in 1988 to reconsider the cardinal rule, and several proposals were advanced for redesigning the bibliographic record. One was to create a composite record for an edition, which would describe its intellectual content (its information) and then enumerate its different versions (the variant embodiments of that information). Another was to create a base record for a given intellectual content to which would be appended partial records for the various versions. The composite-records proposal has been adopted by most libraries for a limited number of document types, those like microforms that are clearly reproductions. But no general solution to the multiple-versions problem was reached.[10] This was a result of two stumbling blocks: (1) a difficulty in defining *version* (does a mono recording and the same recording remastered for stereo constitute the same or different versions?) and (2) a perceived difficulty in using and communicating integrated records in a network environment. The multiple-version problem is complex, and until its ramifications are understood, the conservative stand to maintain the traditional one-one relationship between documents and records is unassailable.

Physicality of Electronic Resources

Electronic resources are distinguished by whether they are local or remote. The former include those that are embodied in carriers, such as disks, cassettes, cartridges, and tapes. They are considered to have physical characteristics, while remotely accessed resources are not. Lacking physical characteristics, they are assumed, at least by *AACR2R,* to require no physical description. It is true that documents in electronic form lack tangibility: there is no physical object to be handled by the cataloger or the user. Nevertheless, there is a sense in which these documents have a physical dimension. The electronic signals that produce the images of characters on a computer screen must act on data in a magnetic or silicon storage medium. Hard disks and computer chips carry information just as do CD-ROMs, floppy disks, and digital tapes. That this is the case is recognized by International Standard ISO 690-2 for citing electronic documents, which uses a medium variable, specifying as possible values online, CD-ROM, magnetic tape, and disk.[11]

Physical Attributes Other Than Medium

It is clear that the medium in which information is embodied is useful for finding and selecting documents. Not so clear, however, is what other physical attributes might be worth mentioning in bibliographic descriptions. In the AACR document language terms indicative of "other physical attributes" are divided into those that designate

- *Extent of item*   The number of physical units an item contains, such as the number of pages in a book;
- *Dimensions*   Size in terms of height, diameter, gauge width, and so on;
- *Accompanying material*   Published-with resources — for example, a CD-ROM might be accompanied by a booklet describing its contents; and
- *Other physical details*   A miscellany category.

The extent and dimensions of the carrier in which information is packaged are attributes applicable to most document types. Usually data of this sort are easily obtainable, though sometimes the recording of them can be time-consuming, as in the case of a set of many maps in a series, each of which has to be measured. Insofar as extent and dimension attributes of documents affect inventory and how the documents are stored on shelves in libraries, they are of housekeeping use to librarians. Insofar as they determine selection (a small amount of information might be desired, for example) or ability to use (gauge width, for example, is dependent on the playback mechanisms available), they are helpful to patrons.

In determining the extent and dimensions of electronic documents, a distinction needs to be made between carriers and files. Carriers can be measured using conventional units, such as those used to describe sound tapes and CD-ROMs. The measurement of files is more problematic; a unit is needed that is both ascertainable and meaningful. *AACR2R* and the *ISBD(ER)* suggest as units simply files or records. The *Guidelines for Electronic Text Encoding and Interchange (TEI Guidelines)* suggest bytes, either the actual number or an inclusive range; words, sentences, or paragraphs; or blocks, disks, or tapes.

The category of accompanying materials is something of an anomaly in that terms in this category do not designate physical attributes. They identify physically separate pieces of information that come packaged with, but are subsidiary to, the item being described. Accompanying-materials information is useful for library inventory control and for user decision making at the time of retrieval. (A CD-ROM containing a computer program that comes with an instruction manual is preferable to one that does not.) For remotely accessed documents, the materials that accompany a focal document may be referenced by the document itself through hyperlinks, in which case they need not be indicated in its description.

The category of other physical details is miscellaneous and open-ended. Before the media explosion, when books were the primary carriers of information, terms in this category pertained largely to illustrative matter, such as the number of illustrations, whether they were colored, and, to a limited extent, what they depicted. With the extension of bibliographic description to nonbook media, this category has expanded to include the following:

• *For sound recordings,* speed, configuration of playback channels, tape configuration and playback, capture and storage data, reproduction characteristics;

• *For motion pictures,* type of color and sound, presentation format (such as wide screen) and configuration of playback channels, aspect ratio, and projection speed;

• *For graphics,* primary and secondary support materials; process used to produce the graphic (such as engraving), method of reproduction (blueprint), and medium (oil).

The assumption that electronic resources lack physicality has led to the corollary assumption that terms indicative of "other physical attributes" need not be included in their description. But this goes against integration. That an image moves, is in color, or is accompanied by sound is required metadata for other media — so why not for electronic media? (Surely it would matter to a surfer whether the images of waves hitting the California beaches were still or moving?) Actually both *AACR2R* and *ISBD(ER)* permit mention of the attributes of color and sound but not motion. However, these data are not recorded in the body of the description, as is done for documents in other media, but are relegated to a notes field. As has happened before in adaptations to accommodate new media, like information is scattered and only at some later date is brought together through integration or harmonization.[12]

It was suggested earlier that an ideal bibliographic record would be so full and accurate that a user would be able to determine the relevance of the document described without physically examining it. Such a record would indeed be ideal, particularly as access to information becomes increasingly virtual and browsing less of an option. On the other hand, some cap has to be put on descriptive sprawl, particularly where the choice objective is concerned. The principle of necessity favors parsimony and requires ample evidence that the physical attributes recorded in a description in fact serve the needs of more than just the occasional user.

Publication Attributes

Purpose
Place and date of publication and publisher's name are space-time attributes that locate documents in the bibliographic universe. As such they serve the finding and identifying objectives and, consequently, are of sufficient importance to be required in traditional citation practice. They are important for other reasons as well. Often a new publication of a work signals a new edition. Thus, publication attributes, which properly pertain only to documents, may at the same time serve as indicators of information content.

Publication attributes are the subject of study in the scholarly fields of textual, historical, and analytical bibliography. In the used-book trade, they are indicators of intellectual and economic worth.

Meaning of Publication

In a bibliographic description documents that are published need to be distinguished from those that are not. Broadly viewed, publication is a means of communicating information. *Publication* is an operation performed on information that makes it manifest by embodying it in documents, which are then made public. Traditionally, publication has entailed submitting a manuscript to a publishing house, where it is put through a variety of editorial, manufacturing, marketing, and distributing processes. A published document differs from one that is unpublished, in that the former exists in multiple copies and is widely distributed, whereas the latter (diaries, journals, letters, theses, legal documents, and so on) are one-of-a-kind documents whose audience is necessarily limited.

Extending the concept of publication beyond books requires some terminological adjustment. When extended to nonbook media like moving pictures, sound recordings, and three-dimensional artifacts, the concept is more appropriately called *production* or *manufacture*. When it is extended to one-of-a-kind (unpublished?) materials that are put on view or made available for circulation, a term frequently used is *release*. The different terminology is needed to reflect the different processes by which information is communicated.

Extending the concept of publication to electronic resources requires more than terminological revision. It requires stretching the meaning of the concept in a significant way. Documents like original manuscripts have traditionally been considered to be unpublished, even if displayed to the public in a museum. But these same documents digitized and made accessible through the World Wide Web are now considered to be published. Publication, once the province of established publishing houses, has with the advent of desktop publishing become everyone's province, as pervasive as free speech. The effect of this on bibliographical control is to dilute the meaning of the concept and thus its usefulness in information retrieval and organization.

Attributes of Publication

The problems encountered in identifying and recording the publication attributes of documents in bibliographic descriptions testify to the ingenuity and inventiveness of the publishing business. In the best of circumstances a document displays only one value for a given attribute variable — for example, the only date appearing on it is 1975. But often there may be no value, several conflicting values, values of different kinds (such as printing and copyright dates or even different copyright dates for different parts of the document), and values that change over time. Despite the variety, however, publication protocols have ensured a reasonable degree of system and method in the way attributes like date and place and publisher's name appear on documents — at least for most traditional book and nonbook media. The variety can be accommodated in bibliographic description without difficulty, but with the inconvenience of having to create many rules. (Variety is a begetter of rules, and code simplification will always founder on the complexities of the objects to be described.) When it comes to the new media, however, and particularly electronic resources, difficulties abound, and it is not clear what rules can be formulated to deal with them.

Publisher

Persons and agencies involved in making a document public include publishers, distributors, producers, manufacturers, and release agents. A *publisher* is a person or agency by whose authority a document is made public. A *distributor* is one from whom copies of a document can be obtained. A *producer* is the person or agency that finances a document, supervises its making, and makes it public. A *manufacturer* is the one who constructs it. And a *release agent* is one who makes an unpublished document available for circulation.[13] The names of some or all of these may appear in bibliographic descriptions.

Even for traditional materials it can be difficult to identify a publisher, as when a document is printed for W, under the aegis of X, supported by Y, and distributed by Z. Sometimes it is difficult to distinguish the publisher of a document from its originator or author. In the online environment identification problems are exacerbated. (Is the person or agency that maintains an Internet list considered to be a publisher?)[14] A Machine Readable

Bibliographic Information (MARBI) committee discussion paper suggests dividing the variety of people involved in the creating, organizing, and making accessible an electronic resource into two groups: producers and distributors.[15] It defines a *producer* as the person or agency who organizes the resource and is responsible for it as a whole. It defines a *distributor* as the one who makes an electronic document available online. It is not clear how often in the electronic environment these distinctions are actual, since frequently the same entity performs all the functions of authoring, producing, and distributing. Most difficult of all, perhaps, is not being able to tell, by looking at the names on a document, who does what. The publishers of online documents are not bound by the same protocols as their offline counterparts. It is not unusual for electronic documents to lack formal publisher statements. When this is the case, bibliographic guidelines suggest that an attempt be made, using internal or external evidence, to infer a publisher.[16] The ISO 690-2 guideline for citing electronic documents suggests that if a publisher is unknown to record instead a network address.[17] But this will not do for AACR-type description, which unlike citation description, must shoulder the burden of bibliographic control.

Place of Publication

Bibliographic control requires fixing a document in the bibliographic universe by its space-time coordinates. The space coordinate marks the place of its publication, production, or manufacture. Of the vagaries exhibited by place-of-publication data shown on documents, the two most common are that no place is shown or several places are shown. In the latter case, traditional practice records the first place and any subsequent place given prominence by layout or typography; further, if none of these is in the home country and a place in the home country is also present, that place is recorded as well. (The home-country clause, while serving the user, militates against standardization on an international level.) This is a problem that affects electronic resources as well, which may be published at mirror sites throughout the world. But for these the problem is further complicated by the fact that their addresses are subject to change over time.[18]

In the case where no place of publication appears on a document, bibliographic practice both for printed and remotely accessed electronic documents is first to attempt to infer it and, failing this, simply to record *s.l.* (*sino*

loco or "without place"). The difference is that for printed documents the use of *s.l.* is only occasional, but for electronic documents it seems to be commonplace. The inability to fix a place of publication undermines bibliographic control. A measure proposed to deal with the problem is to compensate with the address of a contact person. A MARC field (270) has been developed for this purpose.[19] The ISO 690-2 citation guidelines again propose using a retrieval address in lieu of missing publication data. From the point of view of bibliographic control, this solution would be acceptable were a retrieval address coincident with a publication address, but this is not always the case.[20]

Date of Publication

The *date* a document is published is generally understood to be the date of its release or transmission. For static documents (misleadingly called *monographs*), this date is usually ascertainable, but if not, it is approximated by a copyright date or inferred from internal or external sources. For ongoing documents, such as serials, the conventional treatment is, if the document has ceased publication, to record the dates of the first and last issued parts and, if the document is continuing, to indicate this by putting a hyphen after the date of the first issue.

Electronic documents of a continuing nature can be handled by conventional procedures for recording publication dates, again with the difference that the number of documents for which no data exist is disproportionately large. Cataloging guidelines differ as to what to do when publication dates are missing: whether other dates should be used, such as dates of creation or collection *(AACR2R)*, whether approximate dates should be used *(ISBD(ER))*, or whether dates should be omitted (Cooperative Online Serials Program (CONSER)). Actually, for many users the lifespan of a serial, electronic or printed, may be of no great importance; for the purpose of citation they need only to point to a particular fragment of an ongoing publication. (The ISO 690-2 requires date of publication, date of update, and date of citation.) However, for the larger purpose of bibliographic control, fixing a document in time by giving its birth and/or death dates, or approximations thereof, is mandatory.

The problems encountered in describing publication attributes are not new, but the emergence of electronic documents has increased their incidence and fixed attention on them. This is graphically illustrated in a model of publication types developed by Jean Hirons and Crystal Graham.[21] The model uses four dimensions to create publication–type categories:

- Static versus ongoing (this is a continuum, rather than an either-or distinction)
- Determinate versus indeterminate
- Intended to be complete in a period of time versus intended to be continued indefinitely
- Numbered versus unnumbered

With the digital revolution, the way documents are being distributed into the various categories of the model is changing. A website, for instance, falls into the category of a determinate single-part publication, a category that for most of the twentieth century included only loose-leaf publications of limited duration. The category of indeterminate single-part publications was once solely populated by printed serials but now includes online databases.

The changing nature of publication is being paralleled by a loss of bibliographic control. The vital statistics for an embodied piece of information are its progenitor, its birth and death dates, and where it is born. In the past publisher protocols could generally be relied on to provide these data. But such protocols are not forcing for publication on the Internet, where accountability and inventory control are not routinely matters of concern. However, to those whose job it is to keep up-to-date the diary of humankind, the diminishing ability of document languages to describe information embodiments is a serious matter of concern.

Access Attributes

A distinction is sometimes made between *intellectual access* and *physical access,* the former being access to information and the latter being access to the documents embodying it.[22] Intellectual access is provided by work languages; physical access by document languages. Document languages provide physical access to documents by specifying where they are located and the conditions required for their use.

Conditions of Use

Access to documents may be restricted because of *conditions* placed on their use or the hardware and software needed to experience them. Conditions placed on use include having to have a library card, pay an access fee, or use the document on site. Use may be denied because a document is valu-. able, fragile, classified, subject to library rights protection, out of circulation, or lost. Normally there is little need to state conditions of use in bibliographic records, since usually they are library specific and generally understood. The need arises only when restrictions are in some sense surprising, as in having to pay an access fee.

Technical access is a different matter. A century and a half ago, when the foundation of information organization was being laid, the various ways in which technology could affect access to information could hardly be imagined. Fifty years ago, when nonbook materials like motion pictures and sound recordings began to appear, the impact of technology on access was becoming apparent, but it was treated casually. Document languages indicated the need for special equipment by referring indirectly to the technology required for access in statements describing physical attributes, such as VHS, 8 millimeter, and CD-ROM. Today, with electronic media, this does not suffice; an explicit statement needs to be made of the hardware and software required to use information, such as model of computer, amount of memory, operating system and version, software, and peripherals.

Location

The most important information needed to obtain a document is its *location*. In the late nineteenth century, users seeking to obtain a book were given a library-shelf address in the form of a fixed location. The book *David Copperfield* might be assigned the address B347, which would designate the B alcove in the library (the alcove for English literature), the third section, fourth shelf, and seventh book. Such a system (it was argued) had the unique advantage of serving the user who memorized the location of a book and wished to find it in the dark.[23] Users today have to be somewhat more enterprising. They need to be familiar with many different kinds of document locators. These can be grouped by bibliographic domain into those that are used to locate documents or text segments

- Within other documents (analytic locators),
- On library shelves within a local library (shelf locators),
- In national and international libraries (library locators), and
- On the Internet (Internet locators).

Addresses to Text Segments

Book and periodical indexes, analytic bibliographic records, and finding aids are among the tools used to point to information segments within documents. The address information they supply varies "as needed." For a book index, all that is needed are page numbers. A periodical index requires, in addition to these, issue, volume, and number designations. An analytic record that describes a component part of a larger work needs to comprise all bibliographic data critical to identifying the host document, such as the normalized author and title of the work represented by the document as well as the edition, publication information, numerical designations, and page numbers. Finding aids used to locate segments of archival information can be quite elaborate. Generally they point to box locations and are based on locally created classifications that divide documents into fonds (broad sets of documents with the same provenance), which are successively further divided into subfonds, series, subseries, files, and items.

Addressing locations within an electronic document is complicated by the fact that pagination often is lacking. The ISO 690-2 for citing electronic documents advises authors to use pagination if it exists, to use an internal referencing system (such as host-specific designations like line, paragraph, section, or part numbers) if pagination does not exist, and, lacking these, at least to indicate the extent of the segment (such as 35 lines or approx. 12 screens).

Addresses on Library Shelves

When a document itself, and not a segment of a document, needs to be located and this document is housed in a local library, access is provided through a shelf address. For books and many booklike materials shelf addresses take the form of call numbers.[24] A call number for a document consists of a class number (such as a Dewey Decimal Classification number) to which is added a book number, the purpose of which is to individualize the address of that document within the class. A book number consists of coded information indicative of author and/or title and, if necessary, other data such as publication date. Unlike most other document addresses, call numbers are semantically meaningful in that they reference subject content and can be used to create browsable domains of documents. Thus, in addition to their mark and park function, by virtue of the structure built into them they contribute to the navigation objective.

National and International Addresses

To locate documents that exist outside a local library, use needs to be made of document ID numbers. By themselves these numbers do not point to particular sites, but taken together with work and edition identifiers they assist in setting up interlibrary loan structures that map documents to libraries. There are different kinds of document numbers — so many in fact that it is necessary to indicate document-number type in bibliographic descriptions. The most universal document numbers are the standard publication numbers used for universal bibliographical control: for example, for books, the International Standard Book Number (ISBN); for serials, the International Standard Serial Number (ISSN); and for music, the International Standard Music Number (ISMN). For bibliographical control at the national level, country-specific standard numbers are used. Examples in the United States are the Standard Technical Report Number (STRN) issued by the National Technical Information Service and the national bibliography number issued by the Library of Congress. Bibliographic utilities like the Online Computer Library Center (OCLC) and Research Libraries Information Network (RLIN) assign document numbers, as do publishers, in publisher and plate numbers for printed music, publisher stock numbers for sound recordings, and universal product codes for all media types.[25] At the most specific regional level, local systems assign their own document numbers.

Internet Addresses

There is a shifting of emphasis in the description of digital documents from their physicality to the means to access them. This puts a heavy burden on their retrieval addresses, since these addresses become obliged to serve not only for citation and access but also for bibliographic control. Methods of formulating retrieval addresses for electronic documents are still "in process." Generally required is a specification of mode of access (such as Internet, World Wide Web, Gopher, or Dialog) and a network location. Network addresses need to be formulated differently for different types of resources.[26] Andrew Harnack and Gene Kleppinger have developed a model of address formulations for nine different resource types: FTP sites, World

Wide Web sites, Telnet sites, Synchronous communications, GOPHER sites, Listserv messages, Newsgroup (USENET) messages, e-mail messages, and linkage data.[27] Some use a sequence of commands and directory paths, such as Telnet and FTP resources; some use e-mail addresses; and some use Uniform Resource Locators (URLs).

Problems with Internet addresses occur when multiple or mirror retrieval sites exist for a given document. They occur as well when retrieval sites are not distinguished from publication sites.[28] But the biggest problem occurs when addresses change. This problem particularly affects URLs. The URL for a document can change when changes are made in hardware reconfiguration or system reorganization. OCLC has addressed this problem by instituting a Persistent Uniform Resource Locator (PURL) service that tracks changing addresses to provide users with a document's latest address.[29] But this solution is only an interim measure. The changing-addresses problem is more political than technological. To solve it on a political level, an Internet Engineering Task Force is working to develop Uniform Resource Names (URNs) to provide stable long-term access to electronic documents.[30]

Traditional document languages have had the dual tasks of identifying and describing documents. It is hardly surprising that attempts to fit the description of electronic resources into the Procrustean categories used by these traditional languages should meet with difficulties. The difficulties stem from the intangible, fluxible, and distributed nature of these resources and from the lack of reliable identifying attributes in their self-descriptions. The difficulties are complex. They have caused upheavals, necessitated rethinking, and required the making of new distinctions and new categories in the design of document languages. Nevertheless, two verities remain. One is that the purposes and principles of document languages do not change, though the weighting of them may shift over time. The other is that despite the cardinal rule of cataloging that makes the starting point for description the document, document languages that describe the carriers or information are and will always be subservient to the work languages that describe the information itself.

8

Subject Languages: Introduction, Vocabulary Selection, and Classification

Nature and Purpose of Subject Languages

A keyword search for information on a particular subject performed on the World Wide Web may retrieve thousands of documents. For some this may not be a problem; for others, however, it is a serious one, especially if the dump of thousands contains few relevant documents. Though the scale is different, the problem is not new. It can be addressed by using a subject language that incorporates measures designed to improve collocation in retrieval. There are a variety of such subject languages, exhibiting varying degrees of refinement. Using these to retrieve information provides a value-added quality, which, in the case of highly refined languages, can transform information into knowledge.[1] When this happens, the subject language becomes an analog of knowledge itself. As a knowledge representation, it has applications not only in information retrieval but also in other disciplines that reference knowledge structures, like automated language processing and knowledge engineering.[2]

A subject language is used to depict what a document is about.[3] The objectives it serves are primarily those of the *collocation* of documents that have the same information content and the *navigation* of users through the bibliographic universe qua the universe of knowledge.[4] To achieve the collocation objective, the language must be designed so as to facilitate the retrieval of all and only relevant documents, as this is gauged by the twin measures of precision and recall. To achieve the navigation objective, the language must be structured to show relational knowledge.

Alphabetic-Subject Languages vs. Classification Languages

There are two main types of subject languages: *alphabetic-subject languages* and *classificatory subject languages.*[5] The most obvious difference between the two is that the latter use notations, in addition to verbal expressions, to designate subjects. Another salient difference is that they use different vocabulary tools: alphabetic-subject languages employ thesauri and subject authority lists; classificatory subject languages use classification schemes. A third significant difference is in how subjects are displayed and ordered by the two languages: alphabetic languages order subjects alphabetically; classificatory languages order them systematically, first by discipline and, within discipline, hierarchically by topic. For over a century the relative effectiveness of the two languages in ordering subjects was debated, coming eventually to rest in the not surprising consensus that both are needed. Classification schemes require alphabetical indexes, and alphabetical thesauri can be enhanced by displays of terms in hierarchical order. In addition to the obvious differences between alphabetic and classificatory languages, there are less obvious but more significant differences between them that relate to their vocabulary, semantics, and syntax. These are introduced where appropriate in this and subsequent chapters.

Subject Language versus Natural Language

Subject languages are artificial languages, designed for the special purpose of retrieving information. As such they differ in certain essential respects from *natural languages.* In Wittgenstein's formulation, the two languages represent different language games, played with different coins according to different rules.[6] The differences can be illustrated by contrasting subject and natural languages with respect to their vocabulary, semantics, and syntax.

Vocabulary

The chief difference between natural and subject languages lies in the *vocabulary* each uses. The vocabulary of the latter is controlled — that is, normalized. The normalization of a subject vocabulary admits of degree. It can range from the simple enumeration of allowable values for attributes in a specialized database to the complex construction of an in-depth classification scheme. Usually it involves semantically treating terms to restrict their meanings and to make explicit the relationships they bear to other terms. The resulting vocabulary is orderly, in the sense that each term refers to only one concept or object and every object or concept is designated by only one term. As noted earlier, it is only in constructed languages that an isomorphism exists between terms and their referents. Natural languages, by contrast, are replete with synonyms and homonyms that cause a crisscross of many-to-one and one-to-many mappings between words and things. The purpose of normalizing the vocabulary of a subject language is, like the purpose of vocabulary normalization in author-title languages, to straighten out these crisscross mappings and to purge natural language of the ambiguities and redundancies that cause precision and recall failures in retrieval.

Natural- and subject-language vocabularies both employ *lexicons,* but the elements in each differ. Natural-language lexicons (dictionaries) contain words and sometimes phrases. Subject-language lexicons (thesauri or classifications) contain terms. *Terms* are the special-purpose words and word combinations (compound terms) that constitute the technical vocabulary of a subject discipline — the vocabulary used to name its major concepts. Within a given discipline, they are context independent in the sense that they can stand alone as indicators of subject content. Terms usually take the form of nouns (or noun phrases) or the form of verbs that are grammatically equivalent.[7]

Semantics

Category Semantics   Natural languages and many subject languages classify their vocabulary into categories. An important use to which these categories are put is to define the *syntax* of the language. Thus, natural languages class words into parts-of-speech categories, like nouns, verbs, adjectives, and articles. Syntax rules then reference these categories to build noun phrases, verb phrases, adverbial phrases, and so on, which in turn are referenced to build subjects, predicates, and then sentences. Many of the subject languages that classify their vocabulary also use the categories resulting from the classification to construct syntax rules. Subject languages that use a syntax are called *synthetic* and are distinguished from those that do not, which are called *enumerative.* The categories used by an alphabetic subject language that is synthetic are both like and unlike those used by natural languages.[8] Kaiser, who was the first to design such a language, named his categories *concretes, processes,* and *localities.*[9] Concretes and processes correspond roughly to the subjects and predicates of sentence grammar.[10] Other synthetic alphabetic subject languages recognize similar categories. All recognize something akin to the subject of a sentence. The Key System category in Derek Austin's Preserved Context Indexing System (PRECIS) language designates what is talked about, as does the Personality category in Ranganathan's Colon Classification. Most also recognize action categories, which (again roughly) correspond to the verb (part-of-speech) category or the predicate (grammatical) category. Sometimes a conscious attempt is made to model subject-language categories after those used by natural languages. Austin, for instance, includes in PRECIS categories that are strictly functional, like Agent and Object of Transitive Action. On the other hand, there are also dissimilarities. Nearly all synthetic subject languages, classificatory as well as subject, include two categories not recognized in natural languages, those indicative of localities and chronological time periods.

Referential Semantics   Subject language terms differ *referentially* from words used in ordinary language. The former do not refer to objects in the real world or concepts in a mentalistic world but to subjects. As a name of a subject, the term *Butterflies* refers not to actual butterflies but rather to the set of all indexed documents about butterflies. In a natural language the extension, or extensional meaning, of a word is the class of entities denoted by that word, such as the class consisting of all butterflies. In a subject language the extension of a term is the class of all documents about what the term denotes, such as all documents about butterflies.

A character string may have more than one meaning. It may be either a *homonym,* where the different referents of the character string are quite distinct (*bank* as the incline rising from a river and *bank* where one puts money); or a *polyseme,* where the several referents are closely related (the various meanings of the word *system*). Both natural and subject languages disambiguate multireferential character strings, but they do it to differing degrees and use different means. A natural language in its lexicons or dictionaries makes separate entries for the various referents of homonyms but not for those of polysemes. Subject-language thesauri and classification schemes distinguish homonyms and many polysemes as well. They treat each different meaning of a character string as a separate term. The usual but not the only means they use to do this is to create new terms by adding parenthetical qualifiers to the multireferential character strings: thus, Bank (River) and Bank (Financial institution).

Relational Semantics   The *relationships* expressed by subject languages are of three general types: hierarchy, synonymy, and near-relatedness. The first two of these, and to some extent the third, derive from the meaning relationships found in natural-language dictionaries or lexicons. Nearly all definitions in a natural-language dictionary reference hierarchical relationships of the genus-species type. Since Aristotle's time these have formed the backbone of definition. Nearly all indicate sameness in meaning, in the form of synonymy relationships, as well as relationships between terms with overlapping meanings. Thesauri and classifications build on these, but often (despite guidelines proscribing it) go beyond them to include relationships that are syntagmatic or extralexical. Unlike lexical or definitional relationships, which are wholly paradigmatic or a priori, syntagmatic relationships are contingent or empirical. The former express tautological relationships among ideas; the latter express relational knowledge about the real world. A further difference characterizing the relational structures of natural and subject languages is that the latter in their thesauri and classifications express relationships in a uniform and consistent manner, whereas the former observe no system or method (but considerable ingenuity) in their expression.

Syntax

Many subject languages do not employ syntax rules; all allowable expressions in the languages are enumerated. Enumerated subject languages — also called *descriptor subject languages*[11] to distinguish them from *synthetic* subject languages — include those represented by most thesauri. In not using syntax rules to combine terms into larger expressions, they differ significantly from natural languages.

Subject languages that do employ a syntax are in several ways comparable to natural languages. In a natural language the basic synthesized expression is the sentence, which is formed by concatenating words according to natural-language syntax rules. The analogous construction in a synthetic subject language is a string or a heading, which is formed by combining terms according to subject-language syntax rules. Compared to the syntax of a natural language, that of a subject language is simple, uninventive, and finite. In some instances, such as the syntax used in PRECIS, it can even be automated using relatively few algorithms.[12] There are some similarities, however, between the two syntaxes. A. Neelameghan claims that subject languages build on the absolute or deep-structure syntax that underlies natural languages.[13] D. Austin claims that the PRECIS syntax resembles the one that governs passive-voice constructions in the English language.[14]

Automation

The comparison of natural and subject languages is one means of characterizing the latter. But it is more than this. A comparison of this sort is needed as a first step in the practical work of constructing expert systems to map natural-language expressions onto subject-language terminology. Such systems are integral to the sophisticated *automation* of subject retrieval, which, given the Internet-fueled information, is becoming less of an interesting alternative and more of a necessity. To map a natural language onto a subject language, algorithms are needed to

- Extract subject-language terminology from word sequences in running natural-language text,
- Extract and formalize referential and relational semantic information in natural-language lexicons for use in subject language,
- Categorize subject-language terminology into semantic and grammatical categories, and
- Create subject-language strings.

Some progress has been made toward accomplishing these tasks and will be discussed in the following chapters. The remainder of this chapter deals with the first steps in the design of a subject language: vocabulary selection and classification.

Vocabulary Selection

Terminology

The terminology of a subject discipline is obtained by explicating natural-language words and phrases.[15] An explication is a technical definition, whose purpose is to standardize an expression and to hone it to make it more precise. The degree to which different subject disciplines employ a terminology varies. Some soft-language disciplines, where creativity involves redefinition and revisioning, consciously eschew the conformity that would be imposed by a terminology. Many of the disciplines in the humanities and social sciences are of this nature. Scientific disciplines, by contrast, use a more robust vocabulary. No physicist, except perhaps an Einstein, is at liberty to redefine the key concepts in that discipline. In the literatures of scientific disciplines, but not those of the humanities and social sciences, it is easy to distinguish terms from nonterms. In fact, there is some indication that this can be done automatically based on the statistical and lexicogrammatical properties of character strings.[16]

A problem in the design of a subject language is deciding what should constitute a terminological unit. This is the difficult compound-term problem — the problem of deciding how many words it takes to make a term. Sometimes the problem is brushed aside with the observation that since a term designates a concept, it should therefore consist of however many words are needed for this purpose.[17] This approach is straightforward and has the added advantage of being independent of any particular natural language. However, concepts are mental constructs, and, as such, they have unclear boundaries. Do the two terms Information and Retrieval represent one, two, or three concepts? It would depend on who was asked. Yet in the construction of a subject-language vocabulary a decision must be made whether to include both terms, allowing those interested in the retrieval of information to postcoordinate them at the time a search is formulated, or, to include as well, or instead, the term Information retrieval.

Most thesaurus standards provide guidelines for when two words of the form [modifier + noun] constitute a compound term. For example, the two words are to be regarded as a compound term if the modifier

- Has lost its original meaning (such as Lawn tennis),
- Suggests a resemblance (Tree structures),
- Together with the noun does not form a subset of the class designated by the noun (Paper tigers),
- Occurs frequently in conjunction with the noun (Information retrieval),
- Is not used in conjunction with many nouns,
- Is needed to show direction (Fire engine, Engine fire), and
- Is needed for collocation and navigation.[18]

One aspect of the compound-term problem is how many of them to include in a subject vocabulary.[19] When information-retrieval thesauri were first conceived, the accepted wisdom was to restrict terms to as few words as possible. Mortimer Taube went so far as to argue for a uniterm system (one-word terms), his idea being that compound terms could be simulated at the time of retrieval using Boolean operators.[20] It soon became evident that uniterms caused precision failures and also were inadequate for designating the major concepts of a discipline and structuring its vocabulary. While it is clear that some compound terms are needed, it is equally clear that too many of them can burgeon a vocabulary and increase its cost. For instance, one could imagine a hypothetical thesaurus in which a hundred different objects might be modified by any of ten adjectives: Wood bridges, Wood chairs, Steel bridges, Steel chairs, and so on. A thousand terms would be needed just to designate objects by material type. In the design of a subject language this sort of enumeration needs to be contained. The Library of Congress Subject Headings (LCSH) uses an *etc.* device to limit the enumerated number of modifier-noun combinations: Mythology, Armenian [Dravidian, Egyptian, etc.] The Dewey Decimal Classification (DDC) achieves a similar purpose with its pattern headings. Always, however, there are trade-offs. The more redundancy-reducing devices of this sort that are introduced into a vocabulary, the more it assumes the unwanted characteristics of a uniterm vocabulary. Adjusting the balance in a subject-language vocabulary between compound and single word terms is another of those difficult design tasks that must ultimately rely on flair based on experience.

Domain Definition

A subject vocabulary is normalized, first, in that it selects from a natural language a restricted set of words and phrases and, second, in that it treats these terms semantically to fix their referents and establish their relationships with other terms. The first task can be aided by defining a *vocabulary domain*. Defining a domain helps to ensure that day-to-day decisions regarding terms to be added or removed from a vocabulary are made on a consistent basis. It helps also to contain costs. The cost of a normalized vocabulary being roughly in proportion to its size, it is expedient to limit it to only those terms necessary and sufficient to achieve its objectives.

Warrant

Ideally, it should be possible to formulate an abstract characterization of a vocabulary domain so precisely that for any given word or phrase, it should be possible to say unequivocally yes it belongs to the vocabulary or no it does not. But this is not always possible — or, rather it is only more or less possible, depending on the subject discipline in question. In practice, domains tend to be defined indirectly, by specifying criteria for term selection. The traditional criteria used for this purpose are literary warrant, use warrant, and structural warrant.

Literary Warrant

Literary warrant, a concept introduced by Wyndam Hulme in 1911,[21] has the status of a principle. A subprinciple of the principle of representation, it enjoins that the vocabulary of a subject language be empirically derived from the literature it is intended to describe. This means that a literature must be determined. For Hulme, the language in question was the Library of Congress Classification (LCC), and the literature that served as warrant were the books housed in the Library of Congress. For a discipline-specific language, the literature might be defined as the canonical texts in the discipline or as the core set of documents of the discipline, as this is determined by citation frequency. Once the literature of a discipline is defined, then expressions in it indicative of aboutness become candidates for inclusion in the vocabulary of the language.

Use Warrant

Literary warrant is a necessary but not sufficient basis for admitting terms into the vocabulary of a subject language. This is because there is no guarantee that the vocabulary of those who create the literature of a discipline will match the vocabulary of those who search for it. When Cutter wrote that *usage* was the supreme arbiter,[22] he meant the usage not of writers but of those seeking information. Some subject theorists see the usage principle vying in importance with that of literary warrant. Dagobert Soergel, for instance, argues for elevating request-oriented indexing above entity-oriented indexing.[23] But both orientations are needed. It is a matter of course that users' vocabulary must be accommodated, either as lead-in or descriptor vocabulary. At the same time, it is known that users in their attempts to search by subject sometimes find themselves at loss for words. For these users, it is useful to include terms they might never think of but to which they might be directed for the purpose of improving their search requests.

In the creation of a subject language the principle of common usage is often honored in the breach. Seldom is there a systematic attempt on the part of subject specialists to ascertain it. Researchers, however, have taken an interest in common usage and have studied it. On the basis of data extracted from transaction logs of requests put to online databases, they have attempted to measure how well users' vocabulary matches the normalized vocabularies of subject languages.[24] Their findings show that at a lexical level the match is not good. However, at a concept level, which takes into account synonym and generic relations, it is considerably better. This suggests that meeting the common-usage dictate is not so much a matter of identifying the concepts that a user is interested in but of naming of them. As there are many different users with different usages, it follows that a normalized vocabulary needs to include all the names by which a concept is known.[25]

Structural Warrant

Sometimes terms having neither literary nor use warrant are admitted into a normalized vocabulary. They are admitted because they provide a useful *structural* function. Structural terms may be used to supply missing links in a hierarchy or to collocate a set of more specific terms. For instance, in the *Art and Architecture Thesaurus* the term Masonry vaults, used neither by authors nor users, is introduced as a supplied term because it conveniently collocates Brick vaults, Stone vaults, and Tile vaults. Structural terms have the potential to improve both recall and precision in retrieval and also to facilitate browsing.

The more hierarchical a vocabulary, the more likely it is to admit terms that are warranted solely by their structural properties. Highly structured vocabularies, such as those used by classificatory languages, include many subjects designated by expressions no one would think to use in writing documents or searching databases. Examples are headings in the DDC of the type that begin *Kinds of,* such as Kinds of schools (344.071–344.072). Though unsought, these headings by virtue of the structure they impart perform useful collocation and navigation functions. Where structure is a primary consideration, structural warrant tends to override literary or use warrant, resulting in a top-down as opposed to a bottom-up approach to vocabulary selection. Melvil Dewey, a structuralist par excellence, used a top-down approach in his classification that breaks the universe of knowledge down into ten classes, breaks each class further into ten more, and so on. Ranganathan, also a structuralist, also employed a largely rationalistic top-down approach in his Colon Classification, as opposed to an empirical, bottom-up approach based on use or literary warrant. The top-down versus bottom-up dichotomy is not absolute. Neither Dewey nor Ranganathan were idiosyncratic in their approach to classification but relied on relationships among disciplines established by custom. (Custom warrant might be regarded as an entrenched form of literary or use warrant.) Again it is a question of balance. An overemphasis on literary or user warrant (a bottom-up approach) sacrifices structure, while an overemphasis on structural warrant (a top-down approach) sacrifices user convenience. Classificatory and alphabetic-subject languages differ significantly in their placement of this emphasis.

Of such importance is relational structure in a subject language that some thesaurus guidelines ban *orphans* — that is, terms that are not related to other terms. This makes sense if the purpose of vocabulary normalization is to establish connectivity in the form of semantic relationships among terms. It makes sense also if the vocabulary is to be used in conjunction with free-text searching. It would be a needless expense to include in a vocabulary orphans that could be captured by keywords. On the other hand, where the subject vocabulary is the only access to information, such as that used in a paper-based index, it must necessarily include orphans or else important concepts could not be retrieved.

Problems

Defining the vocabulary domain of a discipline is complicated by three problems: a literary-warrant problem, a terminological problem, and a boundary problem. Defining a literature for warrant poses difficulties for certain subject languages. It is difficult, for instance, to define a literature for languages that are used globally. The Dewey Decimal Classification (DDC) is an example. Presently a warrant used for term selection by the DDC editors is WorldCat — the Online Computer Library Center (OCLC)

Online Union Catalog. Although this database is becoming increasingly international, it has not kept pace with the internationalization of DDC, half of whose use is outside the United States. Determining warrant is also problematic for subject languages whose "literatures" are in visual or audio form. The designers of the *Art and Architecture Thesaurus* have dealt with this problem by substituting for literary warrant a principle of *object warrant,* recognizing as acceptable any name any art object might have — a policy so liberal that it lacks the power to limit.[26] There is perhaps a danger that as subject languages become more global and are called on more to describe nonbook documents, the ability of the principle of literary warrant to restrict escalating vocabulary growth (and cost) will be diminished.

The terminological problem in defining a vocabulary domain has already broached. There are disciplines with relatively small technical vocabularies. These tend to be those whose research is point-of-view defined, notably disciplines in the humanities and social sciences. The subject matter of these disciplines — what they speak about — is often lexically indeterminate. It cannot be captured in a word or phrase but may require a paragraph, chapter, or even whole book to express. Lexical indeterminacy occurs also where a subject can be named but not unambiguously defined. The term Culture, which names a subject frequently discussed in the social sciences, has attached to it almost as many meanings as there are scholars who write about it. Where the meanings of words cannot be pinpointed or are unstable — where there is no established terminology — it is questionable whether vocabulary normalization is even worth attempting.

Attempting to fix the boundaries of a vocabulary domain runs into two kinds of problems: how to deal with nontechnical vocabulary that may be needed for subject indexing and how to merge vocabularies for interdisciplinary subject disciplines. Every subject language depends to some degree on nontechnical vocabulary, what might be called *nonterms.* Some admit nonterms but segregate them in special categories, such as the common isolates of the Colon Classification and the common subdivisions of the Dewey Decimal Classification. Some distinguish between the core vocabulary of a discipline and its marginal vocabulary, the former being developed in greater specificity than the latter.[27] Sometimes a subject language is created purposefully to be incomplete or dependent, in the sense that it contains the core vocabulary of a discipline but relies for noncore vocabulary on an already existing universal subject language like LCSH. Perhaps the most usual way to deal with nonterms, however, is simply to intermix them with terms in one vocabulary as needed. The disadvantage here is that it creates a vocabulary domain with fuzzy edges, which, in not being operationally restricted, is in danger of burgeoning unsystematically.

For an interdisciplinary subject, such as environmental studies, the boundary problem lies in deciding which vocabulary to select from the various contributing disciplines. Complicating the decision is the fact that term selection is not an independent operation. Admitting one term into a vocabulary often entails admitting others that are semantically related to it. A more serious complication is that a given term may be used in the literature of several of the contributing disciplines but with different meanings. This is a stumbling block in any attempt to merge specialized vocabularies, both at an interdisciplinary discipline and at a universal level.[28]

Vocabulary Classification: Category Semantics

Facets

Many alphabetic-subject and all classification languages classify the terms in their vocabularies into categories of high generality, often called *facets*. Facets are groupings of terms obtained by the first division of a subject discipline into homogeneous[29] or semantically cohesive[30] categories. To characterize a facet as semantically cohesive is to say that the terms in it have similar referents. For instance, terms in one facet may all refer to processes, like mining, building, or cataloging; in another they may refer to concrete objects, like coal, houses, or books. When a facet is semantically cohesive, terms in it are related by the paradigmatic relationships of synonymy and hierarchy, and the totality of facets used in the subject language are mutually exclusive.

Helpfulness of Facets

Partitioning the vocabulary is helpful in subject-language construction. As mentioned earlier, it is helpful in defining the syntax of a language. Just as in a natural language, syntax rules are defined with respect to sequences of subjects and predicates, which in turn are defined with respect to parts-of-speech and grammatical categories, so for a subject language the syntax rules are defined with respect to well-formed sequences of facet categories.

Another way the partitioning of a vocabulary into facets is helpful is that it creates term groupings of a manageable size. The terms can be structured one by one, within a grouping that limits the domain that has to be combed for paradigmatically related terms. This simplifies and at the same time ensures the correctness of the structuring of hierarchical and synonymous relationships.

In addition to its syntactic and semantic functions, vocabulary partition also has an ontological function. By virtue of being semantic categories, facets are also categories of existence. As such, they determine and limit what is indexable, by predetermining, in Kantian fashion, the perception of what a document can be about. By imposing a constraint on aboutness, facets contribute to defining the vocabulary domain of a subject language: if a candidate term does not belong to one of the facets of the language, it is inadmissible. This same restriction also serves to curtail language subjectivity and inconsistency in indexing.

Semantic Universals

An intriguing question that arises in the design of a subject language is whether the same categories can be used to classify terms in different subject disciplines. Are there semantic universals in subject languages? Ranganathan's answer to this question was an unqualified yes. Enamored of theory and influenced by Hindu philosophy, he constantly sought to find unity underlying diversity.[31] His view of semantic universals was that while at a phenomenal level the facets used to categorize terms in different subject disciplines appear to differ, at a seminal level they can be seen as manifestations of a few fundamental categories, such as Personality, Matter, Energy, Space, and Time. This view was not shared by members of the English Classification Research Group, who, while adopting Ranganathan's techniques of facet analysis, rejected his semantics. The Group's position was that category definition was an empirical matter and, being based on literary warrant, was necessarily discipline specific.[32] The facets used for Soil science, for example, would not be appropriate for disciplines whose subject matter is not physical in nature.

Researchers have looked into the question of whether there are semantic universals underlying subject languages. Among those who have addressed it are Eric De Grolier, who made a survey of the general categories used in classification languages;[33] Ganesh Bhattacharyya, who developed a general theory of subject index languages;[34] Francis Devadason, who studied the deep structure of such languages;[35] and William Hutchins, who analyzed documentary languages from a linguistic point of view.[36] Attempts to answer the semantic universals question, like other questions that involve comparing subject languages, are important as they represent a reaching for high-level generalizations about phenomena and contribute to intellectual foundations. But the question is of more than theoretical interest, in that its answer touches on the practicality and feasibility of merging different subject languages.

Problems with Facets

The biggest problem with facets is that they are difficult to define and, therefore, it is difficult to class terms into them.[37] The difficulties are caused by the fact that language is unruly. There are terms that cannot be categorized exclusively into only one facet and terms that resist categorization because they are ambiguous or abstract. Moreover, attempting to define facets by both semantic and syntactic criteria (as is done) leads to cross- and inconsistent classification. These are fundamental difficulties that strike at "the hidden roots" of many linguistic-based classifications.

Multifaceted Terms

Obviously, terms that are *multifaceted* cannot logically be placed in only one facet. An example of such a term, given by Kaiser, is Bibliography, which since it means book description, would in his subject language logically belong both to a concrete (book) and a process (description) facet. Kaiser's method of dealing with the problem, and one also adopted by some current thesaurus guidelines, was to introduce semantic factoring. Semantic factoring splits a multifaceted term into its logical components. An example is the factoring of the term Thermometer into a device (a thing) + measurement (an operation) + heat (a property). The solution is hardly satisfactory, primarily because it flouts common usage but also because it is not always possible to find factors for a term, which when recombined reproduce the meaning of the original term — for example, the multifaceted term Agriculture has a meaning broader than that of its component factors Fields + Cultivation.

Ambiguous Terms

Another problem in facet definition is caused by the existence of *ambiguous terms*. Examples are terms like Organization and Painting, which being multireferential could be categorized as either processes or entities. Actually, this problem is not serious, as it can be easily addressed by conventional disambiguation methods such as reconfiguring a multireferential into two or more terms. Thus, the term Organization could be split into Organization (entity) and Organization (process). Distinguishing as separate terms the different meanings of a term is a means of facilitating unambiguous categorization.

Abstract Terms

More serious are the categorization problems caused by *abstract terms*. Terms like Love, Truth, and Beauty differ from concrete terms like Chair in that their referents are not physical objects. Lacking concrete, real-world referents they are usually construed as referring to concepts, which, as observed, are mentalistic and therefore fuzzy.[38] Philosophers since Plato have stumbled over the difficulties in classifying abstract terms. (What idea does Beauty participate in?)

It is not surprising then that subject language classifiers should also stumble. Kaiser flatly refused to admit into his subject vocabulary mathematical terms like Coefficient and Factor. Terms like Labor, Power, and Light he unwillingly classed as concretes, giving as a (weak?) rationale that they comprised latent energy. Ranganathan was similarly ill at ease with terms like Morphology, Physiology, and Disease. Originally he characterized such terms as belonging to the Energy category, which for the most part includes action terms, on the grounds that they tended to be associated with problems. Later, because of their use as property terms he moved them to the Matter category, creating there a special subclass of matter-property terms. Austin's approach to abstracts like Foreign relations, Football, and Disease was to class them in a phenomena facet, which he construed as a subclass of his Action facet. Terms belong to this facet if they appear to represent things engaged in action and yet cannot be reduced to an infinitive.[39] (Note the mixture of semantic and morphological criteria in the definition.) As a last resort, the difficulties in classifying abstract terms can be circumvented by introducing a category for abstracts or a category for heterogeneous concepts.[40] Such categories, however, are not semantically homogeneous and are of limited syntactic value; in other words, they vitiate the purposes they were designed to fulfill. Language resists being harnessed, particularly when unmoored from its grounding in existential reality it becomes abstract.

Semantic-Syntactic Terms

Another problem with category definition arises from a semantic-syntactic tension. Facets are defined semantically (as semantically cohesive categories) and then treated as grammatical categories. Doing this assumes some kind of coincidence between a term's meaning and its syntactic function. Kaiser's simple and orderly language comes close to achieving such a coincidence, but most subject languages do not. The conflict in the interplay of syntax and semantics is evident in Ranganathan's admission that his Personality category is hard to define.[41] A term belongs to this category if it focuses on the aboutness of a document; however, what a document is about cannot be constrained semantically. The conflict is apparent also in the PRECIS subject language, which uses both semantic categories (such as Action) and grammatical categories (such as Key System or what a document is primarily about, Object of Action and Agent of Action). The mixture of the two is theoretically unsound since the mode of being of a syntactic category is contingent or accidental and that of a semantic category is existential or essential. The practical consequence is the creation of nonmutually exclusive categories (is Football to be classed as an Action, an Object of Action, or a Key System?).

Some of the problems in category definition are serious, but it does not follow that all categories of terms are affected. Categories of terms indicative of the form or genre of a document, of terms denoting geographical localities, and of terms for chronological time periods are relatively problem-free. It is fairly easy to assign terms to such categories and to construct hierarchies of them and syntax rules that reference them. It is when an attempt is made to go further — to introduce general categories for things,

actions, properties of things and actions, relations between them, and operations on them — that boundary problems arise, categories overlap, and
confusion of purpose, complexity, and redundancy appear.

Automation

This chapter has focused on the processes used to select terms for a subject-
language vocabulary and to classify them into categories. It remains to be
considered to what extent these processes are intellectual in nature and to
what extent capable of being automated.

Term Selection

For more than forty years computers have been used to extract *subject
terms* from documents. In the late 1950s Hans Peter Luhn, the "father of
information science," developed a program to identify words indicative of
subject content in running natural language text. [42] The program was simple. It was based on the absolute frequencies of words in documents, exceptions being made for common words like *of* and for very broad words like
theory.

Luhn's work was catalytic in setting researchers off to pursue more
sophisticated answers to the question (now reframed) of how terms indicative of aboutness differ statistically from those that do not. The answers
proposed were numerous and somewhat contradictory. Content terms
have a higher relative frequency: they occur more frequently in a given document than in the disciplinary literature to which the document belongs.
Or their value as descriptors is directly related to their absolute frequency
and inversely related to how often they are used in indexing. Or they occur
at a frequency midway between that described by Zipf's first law and his
second law. Or they cluster in the manner of a double-Poisson distribution.
The truth of the matter is not clear. A Ph.D. student, defining truth by a
human measure, has found that actual subject terms assigned by indexers
to documents occurred approximately equally in low-, medium-, and high-
frequency ranges, and half of these had frequencies no greater than would
be expected by chance. [43]

Just as for human intellects, so for a machine intelligence, it is a challenge to extract multiword terms from natural-language texts. An early

approach to meeting this challenge was to calculate the absolute frequencies for all word pairs and word triplets occurring in a document, and then to choose as terminological units those that occurred above a certain threshold.[44] More modern approaches supplement statistical measures with linguistic-based algorithms. A good example of such an approach is that taken by NASA's Machine-Aided Indexing (MAI) program. Given titles, or titles and abstracts, of articles, the program delineates candidate terms by looking for thought-ending punctuation, such as periods, colons, and semicolons. Then, using a specially constructed look-up dictionary, the individual words constituting the candidate terms are assigned to syntactic categories. Sequences of words are then vetted against allowable syntactic formats. The process is not wholly automatic in that word sequences passing the vetting test are subsequently subjected to human review.[45] The MAI effort is notable not only for the special-purpose linguistics it developed to extract multiword terms from running text but also for proffering an operational solution to the compound-term problem and for being the first large-scale effort to map a large domain of natural language into an artificial subject language.

Vocabulary Classification

A *vocabulary* can be classed into syntactic, statistical, or semantic categories. The classification done in the MAI program is one form of syntactic classification. The classification effected by linguistic parsing programs is another. If the categories used to group terms in a subject vocabulary were to be defined by syntactic criteria alone, the mapping of natural to subject languages might be within reach. But syntactic categories do not provide the semantic cohesiveness needed to structure subject languages. Statistical categorization of vocabularies are relatively easy to accomplish. Since the 1960s natural-language words and phrases having similar distributions over documents have been grouped to provide clusters of terms intersubstitutable in retrieval.[46] While of use in both retrieval and indexing, such clusters, because they are statistical, are of limited use in the semantic and syntactic structuring of a subject language.

Little progress has been made in automatically classing terms into semantic categories. In part this is because the information needed to do it is not sufficiently formalized or consolidated. Some of the needed information exists in traditional tools, like dictionaries, whose definitions can be exploited to yield primitive concepts or semantic markers, which are not unlike the semantically cohesive categories represented by facets. It exists as well in thesauri, whose relationships can be used to go beyond simple pattern matching to the concept matching needed for accurate classification. Not surprisingly — since this is an information age, and language is the chief embodiment of information — new tools that consolidate and normalize lexical information are being developed at a rapid rate. These tools can be found in the form of lexical databases that combine dictionary and thesaural information, databases mapping natural to normalized language, metathesauri, semantic networks, term banks, and various sorts of knowledge representations. Such tools hold promise for advancing the automation of semantic classification.

Nevertheless, semantic classification will always be difficult, in part because of terms of the kind discussed in the previous section, those that by their nature resist classification. Where a human intelligence cannot unequivocally class a term, a machine intelligence can hardly succeed. That there are difficulties in semantically classifying terms might seem to imply that a subject language cannot really do what it purports to do, which is to represent knowledge in an explicit data structure.[47] But this would be to generalize too broadly. There are many knowledge classifications that are not perfect, but this has not seriously detracted from their general usefulness.

9

Subject Languages: Referential and Relational Semantics

This chapter looks at the semantic treatment needed to transform a natural language into a subject language. As observed in preceding chapters, a subject language is based on a natural language but differs from it primarily in the semantic structures it uses to normalize vocabulary by setting up a one-to-one relationship between terms and their referents. The referential semantics of a subject language deals with the generalized homonym problem. It consists of methods for restricting term referents so that any given term has one and only one meaning. The relational semantics of a subject language deals with the generalized synonym problem and consists of methods for linking terms with similar or related meanings. The referential and relational semantics of a subject language are designed to increase the probability that terms used in search requests will retrieve all and only relevant documents. They are the chief means by which the collocation objective of the language is achieved, and they serve also to further the navigation objective.

Referential Semantics

Purpose

The difficulty caused by homonyms in retrieval is that unwanted documents are retrieved. The use of the keyword Drums in a search intended to retrieve documents on the musical instrument is likely also to retrieve documents on fishes, containers for oil, ears, and the components of a column. To the extent a subject language permits irrelevant material to be retrieved, it has poor precision capabilities.

The need to deal with precision failures is obvious to anyone who has searched the Web. It is not, however, a modern phenomenon. In the middle

of the last century, Samson Low complained that the categories used to classify books were so broad that it was difficult to find books on a specific
subject.[1] His solution to the problem was to eschew traditional classifications and instead to describe documents by the specific words used in their
titles — an approach that today would more likely contribute to, rather
than solve, the problem. The quest for precision in retrieval is so paramount
and of such long duration that it would be possible to frame the history of
indexing over the last hundred and fifty years in terms of the successive
means devised to deal with it.

One of the chief ways to improve precision is to purge the retrieval language of multireferential words. Two classes of such words have been mentioned in preceding chapters: homonyms, which are words spelled or
pronounced alike but different in meaning (as *pool* of water and *pool* the
game);[2] and *polysemes*, which differ from homonyms in that their look-
alikes are related in meaning, either psychologically or etymologically.[3]
Homonyms and polysemes, however, are only part of the precision problem. These constitute rather small subclasses of multireferential words —
too small, in fact, to instigate the large-scale precision failures that cause
concern. These failures come about because most natural-language words
partake of ambiguity in that their meanings vary more or less depending
on the context in which they are used. The degree of their variance is a function of their generality and/or vagueness. The more general or vague a
word, the more its meaning is context dependent and the more normalization it requires when introduced into the controlled vocabulary of a subject
language.

Methods of Semantic Disambiguation
Domain Specification

The degree to which resolving the meanings of multireferential words and
phrases is needed varies. When the controlled vocabulary of a thesaurus is
limited to a specific *domain* of discourse, the domain itself limits the possible referents of its terms. In such cases, disambiguation is attained gratu-
itously: Mercury is a homonym in natural language, but in the context of
an astronomy thesaurus it probably refers to the planet rather than the
Greek god or the metal. Disambiguation through domain specification is
not an option for a general or universal subject language; however, to the

extent that these languages classify by discipline the somewhat analogous method of hierarchical disambiguation can be used (see below).

A problem with relying on the domain of a controlled vocabulary to clarify meaning is that it limits vocabulary compatibility — that is, its ability to be mapped onto, or used in conjunction with, other controlled vocabularies. This becomes an issue in cross-database searching. To address it, one thesaurus guideline advises that even if a multireferential word is used with a singular meaning within a domain-specific vocabulary, it should still be qualified to enhance compatibility.[4]

Qualifiers

The traditional method of disambiguation is to resolve a multireferential term into several univocal terms through the use of parenthetical *qualifiers*, such as Mercury (Greek god), Mercury (Metal), and Mercury (Planet).[5] The qualifier in each of the disambiguated terms is considered to be a component part of the term, both for indexing and searching. Well entrenched as it is, this method has the disadvantage that terms encumbered by qualifiers are not part of common usage. They were designed originally for the manual environment. In book and card catalogs, parenthetically qualified terms were inserted so that users coming across them would realize there were distinctions to be made. This they could do also in a digital environment, although a term like Mercury (Planet) might not in the usual course of searching be discovered by users. Once found it could then serve as an analog for the search prescription Mercury AND Planet.

If a subject language is to develop systematically, rules are needed to govern the selection and formulation of terms used for qualification. There are relatively few such rules and when they are used, they tend to be of a negative or banning nature. Terms used for qualification, for example, should not themselves be homonyms, nor should they be compound concepts that can be expressed by adjectival phrase headings, such as Pile (Plastic).[6] One of the few constructive rules for choice of qualifying terms is the Library of Congress Subject Headings (LCSH) guideline that "qualifiers generally take the form of names of disciplines or categories or types of objects."[7] This rule is appropriate for alphabetic languages but not for classificatory ones. The Dewey Decimal Classification (DDC), for instance, admonishes against the using names of disciplines as qualifiers.[8] The difference is attributable to surface-structure differences between the two languages. Classificatory subject languages have available to them a method of disambiguation not available to alphabetic subject languages — disambiguation by hierarchical or disciplinary contexts. Because of this, they need to rely relatively little on parenthetical qualifiers, and, when they do use them, to avoid redundancy they are obliged to eschew names of disciplines.

Because persons, corporate bodies, and works can function as subjects and because their names can be multireferential, these too need to be qualified. For the most part, rules for qualifying proper names are the province of author-title languages (see chapter 6); however, some subject-language guidelines also include such rules. Ideally, the joint use of the two languages in a given catalog, bibliography, or index should be compatible and not give rise to naming conflicts.[9] In practice conflicts sometimes arise, again partly due to the fact that the two languages favor different disambiguation methods. For instance, a subject language, unlike an author-title language, favors syntactic means for disambiguation. It can fix the referent of a term like London using constructions like Ontario—London and England—London, rather than relying on qualified expressions like London (Ont.) and London (England).

Notes

Another method used to disambiguate multireferential terms is to limit their meanings by *notes*. The general purpose of notes is to explain the use of terms within the context of a given subject language. Notes take different forms, depending on whether they belong to an alphabetic or a classificatory language. In the former, where they are generally called *scope notes*, they are brief, sometimes even formulaic. Their specific purpose is to distinguish closely related terms and to differentiate common language meanings from technical meanings. Occasionally they take the form of full-fledged definitions. In a classificatory language, notes perform these functions and others as well. The DDC uses over a dozen different kinds of notes (such as definition notes, scope notes, class-here notes, class-elsewhere notes)[10] to describe what belongs in a class and to differentiate it from what belongs in closely related classes. The description of what belongs in a class can sometime extend to a miniterminological essay. To the extent that they advise on application and fix usage, notes constitute part of the pragmatics as well as the semantics of a subject language.

Hierarchy

A third method of disambiguating terms is to contextualize them in *hierarchical structures*. Hierarchical structures are used by both alphabetic-subject and classificatory languages, but in differing kinds and degree. While there are several types of hierarchical structures, two are of particular use in disambiguation: genus-species and perspective hierarchies.

Genus-species hierarchies are used in logic and in definition. According to the classic theory of definition, generic terms name classes. Thus, Dog, in its denotational meaning, represents or is the name for the class of all dogs. Dog (the class) is defined by stating first the genus that subsumes it (Canidae) and then the characteristics or differentia that distinguish its members from members of other subclasses of the genus (such as domesticated, descended from the wolf, admitting of a great variety of breeds). The genus-species relationship is the logical relationship of inclusion. Of limited domain and range, it is strictly defined in terms of the properties of reflexivity, antisymmetry, and transitivity. It holds between two classes, A and B, if and only if all members of A are also members of B. The relationship is sometimes represented as the "all-some" relationship — for example, all parrots are birds, and some birds are parrots.[11] (The relationship does not hold between parrots and pets because not all parrots are pets.) The genus-species relationship is one that holds always, in all possible worlds; it is a priori, true by definition, and paradigmatic.

Positioning a multireferential term in genus-species hierarchies disambiguates it by providing its broader contexts. Thus, Mercury might have Element as a broader term in one hierarchy and Planet in another. The relative location of a term in different hierarchies is a form of definition: definition by contextual disambiguation.

Perspective hierarchies generally do not have the logical properties of genus-species hierarchies, except insofar as they include them as subclasses. The value they have in retrieval lies in their ability to provide points of view. They hold between an object (or a concept) and the aspect under which it is considered. For instance, in the DDC, an insect (an object) can be looked at, or studied, from the point of view of agricultural pests, disease carriers, food, art representation, and control technology. The index to the DDC, which is called a *Relative Index,* shows the relative hierarchical locations in which the term Insect is located. While Insect can belong to only one genus-species hierarchy (Arthropoda), it can belong to as many perspective hierarchies as there are aspects of insects to be studied. Perspective hierarchies, for the most part, are not a priori but empirical, contingent, or syntagmatic.

Perspective hierarchies, though they do not contribute to formal definition, do, however, limit meaning by providing context. Such hierarchies tend to be discipline based. Clothing, for instance, can be studied in the disciplines of the arts, home economics, health, and product safety. Each discipline looks at Clothing differently and uses the term with a slightly different meaning. Specifying context contributes to and clarifies meaning in subject languages just as it does in natural languages.

For the purpose of disambiguation, the genus-species relationship is of limited use. A budding zoologist might be interested to know that Insects are generically related to Arthropoda, but the audience for insects is considerably larger than this, including as well persons interested in insects as agricultural pests, disease carriers, and so on. Moreover, the genus-species hierarchy is Procrustean. Terms that are polysemantic, vague, or ambiguous do not fit its mold. (To what genus does Beauty belong?) Not all words convey meaning in the same way. Terms whose meanings are relatively indeterminate (that is, whose meanings depend largely on context) do not lend themselves to logical structuring, but terms whose meanings are relatively context-independent do. The fact that genus-species hierarchies are limited, both in terms of user interest and the vocabulary they can structure, argues for the superiority of perspective hierarchies and thus for classificatory structures over thesaural structures in performing the function of disambiguation.[12]

A practical problem in exploiting perspective information for disambiguation purposes is how to package it for users. Imagine a user, as a first step in an online search, keying in the word Freedom. Ideally, the system would behave like a good reference librarian and respond by asking the user "What kind of Freedom do you mean — Freedom of speech, Freedom of the press, Freedom of religion?" It would elicit perspective information from a universal classification and present it to users in a friendly manner. The possibility of using perspective information in this way has long been understood[13] but has been slow to be realized in practice. There are difficulties. One experiment, which sought to exploit perspective information in retrieval, produced the disconcerting finding that users did not find it helpful.[14] But this may have been due not to the information but to its manner of presentation. In any case, work needs to be done to harness the disambiguating power of traditional classifications for use in online retrieval.[15]

General Issues

Each feature to be included in the design of a subject language can be subjected to a stringent review, which can be formulated as a series of questions: Is the feature needed? What alternative techniques can be used to carry out the functions the feature is designed to perform? How does inclusion of the feature affect the application of the subject language? How does it affect its compatibility? And can incorporation of the feature into the language be automated?

Need

Disambiguation is needed to guarantee collocative precision. But how much is needed? That disambiguation can be overdone is implied by the tradeoff hypothesis that pits precision against recall. Too much of it could have a suboptimization effect and impair recall — for example, a user interested in systems analysis generally might not be served by the distinction between how the term Systems analysis is used in the disciplines of engineering and management. Ideally, where fine distinctions in meaning exist, the retrieval system should be designed in such a way as to give the user the option to accept or reject them.

Indexing Consistency

It would seem that the more closely the meaning of a term is prescribed, the more consistently it would be used by indexers.[16] In fact, it might be supposed that a supercontrolled vocabulary would be one that would take the form of a dictionary of definitions on which is superimposed a formal semantic structure.[17] But recent research has challenged this supposition. Michèle Hudon examined the hypothesis that indexing consistency could be improved by augmenting a standard thesaurus with definitions for each of its terms and found that the hypothesis could not be supported. This is a surprising finding, and while it may be explained in part by the fact that the causes of indexer inconsistency are not well understood, it cannot help but cast doubt on the usefulness of definition. It is possible that too much of it could inadvertently pose a threat to user convenience by producing a vocabulary so artificial and divorced from natural language as to be unusable. To what extent disambiguation should be carried out and which methods should be used to achieve it are as yet unanswered questions.

Nonsemantic Disambiguation

The disambiguation of a multireferential term in a subject language need not be done semantically; it can also be done syntactically by couching the terms in subject language strings. The subdivisions in LCSH strings qualify or present aspects of the topical subject that begins the string. Thus, a term like Reading can be qualified as Reading—Ability testing, Reading—Case studies, Reading—Computer programs, Reading—France, and so on. Syntactic disambiguation methods are powerful. However (another unanswered question), how their cost and effectiveness compare to those of semantic methods for honing the meanings of terms is not known. (Subject language syntax is discussed further in the following chapter.)

Both semantic and syntactic methods for disambiguation were devised for use in a manual environment and have yet to be fully adapted for online use. Any adaptation needs to take into account the fact that disambiguation need not be performed at the time when words are admitted into a controlled vocabulary. It can be achieved postcoordinately when a search is formulated using proximity or AND operators, such as Mercury AND Planet. Combining two or more terms in this manner limits the meaning of each. The advantage of this approach, from the point of view of the subject-language designer, is that it transfers the burden and cost of disambiguation to the user. The user, however, is disadvantaged by not knowing in advance whether or how a term needs to be qualified. But this may not be serious, in that the user is helped somewhat by the disambiguation that occurs automatically in the course of retrieval when, in response to a request, the system displays search terms couched in contexts that resolve meaning, such as titles, subject headings, abstracts, or lists of cooccurring terms.

Compatibility

The provision of bibliographic data, once a largely local operation, is becoming a global. In a global and increasingly interdisciplinary environment, where cross-database searching is the norm, a domain-specific subject vocabulary is of limited use. The more universal the vocabulary, the more useful it will be.[18] A step in the progression toward universality is to merge subject languages, to use them in conjunction with each other, to integrate them through a common command language — in short, to render them compatible. With the need for compatibility comes an increased need for definitional refinement. Terms naturally disambiguated by occurring in a subject language restricted to a particular domain have to be dealt with explicitly when that domain is extended. The task is further complicated when attempting to extend domains across natural-language boundaries (for instance, in the creation of multilingual thesauri), since terms in one language often only partially map to terms in others. The more universal and the more multilingual a subject language, the more disambiguation is need to achieve collocation precision.

Automation

Automatic or semiautomatic methods, similar to those used at the Online Computer Library Center (OCLC) to distinguish homographic proper names, can be used to disambiguate multireferential subject terms. These methods resolve meanings through the use of textual clues. Algorithms to disambiguate homonyms by examining words in their textual neighborhoods were developed for the Biological Sciences Information Services (BIOSIS) system. For example, the word *inmates* in the vicinity of the word *cells* indicates Prison cells is meant rather than Blood cells.[19] Although the BIOSIS algorithms were developed for the purpose of automatically classifying documents, they can be used as well to identify and resolve multireferential terms.

Relational Semantics

Overall Purpose

After terms are selected, classified, and disambiguated, the next step in normalizing a subject vocabulary is to establish meaning relationships among them. The set of meaning relationships for a particular subject language constitutes its relational semantics. A relational semantics is the chief means used to meet the recall requirement of the collocation objective. The amount of effort it takes to bring together all works on the same subject varies from one discipline to another in proportion to which its literature is terminologically inconsistent.[20] A literature is terminologically inconsistent when it uses concepts that can be represented in different ways — that is, if its vocabulary lacks representational predictability.[21]

For minimal subject collocation, all that is required is to set up equivalence relationships among synonyms. Most subject languages, however, go beyond this to establish hierarchical relationships as well as related-term relationships. At first sight going beyond what is absolutely necessary would appear to be an overly generous interpretation of the collocation objective as it relates to subject. However, studies have shown that users are prone to choose search terms that are broader or narrower than, or otherwise related to, the terms used by indexers to describe the subjects of documents.[22] Thus, it is necessary to collocate not only works on *exactly* the same subject but also works on *nearly* the same subject, such as works on a more general subject or on one that overlaps. (Compare the concept of *work,* a device designed to bring together both exactly the same and nearly the same information.) Similarly, to construct bridges between user and system languages, as is required by the navigation objective, requires more relational structure that can be achieved by simple equivalence relationships. For both collocation and navigation, related-term and hierarchical relationships are needed to supplement equivalence relationships.

Equivalence Relationships

Nature and Purpose

Relationships that hold between two or more orthographic variants, word-form variants, syntactic variants, or synonyms are *equivalence relationships*. Equivalence relationships have the properties of symmetry, reflexivity, and transitivity. Terms that stand in such relationships form an equivalence set. They are intersubstitutable in (nearly) all contexts, including that of retrieving information, where the implication is that searching under one will retrieve all documents that could be retrieved by searching under the other(s).

The need to link equivalent terms for effective retrieval would seem to be self-evident, yet it has been challenged with the argument that users are often indifferent to the recall capabilities of a retrieval language, and, if not, they can use Boolean ORs to link equivalent terms. This argument, however, does not take into account the user's right to collocation. It does not recognize the right of the user for whom good recall really matters, such as the historian who wants comprehensive knowledge of an event or the scientist who has to know if his research finding is novel. Even if users want only one document, they have a right to be shown all those that might be relevant to be able to select the best for their purposes. Further, the argument makes the assumption that users are not only aware that relevant material could be missed because of terminological inconsistency but also sophisticated enough to deal with the problem. Undoubtedly users are becoming more sophisticated in devising searches. There is even research to suggest that some may be better able to control vocabulary than some thesaurus designers.[23] Still, there will always be users who are naïve, inarticulate, or desultory, whose needs will not be met if the burden and expense of equivalence linking were shifted to them.

Techniques

The traditional technique used by subject languages to show equivalence is the same as that used by author-title languages: one of the equivalent terms is selected as preferred and the others are mapped to it using *See* or *Use* cross-references. The nonpreferred terms are considered part of the subject language's lead-in vocabulary, the vocabulary whose job it is to map user vocabulary onto system vocabulary. For subjects, as for authors and works, the choice of a preferred term from among a set of equivalent terms is usually and ideally done in accordance with the dictates of the principle of common usage.

Cross-references are not the only means to link equivalent terms. When terms are trivially equivalent,[24] as in the case of the singular and plural forms of a word, it is easier and less costly to establish general rules stipulating when the singular is to be used and when the plural. One of the simpler such rules — and one widely used — is the much-many rule, which distinguishes count from mass nouns. If the question "How many?" can be asked of a term-referent (How many birds?), the term is formulated in the plural. If, on the other hand, the appropriate question is "How much?" (How much grain?), the term is rendered in the singular.

Another technique for handling equivalence relationships is double (or multiple) indexing. For example, in an index to a classification, each of two synonyms can be made to point to the same class number, which obviates the need to link them to each other. In a book index the same technique can be used, each of two synonyms being made to point to the same text passages. Traditionally, indexing with each of the terms in an equivalence set is done only when the number of referents is small; little expense of space or labor is involved, and the user is spared a look-up step in his search. In a digital environment an effect similar to that of linking synonyms through a common referent is achieved by transparent linking.

Common Usage

A difficulty with synonym control has always been to find a *common usage* on which to base the choice of a preferred term. Many usages are common, and often any choice among them can only be arbitrary. Recognizing the limitation of the common-usage principle, Cutter suggested other criteria for choice: a scientific term, for example, should be chosen when the common term is ambiguous or ill defined, and a term should be chosen that brings the subject it names into the neighborhood of related subjects.[25] However, as was discussed in the context of author names, difficulties in finding a common usage become moot in a digital environment where it is possible to link two synonyms transparently and to retrieve the same set of documents no matter which is used in a search. In such an environment equal access can be provided for all "common" usages. But again, the equal-access approach, while a boon to users, does not necessarily eliminate the need on the part of the subject-language designer for choosing preferred terms, since preferences are needed for ordering online displays.

Definition of Equivalence

Another problem in the linking of equivalent terms is how much leeway to allow in deciding when two terms are equivalent. Certain term variants are obviously (nearly automatically) equivalent: orthographic variants (Color and colour), word-form variants (Cove vaults and Coved vaults), and syntactic variants (Egypt, Modern and Modern Egypt). Even some synonyms are obviously equivalent: tradename variants (Kleenex, used in its generic sense, and Facial tissues), dialect variants (Lift and elevator) and scientific-popular variants (Daisy and Bellis perenis). The problem comes with terms that refer to almost the same thing — terms whose denotational meanings overlap. There are few true synonyms in natural language, in the sense of being intersubstitutable in all contexts. Even words that refer to the same thing may not be identical in meaning due to the presence of emotive overtones that color meaning (Guerrillas and Freedom fighters).[26] The problem in retrieval caused by terms close in meaning can be exemplified by the following: Marshes, Bogs, Wetlands, Swamps, and Marshlands. Should these terms be considered equivalent? To do so would improve recall for those users who do not perceive or care about the fine distinctions in meaning among them. But, at the same time, to regard them as equivalent would impair precision for the scholarly user for whom such distinctions matter. Whenever in the design of a subject language there is a choice between a recall- or precision-enhancing feature (and this happens not infrequently), either one or the other must be favored or a way found to accommodate both. The latter course is preferable and in a digital environment also feasible since it is possible to construct a retrieval interface that can query searchers about their precision and recall preferences. Of the many ways the computer is changing how subject languages are designed, probably the most welcome is the means it offers to overcome the trade-off barrier that pits precision against recall.

Sometimes *See* or *Use* cross-references are used to link terms that are clearly not equivalent. For instance, they may be used to link a specific term to a broader one (Plant waxes *See* Waxes). This is done to control the generality level of the subject language and thus the number of terms it contains. *See* references are sometimes used to link antonyms, on the grounds that antonyms represent opposite points on a continuum scale and, thus, really refer to the same concept. However (again), the use of one device for multiple purposes has the potential to cause trouble. In this particular case it has the potential to cause serious miscommunication in retrieval, to deteriorate precision, and to obstruct transparent linking.

Automation of Equivalence Relationships

Automatically linking equivalent and nearly equivalent terms is fairly trivial when the terms are morphologically related. Many search systems already incorporate features that provide this kind of linking. One such feature is automatic searching on singular-plural variants. Another is suffix   dropping, whereby terms with the same stem are coalesced, such as Inform,

Informs, Informing, Information, Informatics. Since it is wasteful to do intellectually and expensively at the level of subject language design what can be done mechanically and relatively cheaply at the system level, it may be expected that even more can be done automatically and that eventually most retrieval systems will incorporate algorithms to equate orthographic, word form, and syntactic variants.

Terms that are semantically but not formally equivalent (terms like Kleenex and Facial tissues) cannot be automatically linked, since the perception of equivalence among wholly different character strings is intrinsically intellectual. However, the design of a subject language or the development of a sophisticated search interface can mechanically mine already existing terminological databases for information about synonymy, such as dictionaries, thesauri, glossaries, and terminological databanks.[27]

Related-Term Relationships
Nature and Purpose
Equivalence relationships shade through a continuum into related-term relationships. The latter can be quite as effective as the former in contributing to collocation, particularly when a search is ambiguously formulated. Also related-term relationships contribute to navigation. As a stimulant to verbal imagination they lead users to effectively articulated search requests. Traditional guidelines for constructing subject languages define related-term relationships vaguely, negatively, and broadly to include all semantic relationships, except equivalence and hierarchy.[28] The only mathematical property possessed by the related-term relationship is that of symmetry: if A is related to B, then B is related to A.

Techniques
The traditional ways to link related terms is through cross-references or by juxtaposition. Cross-references usually take the form of *See also* references or RT (Related term) references, such as Boats *See also* Ships, or Boats RT Ships. The juxtaposition of related terms is shown by their placement in hierarchical and other types of graphical displays. The preferred electronic method to indicate related-term relatedness is through the use of hyperlinks, which is obviously superior to traditional methods in reducing the effort involved in related-term look-ups to a mouse click. Hyperbole has

surrounded the introduction of hyperlinking, even to the extent that some see automatic associationing as a means to extend the intellectual capabilities of the species (as a hammer was able to extend its physical prowess), a means so powerful as to catapult these capabilities to a new level of evolutionary development.[29]

Lack of Rigor

There is a general lack of rigor in expressing conditions under which two terms can be considered related. A quite unbelievable condition used in the early days of LCSH allowed two terms to be related if they occurred in the same monograph![30] The lack of rigor has continued even into recent times — for instance, in the stipulation that two terms are related "if it is believed that the user, when examining one of them, might want to be reminded of the existence of the other."[31] Determinations of relatedness based on conditions such as these inevitably are subjective and lead to inconsistencies in constructing related-term relationships. On the assumption that this inconsistency detracts from their usefulness, current standards are tending to urge strict control be exerted over stating conditions for when two terms are related.[32]

In the interest of rigor, some thesauri use the guideline that two terms are related if one is strongly implied by the other,[33] by which is meant: "one of the terms should always be implied, according to the common frames of reference shared by the users of the index, whenever the other is used as an indexing term."[34] The meaning of *implied* or *strongly implied* is further explicated by the gloss: two terms are related if one is a necessary component in the explanation of the other, as, for example, Birds is used in the explanation of Ornithology.[35] (The gloss could be made even more operational by specifying the source used for the explanation.) The gloss provides formalistic rigor and, at the same time, represents an attempt to construe related-term relationships as paradigmatic. It is possible, however, that what is gained in rigor is paid for by loss in scope and potential, there being more pathways through the bibliographic universe than can be formulated in terms of relationships built on definitions.

Another approach to regularizing the related-term relationship is to replace it with a group of more specific relationships. The more specific relationships can be formalized in terms of schema: two terms A and B are related if "A is presupposed by B," "A uses B," "A causes B," and so on.[36] For a particular discipline, semantic relationships of this kind can be discovered by examining the discipline's literature, the vocabulary tools already developed for it, and the hypertext links users employ when browsing it. The breaking down of generic related-term relationships into groups of more specific relationships would seem to be inevitable in the general evolution of subject languages toward specificity and formalism. Yet the possibility remains that really helpful related-term relationships might actually be those that are lexically indeterminate, those that do not lend themselves to formalization.

Automation of Related-Term Relationships

One approach to the problem of stating conditions under which two terms are helpfully related is simply not to face it — at least not at the point of subject-language construction. This approach, besides being economical, is worth considering in an online environment where alternative means exist for suggesting helpful terms to users. Examples of such means are relevance feedback mechanisms that respond to a user's search request by displaying terms similar to those in the request. The terms may be similar simply by cooccurring in the same citations or in previous search requests,[37] by having a hypertext link worn between them, or by statistically co-occurring in a given database of documents. Using various measures of similarity to operationalize related-term conditions not only is economically attractive but also has the further advantage of defining relatedness empirically in terms of documents retrieved, thus conforming to the stricture that related terms should be established only if they would be required in retrieval.[38]

Hierarchical Relationships
Nature and Purpose

The most philosophically interesting of the semantic relationships are those that are *hierarchical*. They may be the most effective in furthering the collocation and navigation objectives. They are a powerful means for optimizing recall and precision,[39] and at the same time, they are the quintessential means for navigating a knowledge domain. Their efficacy in fulfilling these functions stems from their ability to resolve the retrieval problems caused by the fact that a given object or concept may be referred to at different levels of specificity, such as *furniture, chair, kitchen chair*. Despite the claim that there is a common abstraction level at which most people operate,[40] studies have shown considerable variability in the specificity of users' search vocabulary.[41] Vocabulary specificity is something that needs to be adjusted at the time of retrieval in accordance both with the literature being searched and users' precision and recall requirements. Hierarchical structures facilitate this adjustment by enabling users to move a concept up or down verbal abstraction ladders until the correct expression for it is found.

Knowledge domains are structured hierarchically. Some believe that this may not be a quirk of custom or chance but inevitable. Our brains are hardwired to perceive hierarchical relationships, and, consequently, the only way to comprehend a knowledge domain is through the structure they provide.[42] While this may be debatable, not so is the fact that the hierarchical relationships that structure knowledge domains are paralleled by similar structures in subject languages used for information retrieval. This is what gives these languages their navigation power — their ability to guide users on encyclopedic tours of knowledge domains. Hierarchical structures are of particular help to users with anomalous information needs — for instance, the user who browses the hierarchically ordered stacks of a library looking for a "good book," or the one who browses a hierarchical display in an online catalog looking for a "good" search term. How often serendipitous bibliographic discovery is the result of being invisibly guided by hierarchical structures is not known, but that sort of discovery is why those structures exist.

Hierarchical relationships take a variety of forms. In the previous section the two most important were introduced: genus-species and perspective hierarchies. The genus-species relationship, also known as the *inclusion* relationship, is the classic hierarchical relationship with the properties of reflexivity, transitivity, and antisymmetry. It has another property as well, which in the computer literature is called *inheritance* and in the classification literature *hierarchical force,* whereby what is true of a given class (Furniture) is true of all classes it subsumes (Chairs, Tables, and so on).

Two traditional canons guide class-subclass formation. These are the canons of mutual exclusivity and total exhaustivity. Articulated first by

Aristotle to ensure there would be no cross-classification in nature, the canon of mutual exclusivity requires that the subclasses of a class be nonoverlapping. A corollary to this canon requires that the different characteristics by which a class can be divided be distinguished and applied sequentially. For instance, literature can be subdivided by the characteristics of form, time period, and language, but to incorporate these in a single subdivision would result in cross-classification, such as poetry, nineteenth-century, French. The canon of total exhaustivity requires that in the class-subclass breakdown all subclasses be enumerated. The reason for these two canons is to ensure that there exists a class for every topic — or if it is a shelf classification, for every book — and that every topic, or book, belongs to one and only one class.

Perspective relationships are considerably less strict than genus-species relationships, for the most part neither possessing their properties nor conforming to the canons of exclusivity and exhaustivity. (Often it is incorrectly assumed that what is true of the genus-species relationship is also is true of other types of hierarchical relationships.) Perspective relationships express points of view or aspects from which an object or concept is regarded. In many discipline-based classifications, the point of view is the knowledge domain in which the object or concept is located. As described earlier, an essential difference between perspective and genus-species relationships is that the former hold contingently in particular empirical contexts, while the latter, being a priori and definitionally true, always hold. The genus-species relationship limits a rat to being a rodent; a perspective relationship allows it to be an agricultural pest, an experimental animal, and so on. Philosophically, the distinction between the two kinds of relationship is paralleled by Hume's distinction between two different kinds of knowledge: relations among ideas and matters of fact.

The hierarchical relationships used in subject languages are not limited to genus-species and perspective relationships, although these dominate. Another class of hierarchical relationships, recognized by both thesauri and classifications, are the various whole-part relationships, such as the physical component part relationship (such as between a church and an altar), the conceptual topic-subtopic relationship (between Physics and Mechanics, Optics, Heat, and so on), and the nominal geographic region-subregion relationship (such as the United States and California). Whole-part relationships are not necessarily or logically true, being synthetic rather than analytic. A church may lose its altar, a subject discipline may reconfigure its subtopics, and a geographic region may be of temporal duration. They do not, therefore, have the same logical properties as the mathematical inclusion relationship. Some thesauri standards advise against including the whole-part relationship in the broader-term and narrower-term (BT-NT) set of relationships, preferring to treat it independently as a separate broader-term partitive relationship or including it as a form of related-term relationship.

Traditionally, the whole-part relationships have been difficult to deal with in vocabulary control tools, especially universal tools where many objects have a similar componential breakdowns (such as every animal has an anatomy). To repeat the breakdown into parts again and again (to divide every animal by head, ears, eyes, nose, and so on) would be costly and would burgeon a classification in book form. For this reason the establishing of whole-part relationships is frequently done using pattern rules, such as the DDC rule to construct a class number for a work on the flowers, leaves, or roots of a magnolia tree according to a general pattern for parts of plants. In an online classification, however, whole-part relationships that occur repeatedly may be stored once and automatically displayed whenever appropriate. The fact that they can usefully be stored and displayed differently from genus-species relationships underscores the value of discriminating between them.

For any kind of sophisticated automated information retrieval, as well as expert system development, different types of hierarchical relationships must be distinguished. They call for different management in storing and updating classificatory information and have different roles to play in the dialogue, retrieval, and display functions of online catalogs. Moreover, unless different types of hierarchical relationships are formally distinguished, the programming of automated techniques for perspective searching, transparent linking, and broadening or narrowing searches is thwarted. If inclusion relationships are not distinguished from other types of hierarchical relationships, expert-systems applications are restricted. Most seriously, perhaps, if the different types of hierarchical relationships are not distinguished, any attempt to translate among several classifications or simply to achieve compatibility in retrieval is impaired.

Techniques

In classificatory structures presented as vertical linear displays, hierarchical relationships are shown by successive indentation. In graphic displays they are indicated as branches in tree structures. In thesauri they are shown using BT (broader-term) and NT (narrower-term) links, such as Irish setters BT Dogs and Dogs NT Irish setters. Although different types of hierarchical relationships have different properties and fulfill different functions, they are seldom typographically distinguished in vocabulary control tools. An exception to this is the whole-part relationship, which some thesauri distinguish from generic hierarchical relationships using the two different indicators BTP (broader-term partitive) and BTG (broader-term generic). As yet little innovation has taken place in the graphic representation of hierarchical relationships on computer screens, one problem being how to squeeze the information into a small space. Some experimentation has been done in this area using linearized tree displays in the form of chains.[43]

Choice of Hierarchical Type

The type of hierarchical relationship to admit into a subject language depends on a variety of factors. Chief among these is the nature of the vocabulary to be structured, the purpose for which the structuring is done, and whether the subject language is classificatory or alphabetic (whether its vocabulary control tool is a classification or a thesaurus). Of less import, but still an issue, is whether the option exists to represent hierarchical relationships syntactically as well as semantically.

If the vocabulary of a discipline is soft and includes many terms with linguistically indeterminate referents, it is almost useless to attempt to structure it by genus-species type relationships. Nor does it serve much purpose to force abstract terms like Love, Truth, and Beauty (or for that matter, terms whose meaning are largely dependent on context) into Procrustean genus-species structures. Because it is logical, genus-species structuring works best for terms whose meanings are concrete and relatively well delimited, which is why it is used predominately for structuring scientific vocabularies. Vocabularies that are polysemantic and vague are appropriately and better structured by perspective hierarchies.

Choice of relationship type depends also on the purposes for which the relationships are intended in retrieval. For instance, because it is logical, the genus-species hierarchy is effective for broadening and narrowing searches.

For this reason it is also effective in retrieval strategies that exploit inheritance properties and in artificial-intelligence applications based on knowledge representations. On the other hand, because they lack formal properties, perspective hierarchies are not suited to such applications, but because they provide context, they can assist in navigation. They are ideally suited for disambiguating multireferential terms.[44]

The subject language used, whether classificatory or alphabetic, is also a determinant of hierarchical type. Many thesauri tend (or attempt) to limit the relationships they use to paradigmatic, genus-species type relationships. Classifications, particularly those that are universal and discipline based, while they use genus-species relationships in taxonomic contexts, also make extensive use of perspective hierarchies. To use a term in a disciplinary context is to provide perspective. For instance, Clothing in the DDC is located in nine different contexts: the armed forces, the arts, customs, health, home economics, home sewing, product safety, psychological influence, and social welfare. It would be misleading to suggest that the thesauri used to control the vocabulary of alphabetic-subject languages never make use of perspective hierarchies or that they never locate a term in more than one hierarchy. The difference is one of degree, but the degree is substantial.

There is another structural difference between classificatory and alphabetic subject languages pertaining to the use of hierarchical relationships. This is degree of connectedness, by which is meant the degree to which one term can, by following a path of relationships, be related to another term. Most classifications aim to map a knowledge domain and, in so doing, to show the location of each term relative to all others. This is beyond the ambition of most thesauri. The difference this makes to structure is that the hierarchies in a classification coalesce to form a gigantic upside-down tree, whereas those in a thesaurus resemble more a scattering of small shrubs.[45] It is sometimes asked, If an alphabetic-subject language is used to describe the subject content of documents, why is a classificatory language needed as well? One answer to the question is that classifications, because of their perspective relationships and connectivity, are better designed than thesauri to disambiguate terms and to represent conventional relational knowledge.

Automation of Hierarchical Relationships
Hierarchical relationships, both of the genus-species type and the perspective type, are fundamental to thinking. Genus-species and class-member

relationship are logical, in the sense that they form the basis for syllogistic reasoning. Perspective and topic-subtopic relationships are conventional, in the sense that they have been established by custom to organize thought within a knowledge domain. Whether established by logic or convention, intellectual relationships are the product of human thinking and as such cannot be created automatically — at least not *ex nihilo*.[46] On the other hand, other wholly new kinds of "nonintellectual" hierarchical relationships can be created using automatic means. It is possible, for instance, to cluster terms based on their similar statistical distributions and then to order these clusters hierarchically.[47] Such clusters are proving useful in automatic indexing, but as the hierarchies they create are divorced from meaning, both logical and conventional, they are likely to be of limited use for navigation and semantic collocation.[48]

General Issues

Semantics versus Syntax

Some of the meaning relationships that constitute the relational structure of a subject language can be expressed semantically in the controlled vocabulary or syntactically in the synthesized expressions (strings or subject headings) of the language. The question this poses is which relationships should be expressed where? For enumerative subject languages that do not admit of synthesized expressions, the question is moot. For synthetic languages, there has been a tendency since the time of Cutter to put paradigmatic relationships into the relational structure of the controlled vocabulary and syntagmatic relationships into the synthesized expressions.[49] Cutter purposefully designed a language whose subject headings would be hierarchy-free, so that users might have direct and specific, as opposed to classified, access to information. In 1957 John Metcalfe, attempting to explicate Cutter on this point, distinguished specification from qualification, the former to be expressed semantically and the latter syntactically.[50] A short time later Charles Bernier, who was instrumental in the design of early information retrieval thesauri, argued that thesaural relationships should be permanent rather than transient.[51] A decade later, Derek Austin introduced the *paradigmatic-syntagmatic* polarity to distinguish the a priori information that belongs in a thesaurus from contingent information that belongs in an index language string. Austin was instrumental in drafting thesaurus standards in England as well as internationally, and these standards also advise limiting thesaural relationships to those that are paradigmatic.[52]

The paradigmatic-syntagmatic distinction is difficult to maintain in practice. In fact, it could be argued that to limit thesaural relationships to those that are paradigmatic is to limit their effectiveness in navigation. This may be why in most thesauri quasi-synonyms inevitably creep into equivalence relationships; most related-term relationships are contingent in nature, and of all hierarchical relationships, only the genus-species kind is truly paradigmatic. Actually, even at a theoretical level the distinction is difficult to sustain. This has been observed by philosophers and linguists alike, the former holding that the dualism is untenable and the latter that the two are not mutually exclusive since often a given relationship can be expressed either paradigmatically or syntagmatically.[53] In any case, the issue of the relative roles of semantics and syntax in expressing relational information is an intriguing one and one that needs to be addressed in the design of subject languages. Not to address it runs the risk of inadvertently expressing relational information both semantically and syntactically — thus, introducing synonymy into a language purposefully designed to exclude it. Making the distinction is difficult, however. It may, as J. C. Gardin observes, come down to the practical expedient of expressing straightforward relations (those frequently used in a given domain of knowledge) semantically and expressing unpredictable relations (those that bring forth new knowledge) syntactically.[54]

Compatibility

A major impediment to the compatibility of subject languages is their different semantic structures. Strong compatibility, in the sense of translatability, requires that relational structures be isomorphic. This is clearly an unrealistic requirement, if only because different subject languages use differing degrees of paradigmatic rigor in defining relational structures, an example being when one language defines the equivalence relationship strictly and another allows it to include quasi synonyms. Another example is where one subject language expresses relational information (such as a whole-part relationship) syntactically and another expresses the same information semantically in the form of a hierarchical relationship. Perhaps the most frequent source of contrariety is where one subject language contains relational information and another does not — for example, when different characteristics of division are used in hierarchy construction.

Although two nonisomorphic relational structures cannot be mapped one onto the other, they can be merged, in which case they may be said to be weakly compatible. The merging of the relational structures of two subject languages presumes the prior merging and joint disambiguation of their vocabularies. In the actual merging of structures, each of the contributing terms brings along with it from its source all of its family relations. An example of vocabulary incorporating merged semantic structures is the Metathesaurus created for the Unified Medical Language System. Because merging semantic structures is a labor-intensive undertaking, some metathesauri, such as *The Art and Architecture Thesaurus,* incorporate only the vocabularies of participating languages and stop short of relational integration.

Degree of Semantic Structure

In the design of a subject language a decision must be made as to how much semantic structure to incorporate. The decision has cost-benefit implications insofar as the expense and (in theory) the effectiveness of the language increase with the number and kind of semantic relationships it recognizes. Minimally structured, a vocabulary might recognize as equivalent orthographic variants; at a slightly higher level, singular plural variants; at succeedingly higher levels, true synonyms and then quasi-synonyms. Minimal structure is exceeded when linkages are made between related terms, still more when terms are linked generically, and significantly more when they are linked by perspective relationships. Various measures have been used to describe the degree of semantic structure exhibited by a subject language, the most obvious being simple number counts of the different kinds of relationships. A more descriptive statistic, richness of structure measure, was introduced by G. Van Slype and defined as the ratio of the number of semantic relationships in a thesaurus and the total number of terms contained in it.[55]

Given that there is some leeway in how much semantic structure to include in a subject language, the question of payoff arises. C. Cleverdon, J. Mills, and M. Keen were among the first to address this question in the second Cranfield experiment.[56] To test the effectiveness of semantic structure in retrieval, they compared thirty-three subject languages incorporating varying amounts of structure (called *degrees of control*). The startling result was that a minimally controlled language, one in which only synonyms and word endings were normalized, performed as well or better in retrieval than any other. Although the experiment was methodologically flawed, its result cannot be summarily dismissed. Syllogistic argumentation, taking as its premises the bibliographic objectives, can be used to demonstrate rationally why a highly structured subject language is effective in promoting collocation and navigation. But this does not guarantee that a particular language used in a particular place and time will be effective. Effectiveness depends on many factors, not all of which are easily controlled: how comprehensive the language is, how well it is applied, how well it is manipulated in retrieval, and whether searchers are clever enough to find what they want without it.[57]

10

Subject-Language Syntax

History

In 1955 the Classification Research Group published a classic paper entitled "The Need for a Faceted Classification as the Basis of All Methods of Information Retrieval."[1] It was a manifesto, and its theme was emblematic of what probably has been the most significant trend in subject-language development in the twentieth century — the shift from largely enumerative to largely synthetic languages.[2] The enumerative-synthetic distinction is between languages whose allowable expressions are listed in an authority file and languages whose expressions can be created from a basic core vocabulary using the syntax rules of the language. To illustrate the distinction and its significance, it is useful to review briefly the work of the three theorists who have contributed most to the synthesis movement.

Julius Otto Kaiser

Kaiser published his book *Systematic Indexing* in 1911. He viewed indexing as "the process by which information is made accessible."[3] He defined this process as consisting of two steps: subject analysis and the application of a subject language. The first step was to "take literature to pieces" — that is, to analyze it into kernels or nuclei of normalized information. The second step was to rearrange or synthesize these nuclei into subject descriptions in accordance with prescribed rules. This two-step method of indexing has since come to be called the *analytico-synthetic method* and subject languages employing it *analytico-synthetic languages*.

Kaiser grudged natural language its anomalies, ambiguities, and imprecision. His *Systematic Indexing* was to be a "machinery for regularizing or standardizing language."[4] Though artificial, designed for the special purpose of indexing, Kaiser's index language was nevertheless modeled on the structure of natural language in its use of grammatical categories and rules of syntax. It uses three categories of terms: (1) names of concretes, representing things, real or imaginary (such as money, machines); (2) names of processes, representing either conditions attaching to things or their actions (such as trade, manufacture); and (3) names of localities, representing, for the most part countries (such as France, South Africa).[5]

The syntax rules in Kaiser's language are used to construct well-formed expressions, which he called *statements*. These rules are defined with reference to the grammatical categories of the language, analogously to the way well-formed sentences in a natural language are defined using a syntax that references categories such as subject and predicate. However, whereas a natural language is characterized by a seemingly uncountable number of syntax rules, Kaiser's simple artificial language used only three:

Concrete—Process, such as Wool—Scouring
Country—Process, such as Brazil—Education
Concrete—Country—Process, such as Coffee—Chile—Trade

Kaiser is credited by R. K. Olding for instituting the greatest single advance in indexing theory since Cutter[6] and by J. Metcalfe as being the best mind, in its capacity for scientific and logical thinking, that has applied itself to subject indexing.[7] Little known today, Kaiser nearly a century ago created a blueprint that would chart the course of subject indexing in the twentieth century: first, by introducing the idea of a subject language and working out its particulars, and second, by his forceful articulation of the position that effective information organization requires standardized or canonical representations of information that avoid the inconsistencies of natural language.

S. R. Ranganathan

While Kaiser was its precursor, Shiyali Ramamrita Ranganathan was the bellwether of the analytico-synthetic movement. This came about as a result of an illuminating experience he had in 1924 while attending the School of Librarianship, University College London. At the time he was troubled by the inability of traditional classifications to cope with the constantly expanding universe of knowledge. Pondering how to deal with this problem, he happened to visit Selfridges Department Store, where for an hour he watched a demonstration of a Mecanno set wherein different toys were constructed from a set of uniform slotted strips, wheels, rods, screws, nuts, and pieces of string. Surprised and delighted he saw the Mecanno set as a model for knowledge organization. If a variety of toys could be built from a standardized set of parts, why not build a knowledge classification from the constituent parts of knowledge? The idea of reducing complexity to simplicity, and in particular of reducing the vast universe of knowledge to a set of atomic concepts and certain basic relations among them, captured Ranganathan's mathematical imagination. Witnessing the Mecanno demonstration gave him the idea to design a wholly analytico-synthetic faceted classification, his Colon Classification.[8]

The Colon Classification was designed to overcome the difficulty enumerative languages have in keeping pace with knowledge. Another problem with enumerative languages is that they are uneconomical, as is evident if one tries to imagine describing a natural language like English by listing all the well-formed expressions in it. Much simpler is to classify terms first into categories (nouns, verbs, and so on) and then define a syntax with respect to these categories to combine the terms into sentences. Similarly for a classificatory language, it is economical to classify terms into a few fundamental categories and then to construct syntax rules to combine the categorized terms into the well-formed expressions. The Colon Classification was designed using such an approach. As a classification, it is both dynamic and parsimonious. Consisting of the constituent parts of knowledge, it is capable of expressing all subjects presently existing and those that might be evolved in the future. At the same time it relies on relatively few elements and little machinery, in the form of terms and rules, to accomplish this.

The grammatical categories used by the Colon Classification are Personality, Matter, Energy, Space, and Time (PMEST). Postulated as semantic universals common to all knowledge, they manifest themselves in their particularity as discipline-specific facets.[9] The syntax rules defined in terms of these facets are expressed as formulae using the letters P, M, E, S, and T separated by marks of punctuation called *facet indicators*. (The colon mark of punctuation preceding the Energy category is what gives the Classification its name.) An example of a formula used to construct well-formed expressions in the discipline of Economics is [P] : [E] .[S] '[T]. An instance of the formula is X62:8.44'N5, which stands for Management of banks in India up to 1950. (X stands for Economics, 62 for Banks, 8 for Management, 44 for India, and N5 for 1950.)

A problem in constructing a syntactical formula is to determine a helpful order of components. This is the problem of *citation order,* which writ large is the problem of finding an underlying rationale for subject-language syntax rules. Ranganathan dealt with the problem using a variety of prescriptions — ranging from the simple rule that the order of terms in a well-formed expression should be one of decreasing concreteness to the complex rule that the order of terms should follow the absolute syntax that characterizes the deep structure of natural languages. (The issues raised by citation order are discussed later in this chapter.)

Derek Austin

In 1952 an English Classification Research Group (CRG) was formed to review the principles and problems of classification. The Group was much influenced by the work of Ranganathan and after three years of work issued its manifesto declaring that a successful retrieval system must incorporate a faceted classification. The original members of the Group, which included notables such as Eric J. Coates, Douglas J. Foskett, Jack Mills, and Brian C. Vickery, produced a number of exemplary faceted languages. None, however, was accorded the recognition that attached to that designed by a relative latecomer to the Group, Derek Austin. His Preserved Context Indexing System (PRECIS) language enjoyed great popularity in the 1970s and 1980s and was used to provide subject access to databases as prominent as the British National Bibliography and the Australian National Bibliography.

PRECIS is a universal alphabetic-subject language that differs innovatively from its predecessors in incorporating an automated syntax based on a generative grammar. The crux of its design is that it allows the intellectual part of subject analysis to be done humanly and the clerical part mechanically. The intellectual part consists of selecting, normalizing, and categorizing the concepts that describe the aboutness of a document. The operation of categorizing is accomplished by tagging the concepts with role operators. These are used to designate not only facets but also modifiers, connectives, and certain syntagmatic relationships like the part-whole relationships. As an example of PRECIS indexing, a document on Training of skilled personnel in Canada might be described by the terms Canada, Skilled personnel, and Training. The first term is tagged with (0) to indicate a locality, the second by (1) to indicate the key system (what is being talked about or the object of an action), and the third by (2) to indicate an action:

Canada
Skilled personnel
Training

Role operators serve not only to classify concepts but also as computer formatting instructions. The (0), (1), and (2) tell the computer how to sequence, punctuate, and script terms in an index language string. In the above example, the PRECIS index generator would output three different index entries:

Canada
   Skilled personnel. Training
Skilled personnel. Canada
   Training
Training. Skilled personnel. Canada

The PRECIS automated-syntax routines incorporate three different ordering algorithms. Which one is activated depends on the combination of role operators used in the indexing. The routines are designed to produce coextensive entries that express in summary form the whole subject of a document. Also they are intended to produce entries meaningful in the sense that each term is shown in context and the order of terms in a string is understandable according to common frames of reference.[10]

Kaiser's *Systematic Indexing* is now a period piece; Ranganathan's Colon Classification is used infrequently, even in India; and the heyday of PRECIS is over. Nevertheless, these languages, particularly in the development of their syntax, have served as prototypes in guiding the ongoing development of other languages with better economic backing and survival power.

The Scene Today

The subject languages in widespread use today are the Library of Congress Subject Headings (LCSH), the Dewey Decimal Classification (DDC), the Library of Congress Classification (LCC), and the Universal

Decimal Classification (UDC). These languages can be characterized syntactically along three dimensions: whether they are term or string languages, precoordinate or postcoordinate languages, and enumerative or synthetic languages.

A *term language* is one that does not employ a syntax. Most discipline-specific languages that use thesauri as vocabulary tools fall into this category. (A significant exception is the Medical Subject Headings Language.) A *string language* is one that concatenates terms into larger expressions. In alphabetic-subject languages these expressions are called *strings* or *subject headings* and in classificatory languages *synthesized* or *built numbers*.

The distinction between a term and a string language is similar but not coincident with that between a precoordinate language and a postcoordinate language. *Pre* and *post* reference the time at which terms are concatenated into large expressions. In a precoordinate language, this is done prior to retrieval by a professional in a manner defined by the syntax rules of the language. In a postcoordinate language, it is done at the time of retrieval by a user using a Boolean-based syntax. A concatenated expression in a precoordinate language is a subject heading or a built number; in a postcoordinate language, it is a search prescription.[11] Syntax-free term languages depend more on postcoordination than string languages that come with a built-in syntax.

The distinction between a subject language that uses syntax and one that does not also overlaps the distinction between a synthetic and an enumerative language. A term language is exclusively enumerative: all expressions in it that can be used for indexing or searching are listed in a vocabulary tool such as a thesaurus. A string language, though it employs a syntax, can be enumerative if its constructed expressions are editorially established — that is, established by the designer of the language rather than by the indexers who apply it. It is synthetic to the extent that it provides syntax rules allowing the indexer to create subject strings. The universal subject languages in use today incorporate both enumeration and synthesis. Their syntax can be illustrated using the Library of Congress Subject Headings and the Dewey Decimal Classification as examples.

Library of Congress Subject Headings

The Library of Congress Subject Headings (LCSH) language began in 1898 and was first published as a list in 1909. Its construction followed the precepts laid down by Cutter in his *Rules for a Dictionary Catalog*. Cutter developed a subject approach to information that was in opposition to the then prevalent classified approach, which he regarded as overly generic and suitable only for scholars. His was an approach that permitted specific and direct access to subject information through a string language that was normalized, alphabetic, and precoordinate. For most of the twentieth century LCSH developed as a largely enumerated language. Its expressions, both terms and strings, were for the most part established editorially by those in charge of formulating the language at the Library of Congress. It was not until 1974 that significant synthesis was introduced in the form of free-floating subdivisions that indexers were permitted to append to main headings in accordance with the syntax rules of the language. The LCSH syntax began to grow in complexity, and, at the same time, the work of establishing subject headings began to be distributed outside the Library of Congress. This led in 1984 to the publishing a manual of procedures *(Subject Cataloging Manual: Subject Headings)*.[12] It is a voluminous work, the bulk of which constitutes the LCSH syntax rules.

An LCSH string begins with a main heading that focuses the aboutness of the document to be described. This may or may not be followed by qualifying terms, called *subdivisions*. The LCSH syntax rules specify when these subdivisions can be used and in what order. Like the prototypical synthetic languages designed by Kaiser, Ranganathan, and Austin, LCSH defines its syntax with respect to large semantically homogeneous classes of terms. But it does this only in part. In addition, it employs a syntax defined with respect to smaller, functional groupings of terms, and it also uses an enumerative syntax defined with respect to individual terms.

The facets used in LCSH are Topic, Place, Time, and Form. The most common syntactic constructions in LCSH are[13]

Topical main heading—Place—Topic—Time—Form
ex.: Art criticism—France—Paris—History—Nineteenth century—Bibliography

or

Topical main heading—Topic—Place—Time—Form
ex.: Art—Censorship—Europe—Twentieth century—Exhibitions

and

Geographic main heading—Topic—Time—Form
ex.: France—Intellectual life—Sixteenth century—Periodicals

The functional groupings of terms referenced by the LCSH syntax are either classes of main headings or classes of subdivisions. Syntax rules defined with respect to main-headings types are basically of two sorts:

- Those that list subdivisions permissible for a main heading type, such as names of ethnic groups, corporate bodies, persons, groups of persons, places, bodies of water, and so on, and
- Those that specify a pattern to be followed for a main-heading type, such as languages and diseases. The pattern is shown in the form of a subdivided model heading, which is taken to be emblematic of other like headings — for example, the subdivisions enumerated under English language may also be used under Swedish language.

Of the syntax rules defined with respect to classes of subdivisions, those most frequently used pertain to common or free-floating subdivisions, which can be used to divide any heading, subject to restrictions imposed at the level of the individual subdivision. For instance the subdivision Directories can be used "under names of countries, cities, etc., individual corporate bodies and families, and under classes of persons, ethnic groups, Christian denominations, types of organizations, and topical headings for individual directories containing names, addresses and other identifying data."[14] Subdivision-specific syntax rules are given in the form of notes and references in the authority list of LCSH terms and also in the form of lists of subdivisions and information sheets for individual subdivisions in the Library of Congress *Subject Cataloging Manual: Subject Headings*.

An example of the LCSH syntax defined with respect to individual terms is the editorially established string Food—Labeling; the subdivision Labeling is authorized for use only with the main heading Food. Term-specific syntax is often used with main headings designating countries, such as Sudan—History—Coup d'etat, 1985. Most but not all term-specific syntax is enumerative. An example of a nonenumerative term syntax is the templated phrase (May subd. Geog.) after a term to indicate the next term in a well-formed string can be the name of a geographic locality.

Dewey Decimal Classification

Like the Library of Congress Subject Headings, the Dewey Decimal Classification (DDC) has over the century and a quarter of its existence become increasingly synthetic. However, its syntax has evolved in a more regular fashion than that of LCSH. In a classificatory language, strings are concatenations not of terms but of numbers that stand for concepts. The syntactical process of concatenating coded concepts is called *number building,* and the resultant strings *built numbers.* The DDC syntax consists of its rules for number building.

A DDC built number begins with a base number to which other numbers are affixed. Like LCSH, DDC uses generalized syntax rules defined with respect to large, more or less homogeneous facets of terms as well as rules that reference specific terms. An example of a generalized syntax rule is one that authorizes the notation for terms of a recurring nature to be added to any number unless there is a specification to the contrary. In the DDC recurring terms are called *standard subdivisions* and include, for example, those designating form (Encyclopedias) and approaches to a subject (Research).

An example of a DDC syntax rule defined with respect to a particular term is the following:

Add to the base number 636.5920 (the number for Turkeys) the numbers following 636.0 in 636.001–636.08, such as raising turkeys for meat 636.5920883.

The DDC syntax can also be characterized with respect to where the numbers to be added to a base number can be found. These exist in three locations: in tables preceding the schedules of base numbers, in number spans within the schedules themselves, and in internal add tables preceding sequences of base numbers. Sets of numbers occurring in these different locations are used for different, but overlapping, purposes. The tables, of which there are six, are used to extend base numbers throughout the schedules, usually as-is but sometimes, where context requires, in modified form. They represent facets of varying homogeneity, generality, and applicability. Table 1, consisting of standard subdivisions, which resemble more a collection of facets than a single facet, has general applicability. Table 2 (Geographic Areas, Historical Periods, Persons) and Table 5 (Racial, Ethnic, National Groups) also are generally applicable and, like true facets, are relatively homogeneous. Tables 3, 4, and 6, on the other hand, are designed for use specifically with the disciplines of literature and language. Generalized and term-specific syntax rules authorize the use of numbers in Tables 1 and 2; use of those in Tables 3 to 7 must be authorized by term-specific rules.

Number spans within the DDC schedules are used to provide a patterned breakdown for groups of related topics. A span consists of the subdivisions of one class, which can be used by a dividelike principle to subdivide other classes also. For instance, in the add instruction illustrated above for Turkeys, the span 636.001–636.08 in Animal husbandry includes a variety of operations applicable to domestic animals in general, such as selection, breeding, care, and feeding. (Feeding of turkeys is 636.592084.) The span functions as a minifacet specific to domestic animals. In mini-facets like this, concepts are enumerated to the specificity needed to provide a suitably expressive base number and yet can be referenced at less depth if so required for the purpose of number building.

Add tables preceding sequences of base numbers are used to ensure uniformity in the sequencing of facets in a built number. They are placed at the beginning of the span of the base numbers beginning the sequences. For example,

748–788 Instruments and their music
  Add to each subdivision identified by * as follows
    01–09 Standard subdivision
      Notation from Table 1 as modified under 780.1–780.9
    1 General principles, musical forms, instruments
    11–17 General principles
      Add to 1 the numbers following 781 in 781.1–781.7
    18–19 Musical forms and instruments
      Add to 1 the numbers following 784.1 in 784.18–784.19.
In building numbers, do not add by use of 0 or 1 (alone or in combination) more than twice.

As the DDC has become more synthetic, it has made increasing use of facet indicators. Functioning as mnemonic repeaters, facet indicators signal that a syntax rule has been applied; semantically they herald a switch in aspect of the subject being treated. In the DDC, facet indicators take the form of digits. At first only zeros were used, to signify standard subdivisions and to announce add-ons from other tables. In 1989 when the highly faceted music schedule was developed for edition 20, the indicator 1 and subindicators 1x were introduced to signal facets such as musical form and size of ensemble. In 1996 when the biology schedule was developed for edition 21, four discipline-specific indicators were introduced (with certain exceptions): for animals, for plants, for when one topic in physiology is studied in another, and for biochemistry of specific physiological systems in animals and plants. Digits being in short supply, it is not possible to use facet indicators with consistent meaning throughout the DDC schedules and at times not even within the schedule for one discipline; however, their use and meaning are clear in context.

Problems and Issues

Term-String Synonymy

Sometimes it is possible to express a concept either as a term or a string, in which case a decision needs to be made to choose one or the other. For instance, should the concept of fertilizing flowers be expressed as the phrase Fertilization of flowers or as the syntagma Flowers—Fertilization? (The expressions Flower fertilization and Fertilization, Flower also have to be considered.) Ideally, this is a decision that should be made when index language design is initiated and when generalized guidelines are formulated as to what constitutes a term in the language. But this seldom happens. Terminology is difficult, particularly for nonscientific disciplines, and in practice on-the-spot decisions frequently are made at the moment when a term is admitted into the language. There is no general rule in the LCSH language for when a term in the form of a noun phrase heading is to be preferred to a string consisting of a main heading and a free-floating subdivision, only a nonbinding guideline that the former might be preferred if it seems better or if the subdivision is of limited applicability.[15] While not having to deal directly with the problem of what constitutes a term, designers of classificatory languages face similar enumeration versus synthesis decisions.

As an enumerative language becomes incrementally more synthetic, there is always the danger that a given concept may inadvertently be used in the language both as a term and as a string, creating the synonymy that controlled languages are specifically designed to eliminate. This happens, for instance, in the Universal Decimal Classification where some of the concepts designating Economics in relation to Mineralogy can either be found enumerated or be created by synthesis. One way to prevent synonymous constructions is to introduce more rules. LCSH, for instance, has a rule stating that a standard subdivision cannot be applied if the result would duplicate an established term heading. For example, the subdivision Research cannot be applied to Psychology (as Psychology—Research) because the term Psychological research exists in enumerated form. The subdivision can, however, be applied to Physics or Sociology. The DDC in its schedules and tables offers opportunities for synonymy, but its number-building rules are scrupulously constructed to forestall it.

Citation Order

There are two issues relating to *citation order,* or the order in which terms are concatenated in a string or heading: its rationale (why one citation order is preferable to another) and its regularity (whether the syntax used to produce it is algorithmic).

Rationale

Various principles have been offered to explain the ordering of terms in the synthetic expressions of a subject language.

- *Principle of decreasing concreteness*   First expressed by Ranganathan, this principle states that a set of terms should be sequenced from the most physical to the most abstract. A related principle is that of significance order, as explicated by Coates, wherein the most significant term is the one that is most readily available to the memory or the one that evokes the clearest mental image.[16]

- *Wall-picture principle*   Also introduced by Ranganathan, this principle figuratively expresses a dependency. It states that "if two facets A and B of a subject are such that the concept behind B will not be operative unless the concept behind A is conceded, even as a mural picture is not possible unless the wall exists to draw on, then the facet A should precede the facet B."[17] Similar to this is the time of conceptualization principle that Jutta Sørenson and Austin use to explain the PRECIS syntax, the "time" in question being not real but logical time. In Planning medical research, for example, the planning cannot be initiated until the concept of medical research exists.[18]

- *Principle of absolute syntax*   Another Ranganathan principle, this one prescribes that the order of terms in a subject string should mirror the seminal or deep structure underlying syntactic constructions common to all natural languages. A function of hard-wiring in the human brain, absolute syntax parallels the process of thinking, irrespective of the language in which these thoughts are expressed. Sørenson and Austin construe the PRECIS syntax as also conforming to this principle and, further, on its basis argue the adaptability of PRECIS to multilingual information organization.[19]

• *Principle of common or normal frames of reference* The meaning conveyed syntactically by the order of terms in a synthetic expression should be understandable to a majority of users, as evidenced by the manner in which they communicate about a subject. A corollary to this is that the syntactic meanings of subject strings should derive from syntactic meanings implicit in natural language. Both PRECIS and LCSH subscribe to this principle.

• *Principle of literary warrant* The order of terms should as far as possible conform to how the literature of a discipline is studied, searched for, or created. This is the rationale underlying the preference for processes or structures over organisms in the newly devised DDC schedules for biology. It is also the rationale assumed by one of the few studies undertaken to evaluate the comparative effectiveness of different syntaxes.[20]

It should be simpler to generalize about the syntax of subject languages than that of natural languages. Nevertheless, generalizations are hard to achieve. One generalization, noted in the preceding chapter, is that there is a tendency, at least in Western countries, to use the syntax of a subject language to express relationships among ideas that are syntagmatic rather than paradigmatic. Limited generalizations can be made about sets of terms that are syntactically homogeneous, insofar as they have similar distributions in subject-language expressions. Some of these sets of intersubstitutable terms can be characterized semantically, for instance, as indicating form, time, or place and (sometimes) things and processes. However, as yet such generalizations as can be made are too weak to yield satisfactory explanations, principles, or rationales.

Regularity

Over its hundred years of development, the LCSH syntax has evolved unguided by principles that might have ensured consistency and economy of expression. It is a syntax that contrasts dramatically with the simple routinized syntax of Kaiser's *Systematic Indexing,* Ranganathan's Colon Classification, and Austin's PRECIS. In 1992 a conference was convened to consider the future of the LCSH syntax, which, as noted, was becoming increasingly complex. One of the recommendations was that it be regularized to use a standard citation order of facets under topical main headings: Topic—Place—Time—Form.[21] The recommendation met with resistance on the grounds that implementing it could easily result in loss of meaning. This would particularly affect the disciplines of art, literature, history, and law. For instance, where the subdivision History is located in a string defines the meaning of the string. Music—Brazil—History and criticism, for example, has a meaning different from Music—History and criticism—Brazil. A study was done to see if implementing the proposed standard order would affect users' perception of meaning.[22] It was found that it would neither increase nor decrease it. The upshot was not to introduce the standard order and to maintain the expressiveness of LCSH, even at the cost of complexity.

What most characteristically distinguishes the LCSH syntax from that of the prototypical synthetic languages is that it is not defined exclusively with respect to large facets of homogeneous terms. It also references groupings of syntactically intersubstitutable terms (such as the standard subdivisions) and of individual terms (Food). A labor-intensive syntax, it nevertheless has the advantage of providing custom-tailored specificity and expressiveness. It can, for instance, customize the breakdown of a country, gearing it to the major events marking that country's history, as was shown above in the Sudan example.

While the DDC syntax is more regular than that of LCSH, it is not less complex. Like LCSH, it too is defined with respect to individual terms and groupings of terms in the form of facets and minifacets. Like LCSH it evolved in a somewhat pedestrian manner, introducing synthetics whenever they seemed to be warranted by recurring patterns of thought. And like LCSH it has the advantage of being more expressive than the boilerplate syntax of more rigorously faceted classifications.

Although Ranganathan argued that a synthetic language is more expressive than an enumerative one, it could be argued that a wholly synthetic language is actually more limited in what it can express because of its boilerplate syntax, that is, a syntax defined exclusively in terms of facets of high generality. Ranganathan's delight in viewing the Meccano set as a model for knowledge organization is reflective of a mathematician's passion for reducing complexity to simplicity — for reducing the vast system of the universe of knowledge to a set of atomic concepts and certain basic relations among them. But the universe of knowledge is not simple; it *is* complex, and too much atomization can result in a uniformity that fragments and falsifies.

A syntax can be regular in the sense of producing parsable expressions without relying on a facet- or role-defined syntax. The DDC syntax is an example of this. Much of it is defined with respect to individual terms and small classes of syntactically equivalent terms, which results in a great many number-building rules, but overall its use is systematic. Songqiao Liu in his Ph.D. dissertation demonstrated that the DDC syntax rules can be classified into ten basic types and then went on to demonstrate that it is possible to decompose DDC-built numbers into their constituent parts, automatically and unambiguously.[23]

Automation

A synthetic expression that can be automatically decomposed can also be constructively composed. A great advantage of an algorithmic syntax that can be applied automatically is that it spares the indexer the often complex and burdensome work of building expressions from atomic concepts. Of the major subject languages in use today only the DDC has been demonstrated to have such a syntax, a property that augurs well for its future. The survival of controlled synthetic subject languages depends on their continuing to be cost-effective, particularly in their application. Automation must be plumbed for what it is worth. General programs for automatically indexing and classifying documents have become increasingly sophisticated, particularly those that use controlled indexing to describe a document based on its similarity to documents previously indexed by human indexers.[24] Once index terms have been automatically applied, it should not be difficult to go further and use an algorithmic syntax to combine them into synthesized expressions in the form of strings or built numbers.

Precoordinate versus Postcoordinate Syntax

Normally only one DDC number is assigned to a document. To the degree the language allows, this number is expressive of the subject of the document. LCSH was originally designed to be single-entry specific — to produce subject headings conceptually coextensive with the documents they describe.[25] PRECIS aims to produce entries in the form of summaries of the complete topic of a document. Made-to-measure coextensive headings represent one interpretation of what Cutter meant when he stipulated that the subject heading applied to a document should be as specific as possible.[26]

The need for specificity is both reaffirmed and questioned periodically.[27] At the 1991 conference on the future of the LCSH syntax, overdoing specificity was cited as a contributing cause to the complexity of the LCSH syntax. This led to a proposal to shorten LCSH headings by removing from them terms belonging to the Time, Place, and Form facets.[28] These terms would still be used in indexing but not as component parts of topical headings. The proposal was not adopted, one problem being that doing so would cause retrieval and display difficulties when attempting to link a given topical heading (where there were several) with a given time, place, or form term.

The pros and cons of coextensivity are the pros and cons of a more basic issue — whether subject languages need to employ a syntax at all. This issue was first raised in 1951 when the potential of the computer in information retrieval was first discussed. Mortimer Taube, an early visionary, proposed replacing the relatively complex grammatical syntax used to construct subject headings with a simple logical syntax.[29] Taube called this simple logical syntax *coordination;* it is known now as *Boolean coordination.* To explore the implications of his proposal, Taube developed a uniterm subject language — a syntax-free language whose vocabulary consisted almost entirely of one-word terms. He then evaluated his language with respect to other subject languages, empirically and analytically.[30] The empirical evaluation took the form of a retrieval experiment — an experiment that in embryonic form prefigured the landmark Cranfield experiments of several years later. The analytic evaluation consisted of comparing subject heading and uniterm languages according to sixteen evaluation criteria, among them simplicity, speed in cataloging or indexing, vocabulary size, vocabulary growth and obsolescence rates, cost, universality compatibility, specificity, and suggestibility.

Now, nearly fifty years later, the issue of "precoordination or not" or whether to employ a subject-language syntax is still unresolved. As with many bibliographic dilemmas, this one comes down to costs versus benefits. The pros and cons can be summarized using some of Taube's original criteria as well as other criteria that derive from the collocation and navigation objectives:[31]

- *Specificity* Cutter's injunction to use the most specific heading possible is the foremost rule in indexing. The concept of specificity is an elusive one.[32] In part this is because there are different ways to achieve specificity. The specificity achievable by a postcoordinate language using the Boolean syntax of intersection and coordination is different in kind from the specificity that can be achieved by a precoordinate language using a subject-language syntax. Taube argued that the former is superior to the latter, at least for scientific subjects. But he did not demonstrate this, and, in fact, it unlikely it could be demonstrated since a common criticism leveled against postcoordinate languages is their inability to express relationships more specific than those expressible by the AND, NOT, and OR operators.[33] Precoordinate languages have a more sophisticated syntax and as such are more expressive. (PRECIS, for instance, boasts of its ability to distinguish the biting of dogs by children and the biting of children by dogs.)

• *Precision*   This post-Taube measure is the degree to which a subject language is capable of deselecting irrelevant documents in retrieval. To the extent that precision is a function of the specificity and expressive power of a subject language, precoordinate languages also score better here. Generic Boolean relationships foster false drops: a search for information on the history of philosophy using the search prescription History AND Philosophy may also retrieve material on the philosophy of history.

• *Contextually*   Related to specificity and expressive power, contextuality is the ability of a subject language to recognize distinctions in meaning. Since the task of vocabulary disambiguation is not limited to homonyms and polysemes but extends to all words whose meaning is in part contributed to by context, context is needed for making distinctions in meaning. The contexts shown by Boolean intersections of terms are relationally indiscriminate and therefore cannot disambiguate sufficiently to achieve acceptable precision. Precoordinate strings, by contrast, offer a wide variety of contexts that can be used to pinpoint meaning.

• *Suggestibility*   Often users do not know what to do when they retrieve too many citations. They find it difficult to think of appropriate qualifiers. A precoordinate language addresses this problem by displaying to users the different strings in which their search terms are embedded. The association of ideas triggered by such displays helps users to imagine what they cannot clearly articulate a priori. It was only in the matter of suggestibility that Taube conceded that subject-heading languages with their long phrases and topical subdivisions might be superior to his uniterm language.

Natural-Language versus Subject-Language Syntax

Context is needed for disambiguation, suggestibility, and precision. Immediately, the question of exploiting the richness of natural-language contexts in retrieval arises: why incur the expense of creating artificial subject-language contexts? Natural-language contexts have long been used in indexing, at least since the middle of the last century when Samson Low and Andrea Crestadoro introduced title-term indexing,[34] a precursor of *keyword indexing,* introduced a century later by Hans Peter Luhn.[35] There are various forms of keyword indexing. Relevant to the present discussion is keyword-in-context indexing (KWIC). In a KWIC index document titles are algorithmically rotated to bring each of its keywords to a selected eye-catching position. Simple in its conception and execution, KWIC spawned a progeny of more complex string index languages whose syntaxes are algorithmic permutations of natural-language syntax.[36] Using an index string generator, they transform a natural-language input into an output consisting of a set of index strings. Examples of such languages are Michael Lynch's Articulated Subject Indexing and Timothy Craven's NEPHIS.[37]

KWIC-derived languages were designed for printed indexes and are infrequently used today. However, most retrieval systems exploit natural-language contexts in their displays. Typically, a first-stage response to a user's query is to display his search terms in a syntagmatic context, such as in title statements, abstracts, or other text fragments. Contexts such as these are helpful in suggesting additional search terms and in narrowing searches to improve precision. An important question is whether they are any more or less helpful than the more pricey contexts afforded by subject-language syntax.

It can be argued that the relative uniformity of a subject-language syntax and the type of specificity it provides allow it to create better browsing domains than a natural-language syntax. In card-catalog days subject headings were subdivided to ensure that not too many cards would file behind a single heading. This was a simple and expedient means to improve browsability and also precision. The bunching of large numbers of cards behind a single heading in a card catalog has its online analog in large retrieval sets. These must somehow be managed. One way to do this is to order retrieved text fragments according to the frequencies of occurrence of search terms in them. But the resultant ordering, being statistical rather than semantic or conceptual, does not, like subdividing a card file, create a browsable domain.

The syntax used in subject languages offers a means to organize large retrievals conceptually. It does this by chunking, compressing, and layering subject descriptions of the retrieved items. A keyword-in-*title* search on a widely used term like Art would in many online catalogs result in an unmanageably large retrieval. A more focused strategy would be to perform a keyword-in-*subject heading* search on the term. (Even this more focused search would in the UCLA ORION 1 catalog retrieve around 8,000 subject headings.) The focused strategy offers a better guarantee of relevance, since the indexing is intellectual rather than mechanical. Moreover, and more to the point here, is that what is retrieved is conceptually browsable. The syntax used to create headings can also be used to order them in a systematic manner. While the ordering of subject headings in most catalogs today is distorted by the use of computer filing, it is in principle possible to order them automatically and neatly by geographical, form, chronological, and topical facets. The conceptual ordering could be further refined by grouping topical headings into larger classes — for instance, by organizing them by discipline.[38] Browsability could be enhanced by consolidating headings containing like information. For instance, headings such as Art, Modern—Nineteenth century—Austria; Art, Modern—Nineteenth century—Belgium; and Art, Modern—Nineteenth century—Brazil could be consolidated as Art, Modern—subdivided by geographic area, which then can be opened when needed by a mouse click.[39] A subject-language syntax, then, is superior to a natural-language syntax insofar as it can organize large sets of citations by layering and chunking. The effect of assigning precoordinate subject headings to documents is to pack them, or rather their surrogates, into an orderly sequence of Chinese boxes.

The creation of a meaningful order is equally as important in information organization as the grouping of documents into classes. In the precomputer age filing rules could be relied on to order bibliographic records in a systematic manner. Computer filing can produce orders based on statistical, alphabetical, and numerical data but cannot without assistance produce orders that are semantically meaningful. Imposing structure on the material to be ordered is a way of providing that assistance, which is what bibliographic languages, author-title languages, as well as subject languages can do by virtue of their syntax.

A second answer to the subject-language versus natural-language syntax question is the answer given to the more familiar question of free-text versus controlled-vocabulary searching. The answer turns on the need for normalization: a searching vocabulary needs to be normalized and so does the syntax used to create synthetic search expressions. Without normalization there will be recall, precision, and navigation failures in retrieval. This does not have to be demonstrated empirically, since it is logically deducible from the fact that natural languages contain synonymy and homonymy at the level of both vocabulary and sentence structure. Ridding a natural language of its surface-level anomalies amounts to reducing the variety exhibited by phenomenal language to its seminal or deep structure. The reductive analysis pursued in linguistics for the purpose of explaining and generalizing about natural languages, in bibliographic practice, serves the more practical purpose of intelligent information organization.

Afterword

The intellectual foundation of information organization is a fascinating and worthy study. The laying of the cornerstone of this foundation in the second half of the nineteenth century and its subsequent fortification during the twentieth in the face of the challenges posed by internationalism, the new media, and the digital revolution make for a dramatic history. And while a good drama needs no epilogue, this one remains unfinished, and it is tempting to speculate on how it might go on to unfold.

New information technologies can be imagined, but how and whether they will be applied — and, if applied, whether they will succeed — are imponderables. The direction in which information organization will develop commercially and as a scholarly discipline is subject at times to irrational forces and cannot be anticipated. Political events — constructive ones (like the adoption of a standard that advances universal bibliographical control) or those that are destructive (could an act of terrorism destroy large systems of organized information?) — cannot be predicted. The economic factors that could affect funding for research and the implementation of new methods to organize information cannot be foreseen. Despite what cannot be known, however, an ivory-tower kind of speculation is possible, one that looks at the future of systems for organizing information in terms of what would be useful, possible, and also likely, based on an observation of developing trends.

Two trends appear to be dominating current research and development. One is the increasing formalization of information organization as an object of study through mathematical and entity-relationship modeling, linguistic conceptualization, definitional analysis of theoretical constructs, and empirical research. The second is the increasing reach of automation to develop new means to achieve the traditional bibliographic objectives, to design intelligent search engines, and to aid in the work of cataloging and classification. Other things being equal, it seems likely that these trends will continue. The former is a trend pervading scholarly disciplines generally and is said to be a defining characteristic of the present information age. The latter would seem to be inevitable on economic grounds. Some observations relating to formalization, as expressed through linguistic conceptualization, and to the automation of information organization follow.

General Observations Relating to Linguistic Conceptualization

1. Heading the list of desiderata pertaining to information organization, regarded as an object of scholarly study, is the development of a special-purpose linguistics within information science. Linguistic concepts — such as vocabulary, semantics, syntax, and pragmatics — are useful for evaluating and comparing systems for organizing information and for developing frameworks for research, which can improve such systems and lead to formulating scientific generalizations about them. Though introduced nearly a century ago, many of these concepts still exist in an embryonic state, in the sense that they are still on loan from other fields and not honed specifically to the task of organizing information. Indicative of the type of honing that is needed to produce a custom-tailored information-science linguistics is the machine-assisted indexing system used by NASA.

2. The era of local in-house thesauri, which began in the mid-twentieth century, is likely to wane as bibliographical control expands to achieve interdisciplinarity and universality. The situation where users searching for information must translate their search terms into the vocabularies of a number of different retrieval languages is no longer tolerable. Until better alternatives are developed, users will cross-database search using natural language. But better alternatives are surely in the offing. An example of a better alternative is a bibliographic language that merges the various sublanguages of a discipline, such as the Unified Medical Language System being developed at the National Library of Medicine.[1] For interdisciplinary searches, a better alternative would be a universal, multilingual controlled language, a language broad enough to describe any document and to accommodate the vocabulary of all users, regardless of their nationality or culture. Colossal labor is needed, much of it highly intellectual, to develop merged and universal languages.

3. Because bibliographic description, when manually performed, is expensive, it seems likely that the "pre" organizing of information will continue

to shift incrementally toward "post" organizing. This shift (surely paradigmatic) was heralded in the early 1950s when Taube urged replacing traditional subject-language syntax with an automated Boolean syntax. The shift today is reflected by a changing research emphasis from the design of bibliographic languages to the design of search engines. While in the past the shift has been accompanied by a shift from controlled vocabulary to free-text searching, the association is not a necessary one, nor need it persist. As the processes by which information is organized become increasingly automated, it should become feasible to incorporate some of the information control structures, devices, and stratagems used in traditional bibliographic languages into the design of sophisticated "post" organizing search engines.

Observations Relating to the Vocabulary, Syntax, Semantics, and Pragmatics of Bibliographic Languages

1. *Vocabulary* The requirements for a universal bibliographic language and for sophisticated search engines dictate that the single most important direction for vocabulary development is toward the large-scale mapping of natural-language vocabulary onto controlled vocabularies. The word *large-scale* is operative here. Vocabulary mapping, in the form of authority structures such as thesauri, has always been a part of intelligent information organization. However, the entry vocabularies provided by many traditional tools have been limited. For automating information organization and for multilingual and cross-database searching, universal entry vocabularies encyclopedic in scope are required, vocabularies that contain names of all subjects, persons, corporate agencies, and places. The creation of encyclopedic knowledge in the form of semantic nets and thesauri-dictionaries is a burdensome, plodding, and largely intellectual task, one of Herculean proportions, one that amounts to creating a *characteristica universalis* for information retrieval. But it is a task that can be accomplished step by step, and in some limited lexical environments steps are being taken (at NASA and at the National Library of Medicine) and may be expected to continue to the extent that money and disciplinary infrastructures permit.

2. *Syntax* Given its importance in designing intelligent ordered displays of bibliographic information and providing systematic contextual environments for search-term disambiguation, bibliographic syntax is likely to continue to be of theoretical and practical interest. Of theoretical interest is research that seeks to generalize about the syntax of existing bibliographic languages — for example, to discover whether indeed they reveal an underlying structure indicative of a universal or absolute syntax. Such

research would be of potential practical use as well in pointing a direction for the development of syntax algorithms in the form of string generators. String generators have the potential to significantly improve automatic systems for organizing information. An example of an improved system would be one that would map the natural language of documents to a controlled vocabulary and then automatically create complex descriptors in the form of Dewey Decimal Classification (DDC) numbers, index-language strings, or bibliographic entity identifiers.

3. *Semantics*   To the extent that vocabulary classification is useful for creating semantic structures and developing automatic string generators, it is likely that the interest in category or facet semantics will continue. But this is an uncertain research front, and how far progress can be made will depend on the success of attempts to deal with term classes that are fuzzy, overlapping, and not mutually exclusive. Relational semantics has a more visible future. This is apparent in the drive to extend, refine, and formalize relationships among terms toward the ultimate goal of facilitating a memex-style navigation of the bibliographic universe. That this drive is part of a trend can be seen in the increasing specification of bibliographic relationships since the beginning of the twentieth century, from simple *See* and *See also* relationships to broader, narrower, and related-term relationships, to a breaking out of a variety of subtypes of these, to hypertext relationships. Semantic structures are the chief means to chart the universe of knowledge, and as this universe is ever expanding, so the work of semantic structuring is never ending.

4. *Pragmatics*   Given the research directed toward automatic classification and cataloging, it would seem that bibliographic pragmatics — how indexers and catalogers apply descriptors to documents — ought to be a serious research focus. But this does not seem to be the case. What has been written on the topic deals mostly with indexer and cataloger inconsistency, although some researchers have studied human indexing behavior with a view to whether machines can mimic it (or vice versa). With few exceptions, the study of bibliographic pragmatics has not led to actionable results, but conceivably it could. It could lead to an improvement of the rules for the application of bibliographic languages and an understanding of concepts like *aboutness, semantic relatedness,* and *bibliographic significance* that could inform efforts at automation.

Observations on Directions for Automation

1. It is certain that automation will continue its juggernaut advance. An important path along which to advance is the devising of new means to

achieve the objectives of systems for organizing information. In the previous chapters, isolated examples have been given of how computer potentialities could and have been harnessed for this task. For instance, by virtue of its ability to present instant access to different views of the same information, it can be used to resolve the conflict between the principle of standardization and that of user convenience. And by virtue of its ability to make inferences based on similarity matching, it can aid in automatically normalizing vocabulary and imposing post hoc quality control on bibliographic databases. It can be hoped and expected that the future will see a widespread actualization of these potentialities.

2. A second path along which automation research is proceeding is toward the development of increasingly intelligent search engines. Here again it is the viewpoint switching and inference abilities of the computer that harbor the seeds of progress. The former is of use — indeed is being used — to develop multilingual retrieval interfaces, a necessary concomitant of universal bibliographical control. It is of potential use as well in providing different views of a database, custom-tailored to users' search requirements, whether for precision, recall, or navigation. The computer's ability to draw inferences based on similarity matching has since the 1960s been exploited to help users expand queries — for example, to find documents similar to a given document and to order bibliographic information in display. For the most part, automatic techniques for query expansion and document ordering have relied on frequency calculations and numerical or alphabetical sequencing algorithms. A logical direction for future development would be to introduce into these mechanisms some of the semantic structures to be found traditional bibliographic systems.

3. A third path for automated research, also a continuation of a path already begun, is toward the development of machine-assisted systems to catalog and classify documents. Today that path has signs along it pointing in the direction of expert systems that incorporate semantic knowledge to impose order on massive amounts of information. A prototype system suggestive of this direction is the U.S. Census PACE (Parallel Automated Coding Expert) system. This system was created to classify census data, consisting of 22 million responses to work-related questions into 800 industry and occupation categories. At ten responses per second, the system was able in three months to classify the 22 million responses, a task that if done manually would have incurred $15 million in labor costs. The system, which uses the computer's ability to make inferences based on similarity comparisons, took less than two months to develop and was reported to perform with an accuracy rate of above 86 percent. The continued improvement of systems such as these is as important as any automation research of the future, particularly for their potential to

organize documents on the Internet and particularly as they might do this using a universal bibliographic language.

4. Automation research raises the question of which aspects of the procedures used to organize information are algorithmic in nature (and thus amenable to automation) and which are truly intellectual (and thus the domain of thinking beings). This question, formulated half a century ago, still awaits a satisfactory answer. In partial answer, it can be said that automation efforts can proceed only so far before coming up against a semantic barrier. At this barrier questions of meaning and significance intrude, which means that efforts to automate the organization of information must then fall back on lexical information intellectually compiled and structured. While it is possible to build semantic structures from scratch, doing so would take a long time — as long as it has taken to create the authority files, multilingual thesauri, and classificatory structures developed in the context of traditional bibliographic systems. It would make better economic sense to adapt traditional structures to this purpose, but, however it is done, it will have either to reference or to recreate the intellectual foundation of information organization.

Notes

Chapter 1

1. Carpenter (1994, 107).

2. Brault (1972, 3–11).

3. *Bibliographic* is used in this book in an extended sense. Bibliographic objects are all objects embodying information and not just those in biblio or book form. Bibliographic systems for organizing information include the traditional systems for cataloging, classification, and indexing, as well as modern systems for automatic clustering, partitioning, and indexing.

4. Santayana (1932, 1:284).

5. Cutter (1904, 5).

6. Coffman (1998).

7. Bertalanffy, von (1972).

8. Cutter (1876a, 1876b).

9. Miksa (1977).

10. In the context of cataloging rules, this concept has recently been expressed by Taniguchi as "oriented-ness." Taniguchi (1999).

11. Bridgman (1938).

12. Eddington (1929, 251).

13. Waples (1931).

14. See *The Encyclopedia of Philosophy* (7 and 8: 240–246).

15. Wittgenstein (1953).

16. Kaiser (1911).

17. See, for instance, Foskett (1996).

18. Like the statistical concept significance, information is associated with improbability and the removal of uncertainty. Various attempts have been made to incorporate the Shannon-Weaver definition of information into other disciplines, but since it is statistical, rather than semantic, most have been unproductive.

19. *Webster's Third New International Dictionary*, s.v. "information."

20. Wilson (1968, 17).

21. Drucker (1988, 46).

22. Langer (1949).

23. There are of course exceptions. The *AACR2R* presents rules for describing realia, which includes "naturally occurring entities."

24. Quoted in Lubetzky (1969, 1) from *The Home Book of Quotations*, 6th ed., rev., edited by Burton Stevenson (New York: Dodd, Mead, 1949), attributed to the Rev. George Dawson, who used it in his *Address on Opening the Birmingham Free Library*, October 26, 1866.

25. Since this book is concerned with messages that are recorded (that is, documents), the term *message*, having served its purpose by bringing the discussion to this point, will not be used much in the rest of the book.

26. As early as 1907, Paul Otlet defined a document as "whatever represents or expresses an object, a fact, an impression by means of any sign whatever (writing, picture, diagrams, symbols)." See Rayward (1997, 32).

27. *Webster's Third New International Dictionary*, s.v. "document."

28. Pettee (1936, 80). Pettee's statement has been challenged by de Rijk (1991).

29. For instance, it may be inferred from this statement: "A reader may know the *work* he requires; he cannot be expected to know all the peculiarities of different *editions;* and this information he has a right to expect from the catalog." Commissioners Appointed . . . (1850), Q 9814. Note: Question numbers reference the *Minutes of Evidence*.

30. Pettee (1936).

31. Ranganathan (1955).

32. In the early 1960s Lubetzky opposed works sometimes to editions and sometimes to publications. His most forceful expression of the work-versus-book distinction is in his *Principles of Cataloging* (1969, 11–15).

33. Quoted in Pettee (1936, 79).

34. Commissioners Appointed . . . (1850), Q 5103.

35. The problem of operationalizing work is discussed further in Chapter 3.

36. Commissioners Appointed . . . (1850), Q 9814.

37. McLuhan (1964).

38. Exceptions always cause problems, as when a long document runs over several physical objects or one physical object contains several different documents. But problems like these are relatively easy to handle.

39. Attributed to Heraclitus. *The Encyclopedia of Philosophy* (3 and 4: 479).

40. Leibniz (1951).

Chapter 2

1. Cutter (1876b, 10).

2. In a note to the second edition of his *Rules,* Cutter observes that his statement of objectives, which he followed also by a statement of means, "has been criticized; but as it has also been frequently quoted, usually without change or credit, in the prefaces of catalogs and elsewhere," he supposes it has on the whole been approved. The fact that this statement of objectives is also quoted frequently today, more than 100 years later, testifies to their stability and to the endurance of their intellectual foundations.

3. Lubetzky (1960, ix).

4. IFLA (1962, 91–92).

5. IFLA (1998, 82).

6. Wilson (1983, 6–8).

7. The IFLA model distinguishes also other entities not recognized in earlier statement of objectives. One of these is expression, which is the set of all intellectual, as opposed to physical, realizations of a work "in the form of alpha-numeric, musical, or choreographic notation, sound, image, object movement, etc., or any combination of such forms" (IFLA, 1998, 18).

8. Butler (1953, 7). The concept of navigating the bibliographic universe, if not the word "navigation," has figured in the library and information science literature throughout the twentieth century. See, for instance, Rayward (1997, 27).

9. Belkin (1982).

10. Identified as a group first in 1980, the navigation rules in the Anglo-American Cataloging Rules (AACR) have several times since been the focus of empirical study. In their doctoral theses, Barbara Tillett (1987), Richard Smiraglia (1992), and Sherry Vellucci (1995) have studied and classified them not only as represented by AACR rules but also in terms of their frequency of cooccurrence in bibliographic descriptions. Michèle Hudon has written about subject relationships in her dissertation (1998, 612–667); Margaret Willetts has written an article about them (1975).

11. The IFLA model distinguishes also other entities not recognized in earlier statements of objectives. One of these is expression, which is the set of all intellectual, as opposed to physical, realizations of a work "in the form of alpha-numeric, musical, or choreographic notation, sound, image, object movement, etc., or any combination of such forms." IFLA (1998, 18).

12. O'Neill, Rogers, and Oskins (1993).

13. Cleverdon (1962).

14. Carlyle (1994).

15. Cutter (1904, 15) .

16. See, for instance, Cromwell (1994).

17. Carlyle (1994). See also Subramanyam (1998) and Baker (1994).

18. Numerous exceptions to this generalization can be found. Library catalogs provide analytic access to individual items on sound recordings. On the other hand, they may treat many individual, physically discrete documents as a single object of description. Legal indexing frequently takes as its objects of description sections of documents, as does the indexing provided by the *Guidelines for Electronic Text Encoding and Interchange (TEI Guidelines)* (see Sperberg-McQueen and Burnard, 1994).

19. Its creators intend that the Dublin Core element should map onto the Machine Readable Cataloging (MARC) format; however, this is possible only to the extent that isomorphisms can be set up between the two. In theory this is possible only if the same distinctions are recognized by both; however, by its very nature, the Dublin core consists of few elements, whereas the MARC format consists of a great many. Also it is intended that the Dublin Core be adopted as a standard. It is not clear what political, economic, and social infrastructures are required to make this happen.

20. Svenonius (1986).

21. Cleverdon, Mills, and Keen (1966).

22. For a brief summary of these, see Svenonius (1986).

23. Seal, Bryant, and Hall (1982). See also Seal (1983).

24. The short entries were lacking statements of responsibility, edition author statements, distribution type information, series information, notes, and ISBNs. They also abbreviated the forenames of authors to initials.

25. Luhn (1959).

26. See Wilson (1983, 16).

27. Bishop (1916). See also Panizzi (1850) and Mann (1991).

28. Matthews, Lawrence, and Ferguson (1983). See also Kaske et al. (1983).

29. Pettee (1936, 76 ff).

30. Jewett (1853).

31. The creators of the Universal Decimal Classification, Paul Otlet and his colleagues, were particularly eloquent and hopeful about the possibility of the universal bibliographical control of all knowledge. See Rayward (1976).

32. Some credit is due as well to OCLC, whose database of nearly 38 million records (at the end of 1997) has by expansionist force increasingly assumed the character of a global catalog. For an account of standardization efforts in the name of universal bibliographical control, see Delsey (1989) and Schmierer (1989).

Chapter 3

1. *Webster's Third New International Dictionary,* s.v. "ontology."

2. Quine (1980, 103).

3. See, e.g., Svenonius (1992) and IFLA (1998).

4. This trend, now evident in many disciplines, was predicted by Daniel Bell (1976).

5. *Webster's Third New International Dictionary,* s.v. "intelligence."

6. Simon (1978, 16).

7. Eddington (1929, 251).

8. See chapter 1.

9. Documents on the Internet, which seem to have insubstantial existence as flicks of light on a screen, nevertheless have embodiment in magnetic and silicon media.

10. The concept of work is reflected in the filing arrangements of early catalogs and even in the cataloging literature prior to Lubetzky's writing. Pettee claimed that the originator of the concept was Sir Thomas Hyde, who produced a *Catalogue of Printed Books* for the Bodleian Library of Oxford University in 1674. For a discussion of this claim, see de Rijk (1991). A. Panizzi recognized the concept, as his quoted remark on p. 11 testifies, as did C. C. Jewett a few years later in 1853 (10–11). C. A. Cutter referred implicitly to the concept when he states an object of the catalog is to assist in the choice of a book as to its edition (bibliographically) (1876, 10). Pettee, writing in 1936, discusses the concept under the name *literary unit,* a term later adopted by Eva Verona (1963). Ranganathan introduced the term in 1955 with the meaning of "expressed thought" and contrasted it with *document,* which he defined as "embodied thought" (Ranganathan, 1955, 26, 43). In more recent times, writers who have tackled the definition of work include Akòs Domanovsky, Patrick Wilson, Michael Carpenter, Richard Smiraglia, Edward O'Neill and Diane Vizine-Goetz, and Martha Yee (see the Bibliography).

11. Lubetzky (1969, 11).

12. Ibid.

13. A work set can consist of only one item, such as a one-of-a-kind work of art that is not reproduced in any form.

14. Referencing can be done without hypostasizing works. The referencing systems used by the *Guidelines for Electronic Text Encoding and Interchange (TEI Guidelines)* are examples. See Sperberg-McQueen and Burnard (1994). These systems link documents rather than works. The problem here is that referencing often needs to have as its object not a particular document but a work. For instance, the entity that *West Side Story* is based on the generic (or work) *Romeo and Juliet,* not the manifestation of *Romeo and Juliet* as it appears in Shakespeare's first folio.

15. This attribute — descent from a common origin — has, since Domanovsky's time, been used by several authors to define work sets (see O'Neill and Vizine-Goetz, 1989, and Wilson, 1989a). It has also been used to define other sets, such as the set of derivative works (see Smiraglia, 1992) and the set, called a *superwork,* of all documents related in any fashion to a given ur-document.

16. Domanovsky (1975, 100).

17. At least in the Anglo-American cataloging tradition, these operations are assumed to preserve identity.

18. Wilson (1968).

19. Elizabeth Betz (1987) has observed that the most notable difference between describing books and graphic materials is the discretion that is given in determining what will constitute a work. The observation suggests that perhaps another concept, more appropriate than work, might be devised to perform for nonbook materials roles analogous to those performed for books by work.

20. See Svenonius, Baughman, and Molto (1986); Jeng (1987); and Molto and Svenonius (1991).

21. R. Smiraglia, who has written extensively about this entity, calls it a *bibliographic family* (1992).

22. See, for instance, Genette (1982). I am indebted to an unknown reviewer of my manuscript for this citation.

23. Panizzi (1850), in Carpenter and Svenonius (1985, 21).

24. Patrick Wilson (1989a) raises the question whether works should figure as the primary referents of the bibliographic record. This would make sense if the collocating function of the catalog were to be emphasized over its finding function. However, insofar as the finding function coincides better with the inventory function of a library, it is unlikely to receive such emphasis.

25. *AACR2R* (1988, 617).

26. *AACR2R* (1988, 30).

27. Yee (1993).

28. Sperberg-McQueen and Burnard (1994); IFLA (1997).

29. Sperberg-McQueen and Burnard (1994, 51–52).

30. Pierce (1946).

31. Yee (1993).

32. Terminology is difficult here. The term *subedition* was introduced by Bowers (1949) and reintroduced by Tanselle (1984). By *subedition* Bowers meant, first, an impression with a different publisher's imprint. But he also regarded the making of changes deemed insubstantial with respect to intellectual content as triggering new subeditions, such as the introduction of a critical preface or a small amount of additional matter in a collection of poems. Tanselle was troubled by Bowers's definition of *subedition* because it incorporates publishing considerations into the edition-impression classification, whose characteristics of division are based on printing considerations. The IFLA *Functional Requirements* paper distinguished intellectual from physical or embodiment differences using *expressions* for the former and *manifestations* for the latter (IFLA, 1998). The problem with this terminology is that *expression* lacks use warrant and the use of *manifestation* runs counter to use warrant, which regards a manifestation as any embodiment of a work, whether intellectual or physical in nature. In this text, *subedition* is used to refer to a different publication of a given edition where the intellectual content is unaltered.

33. A (rare) exception to this practice is when separate full bibliographic descriptions are made for component parts of physical documents — for instance, when two or more novels are bound together as one physical object.

34. Graham (1990).

35. The *ISBD(ER)* in its explication of "change in intellectual content" quite clearly states "Differences that do not constitute a new edition include: a difference in the type of physical carrier (e.g., from disk to cassette) and/or the size of the physical carrier (e.g., 14 cm to 9 cm disk)." IFLA (1997, 52).

36. Exceptions are obvious reproductions, which some libraries describe not as objects in themselves but as objects dependent on the originals from which they derive.

37. See Association for Library Collections and Technical Services (1992).

38. See, e.g., OCLC (1992).

39. Some writers recommend dropping the inventory function of the bibliographic record and using the record to denote conceptual entities such as works and editions. See Wilson (1989a) and Heaney (1995). The bibliographic record is further discussed in Chapter 6.

40. Cutter (1904, 14).

41. American Library Association (1949, 3).

42. Pettee (1936).

43. Domanovsky (1975).

44. Verona (1975).

45. Cited by Piternick (1989, 31). Because credit for publication is needed in academe, abstracting and indexing guidelines tend to be more generous in their recognition of authorial status than cataloging codes.

46. See, e.g., Croghan (1972), IFLA (1987), Tillin and Quinly (1976), and Library Association (1973).

47. The line is a quote from Beckett in Foucault (1979, 141).

48. Wilson (1983).

49. Lubetzky (1969, 29). See also Carpenter (1981) and Wajenberg (1989).

50. See, e.g., Svenonius and Molto (1990) and Molto and Svenonius (1991).

51. See Svenonius (1990a).

52. Cochrane (1983).

53. Russell (1982); Todd (1992).

54. Maron (1977).

55. Fox and Norreault (1980).

56. Aboutness is relative not only to the language used by documents but also to the index language used to describe them. See Chapter 8.

57. See Svenonius (1994).

58. Bhattacharyya (1979).

59. Kaiser (1911).

60. Vickery (1966, 132).

61. Kintsch and Van Dijk (1978).

62. Wilson (1968, 77).

63. Hutchins (1975, 80).

64. Wittgenstein (1953, 19).

65. Normally the word *language* is understood to mean verbal language, either written or spoken. However, because language is a system of symbols used for communication, it is possible to speak of other languages, such as the language of flowers and the language of music. See Svenonius (1994) for a discussion of the visual and musical languages.

66. Ryle (1959).

67. Carlyle (1902, 78).

68. Gopinath (1970, 58).

69. Cutter (1904, 67).

70. Miksa (1983, 38 ff).

71. An exception is when a novel is clearly focused on a nameable topic, such as the Civil War in the case of *Gone with the Wind*.

72. *Genre* is a difficult term to define. It tends to be defined differently for different types of materials. In fiction books and films, it is often defined in terms of story type or approach, such as mystery, western, or *film noir*. In painting, it may be defined in terms of material used (oil painting), object that is painted (still life), the period of creation (modern), or painterly approach (cubist). For a discussion of indexable attributes of images, see Layne (1994).

73. Ranganathan (1957, 25).

74. Wilson (1968, 9 ff).

Chapter 4

1. There is an essential difference between organizing information to compile an encyclopedic compendium of knowledge and organizing it for the purpose of information retrieval. In the former, what is ordered and arranged is the information itself; in the latter, it is the documents embodying information (such as books systematically arranged on library shelves) or their surrogates (such as catalog cards alphabetically arranged in a catalog). In the context of information retrieval, the modus operandi of information organization is not compilation but description.

2. *Webster's Third New International Dictionary*, s.v. "description."

3. The current view on authors is that they do not include corporate bodies. Corporate bodies are rather regarded as emanators. For economy of expression, in

this text the tem *author* will be used in an extended and generic sense to include both persons and corporate bodies.

4. Analogously, work and document languages could be subdivided by the bibliographic relationships each recognizes.

5. *Webster's Third New International Dictionary,* s.v. "vocabulary."

6. Svenonius (1992, 8).

7. Svenonius (1990c, 92–100).

8. In a subject language, facets are also used to define vocabulary domains. As such they determine what a document can be about. They are used as well in constructing the relational semantics for a subject language insofar as relationships are defined as holding within or across facets.

9. Kaiser (1911).

10. An exception to this statement is keyword languages.

11. For exact citations see the Bibliography under International Federation of Library Associations and Institutions; International Organization for Standards; Library of Congress; and Online Computer Library Center.

12. Throughout the text *AACR* will be used to mean the Anglo-American cataloging rules generically understood and not the publication that constitutes the first edition of these rules. This is because the points being made for the most part apply to traditional Anglo-American cataloging generally and not to a particular manifestation of it. When specific reference to the current edition of the rules is needed, *AACR2R* (*Anglo-American Cataloging Rules,* second edition, revised) will be used.

13. That Bradfordian distribution characterizes the use of cataloging rules was first notice by Ann Fox in 1972. More recently, it has been demonstrated in a small study by Abrera and Shaw (1992).

14. Molto and Svenonius (1998).

15. Fidel and Crandall (1988); see also Molto and Svenonius (1991).

16. Ibid.

17. Using an object-oriented approach Michael Heaney (1995) suggests segregating attributes pertaining to works (texts), publications (manifestations), and items, respectively, and, by implication, the rules specifying them.

18. Osborn (1941, 395–399); Pettee (1936, 290).

19. Tillett (1987); Svenonius (1996); Lubetzky (2000). Another example of role confusion is the treatment of the part-whole relationship, which in present online catalogs (admittedly in card catalogs as well) are shown in some instances by added entries, in some instances by cross-references, in some instances by analytic entries, in some instances by multilevel records, in some instances in holdings records, in some instances implicitly in the physical description of an item, in some instances in listings of contents, in some instances as links in linking entry fields, and in (many) instances not at all.

20. In the interest of catalog-code reform, Lubetzky launched a campaign for eschewing sui generis rules and returning to principle, heralding it with the celebrated question "Is this Rule Necessary?" (Lubetzky, 1953, 1).

21. Tadayoshi (1989).

22. See, e.g., Tillett (1997). See also the essays in Svenonius (1989).

23. The word *reasonable* is key. An often quoted remark is the first sentence in Cutter's *Rules:* "a code of cataloging rules could never be adopted on all points by everyone." Still, standardization requires a reasonable amount of uniformity. For an example of an evaluation that focuses on uniformity, see Cook (1977).

24. Lubetzky (1953, 61–62).

25. *Catalogue of Printed Books in the British Museum,* vol. 1 (1841).

26. Commissioners Appointed . . . (1850, 389).

27. Sometimes several cards were used in the description of one document, and occasionally one card with dashed-on entries was used to describe several documents.

28. Lubetzky (2000).

29. Yee, M. M., and Layne, S. S. (1998), pp. 144–45.

30. Lubetzky (2000).

31. Wilson (1989a).

32. Heaney (1995).

33. Multiple Versions Forum (1990).

34. Ibid.

35. Attig (1989).

36. To deal with the problem, it has been suggested that records should be embedded in or linked to multientity records to show what a given library has. Multiple Versions Forum (1990).

37. Green (1996).

38. Sperberg-McQueen and Burnard (1994); ISO (1986b).

Chapter 5

1. Lubetzky (1953, 61–62).

2. IFLA (1999, 9).

3. *Oxford English Dictionary,* s.v. "principle," 7th meaning.

4. Ranganathan (1957, 52).

5. Ibid.

6. Haykin (1951, 7–9) uses the expression "The Reader as Focus" and "Usage" to express the user convenience principle.

7. Cutter (1904, 6). Miksa (1983, 73) suggests that Cutter did not intend usage alone to guide practice, there being situations where practice was better served not by the vagaries of usage but by systematic rules.

8. Cutter (1876a, 541, 548).

9. See Metcalfe (1959, 51). For an extended discussion of Cutter's psychology of the public, see Miksa (1983, 77–82).

10. Cutter (1904, 69).

11. Cutter (1876a, 537).

12. Ranganathan (1957, 35, 36).

13. IFLA (1997, 8). This document also illustrates the use of this principle in various subject heading languages (145 ff). Many theorists have written about this principle. See, for instance, Hanson (1909), Haykin (1951), and Miksa (1983).

14. Cutter (1876a, 536–537).

15. Library of Congress, Cataloging Distribution Service (1989–, LCRI 22.3)

16. Skrobela (1980, 2).

17. Ranganathan (1957, 52).

18. Tillett (1990, 1997); Gorman (1992). The dilemma is not avoided entirely, since even in a sophisticated online catalog a single form of name would continue to be needed for display and citation.

19. See, for instance, Krikelas (1980).

20. Bradford (1948). A Bradford distribution is one characterizing the use of a set of objects — such as letters of the alphabet, books in a library, journals cited in a bibliography, or objects for sale in a grocery store — so that a few of the objects account for a majority of the use, and most are used infrequently.

21. Matthews, Lawrence, and Ferguson (1983).

22. See, for instance, Carlyle (1989) and the bibliography at the end of her article.

23. A description can be regarded as inaccurate for reasons other than transcription failures. For instance, it can be too brief, or it can be a result of the misapplication of rules.

24. Library of Congress, Processing Department (1946, 26).

25. Blackburn (1884, v).

26. Lubetzky (1953, 41).

27. Ravilious (1975, 33).

28. Cutter (1904, 24).

29. Ravilious (1975).

30. Lubetzky illustrates his point by saying how when Winston Churchill brought a draft to King George VI for him to use as his Speech from the Throne, the King "reflected wistfully upon his delivery of a prime-ministerial statement as a Speech from the Throne." Churchill is said to have replied sensitively: "Your

Majesty, anyone can write a check, but only the one who signs it can validate it." See Lubetzky (1969, 28).

31. See Wajenberg (1989). Wajenberg brings up the interesting case of a document purporting to be written by a computer.

32. Commissioners Appointed . . . , Q 4100. Quoted in Brault (1972, 42).

33. Library of Congress, Processing Department (1946). Both Herman H. Henkle and Luther Evans credit Lubetzky with the substance of this report.

34. See the discussion on empirical methods of determining necessity in the next section.

35. This is not necessarily true. Some data elements are more expensive than others: for example, assigned or organizing data elements are more expensive than derived data elements that are merely descriptive. See Svenonius (1992).

36. Lubetzky (1953, 1).

37. Lubetzky (1953).

38. Library of Congress, Processing Department (1946, app. D).

39. O'Neill, Rogers, and Oskins (1993).

40. Seal (1983).

41. Library of Congress, Cataloging Distribution Service (1989–, LCRI 2.5C1, 2.5C2).

42. Library of Congress, Program for Cooperative Cataloging (1999).

43. Library of Congress, Serial Record Division (1994).

44. IFLA (1998).

45. O'Neill, Rogers, and Oskins (1993).

46. Ranganathan (1957, 55).

47. Hagler (1989, 199).

48. Jewett (1852, 8).

49. *Webster's Third New International Dictionary,* s.v. "standardize."

50. Delsey (1989).

51. IMCE (1970, 15–16).

52. Cutter (1904, 6).

53. Cutter (1904, 11).

54. Hanson (1939, 134).

55. Osborn (1941).

56. Lubetzky (1953, 1).

57. Dunkin (1969).

58. This has happened, for instance, in the changes introduced to bring about format integration. See chapter 7.

59. Hagler (1977, 611).

60. See the discussion in the section on sufficiency and necessity.

61. See the discussion in the section on common usage.

62. Hagler (1977, 617).

63. National Education Association, Department of Audiovisual Instruction (1968).

64. Gorman (1980, 42).

65. It has been found that of the art works that would be relevant to the work of art historians, 29 percent lack distinctive titles in the sense of having proper names. See Layne (1997).

66. IFLA (1997, 61).

67. See chapter 7 for a further discussion of these issues.

Chapter 6

1. According to Michael Gorman, Sumner Spalding used the term *nominal* to refer to such attributes (Personal communication, April 18, 1998).

2. An exception is assigned vocabulary in the form of ID and control numbers.

3. The activity of introducing vocabulary control is, in the context of descriptive cataloging, called *authority work* and its output an *authority record*. The authority record shows the established or authorized name for a given entity, as well as all other names it is known to have. In accordance with the principle of accuracy, the record also shows the source from which the authoritative form of the name is taken.

4. *AACR2R* (1988, 381).

5. *AACR2R* (1988, 381–382).

6. *AACR2R* (1988, 449).

7. Ibid.

8. *AACR2R* (1988, 450).

9. While not linked using the device of a uniform title in conjunction with a *See* reference, the two titles would presumably be linked in a note in the bibliographic description. See the final section of this chapter on bibliographic relationships.

10. *AACR2R* contains an optional rule suggesting that birth-date qualification might be used even if the name is distinctive. This is a useful hedge against the name becoming nondistinctive in the future. *AACR2R* (1988, 415).

11. Wendler (1995, 5).

12. Wendler (1995, 7).

13. Thomas (1984, 397).

14. When *AACR2R* was first published in 1981, the need for distinctive serial titles was overlooked. Rules for supplying them were added in the form of rule interpretations.

15. When technology changes, so do means to ends. It can happen that one of the functions performed by a multifunctional device could be better accomplished by other means. Introducing a new means invariably introduces inconsistency. This happened when added entries replaced cross-references and when broader and narrower terms replaced *See also* references.

16. Neither the philosophy behind the concept of identity in Anglo-American cataloging nor its impact on the practice of organizing information is particularly well thought out. This has resulted in inconsistency. Not all pseudonymity is treated in the same way (contemporary authors are treated differently from noncontemporary ones), and it is not clear the difference in treatment can be defended on other than economic grounds. It has also resulted in complexity. When a person writes under a great many names, the cross-reference structure becomes messy.

17. The complicated semantic linkages could be avoided if the corporate body were designated by its full-form rather than its commonly known name.

18. A few works do not have identifiers. This happens when uniform titles are not assigned. See the caveat above in the discussion of uniform titles.

19. See Fattahi (1995) for a review of the controversy.

20. Domanovsky (1973, 196–197); Chaplin (1966, 10–11).

21. Pettee (1936); Matthews, Lawrence, and Ferguson (1983).

22. Hamdy (1973, 17 ff).

23. Alternatively, the relationship between variant and authorized names of works can be shown implicitly by including both (or elements of both) in the bibliographic description of a document manifesting the work.

24. It is likely the future will see an increase in multiply-manifested works. See Wainwright (1991).

25. For any work manifested in multiple editions, the assignment of edition identifiers would serve to organize bibliographic displays. To some extent premachine filing rules were able to achieve such displays without the use of explicit identifiers. The order of sorting was specified by rules identifying a sequence of elements.

26. Thus, the uniform title for the 1959 publication of the Revised Standard edition of the Bible is Bible. English. Revised Standard. 1959. Through its first element it designates a work, through its second two elements an edition, and through its last element a publication.

27. Smiraglia and Leazer use the expression *bibliographic family* to designate a set of related bibliographic works derived from a common progenitor. See Smiraglia and Leazer (To be published).

28. Tillett (1992b).

29. Most of the examples in this chapter are taken from *AACR2R*. *AACR2R* itself does not authorize the used of coded information. However, they are used in MARC-formatted *AACR2R* descriptions.

30. It has been suggested that the bibliographic record be redesigned to reference a single bibliographic entity (Heaney, 1995). Such records would be tidier and more

in line with current database design views than those incorporating emblematic descriptions. In a manual environment, however, such an approach would be unconscionably expensive, increasing both the amount of labor and the number of records required. Whether the approach could be justified in an electronic environment remains to be seen.

31. Tillett (1987); Smiraglia (1992); Vellucci (1995); IFLA (1998).

32. At a physical as opposed to intellectual level, it holds as well between publications and editions and between versions and publications. See Chapter 7.

33. See chapter 3 for a discussion of work-preserving relationships. While in a strict sense, these relationships hold between items, as when one item is a translation of another, in common parlance they are spoken of as holding between the sets to which they belong.

34. Wilson (1989b). Using traditional bibliographic devices, one or other of the finding or collocating objectives is favored in catalog structure.

35. *Guidelines for Electronic Text Encoding and Interchange* (Sperberg-McQueen and Burnard, 1994).

36. An example of a physically defined aggregation relationship is the accompanying relationship.

37. There is a conundrum here. The editions of a work supposedly do not differ essentially with respect to content (by definition), and yet it is possible for editions of the same work to have different works as their component parts.

38. In the context of descriptive cataloging, these would be called *added entries for the component works.*

39. McCallum (1982).

40. In the context of descriptive cataloging, such descriptions are known as *analytics.*

41. There is a certain redundancy in this maneuver insofar as a description for *The Two Towers* will include as an organizing field the comprehensive title *Lord of the Rings*. As a result the user searching under *Lord of the Rings* for *The Two Towers* is, on the one hand, told to look elsewhere and, on the other hand, told "here is what you want." The use of alternative ways to express the same information, here relationship information, not only creates redundancy, which is uneconomical and theoretically unsatisfactory, but also is user-unfriendly.

42. Tillett introduced this relationship and named it the *descriptive relationship.* The term *commentary* is used instead here in an attempt to restrict the number of meanings attaching to *description.*

43. Self-parody is a relationship deemed unnecessary to represent in a bibliographic description.

44. Wainwright (1991).

45. Added entries are secondary access points for works, as contrasted with main entries, which are primary access points. Like main entries, they are normalized data elements entered into organizing fields of a bibliographic description. An example

of an added entry is a joint author of a work. In the move from book to card catalogs, added entries were in many cases substituted for the *See* cross-references that
directed a user from the name of a secondary author of a work to the work identifier. The substituting of added entries for cross-references was seen as a way to provide more information at less expense. However, two problems resulted from the
substitution. First, it could happen that a secondary author was associated in display only with a particular edition of a work (the one to which he contributed) and
not with other editions of the work. Second, the relative roles of added entries and
cross-references were not clearly delineated. Not only is it theoretically unsatisfactory when different devices are used to serve the same function; it is also unsatisfactory, from the point of view of the user, simultaneously to be given direct and
indirect access to information.

46. Carlyle (1994).

47. Sperberg-McQueen and Burnard (1994).

Chapter 7

1. Howarth (1998).

2. American Library Association et al. (1988, rule 0.24, p. 8).

3. Wilson (1989a). The challenge has forced in some instances a reexamination of
present practice, and in some libraries bibliographic records surrogate works, rather
than documents.

4. Exceptions occur where these are still being worked out, which is the case for
some electronic documents.

5. Carlyle (1999).

6. Library of Congress, Prints and Photographs Division (1995).

7. Helmer (1987).

8. Cutter (1904, 69).

9. Library of Congress, Prints and Photographs Division (1995, 482).

10. A recommendation emanating from the conference was to use a two-tiered hierarchy, whereby metadata indicative of information content would be recorded on
the bibliographic record, and carrier information would be recorded on a linked
holdings record. However, none of the libraries participating in the conference followed through with the recommendation.

11. International Organization for Standards (1998).

12. As bibliographic descriptions evolve to embrace new media, like information
is being scattered throughout the record. Document-type information, for instance,
can be found in the MARC record in at least seven different fields.

13. Definitions are from Sperberg-McQueen and Burnard (1994, sec. 5.2.4).

14. Harnack and Kleppinger (1996).

15. Library of Congress, Network Development and MARC Standards Office (1998).

16. Library of Congress (June 1998).

17. International Organization for Standards (1998).

18. See the discussion of Persistent Uniform Resource Locators (PURLs) later in this chapter.

19. This measure has not been authorized by *AACR2R* or *ISBD(ER)*.

20. Harnack and Kleppinger (1996).

21. Hirons and Graham (1998).

22. In the electronic environment, the acquisition of a document does not necessarily entail a hands-on use (though it can if printed out); it still is physical in the extended sense of being eye-legible.

23. Comaromi (1976, 94, 95).

24. The qualification is introduced because in many libraries nonbook media are organized on shelves by acquisition numbers or numbers deriving from special numbering systems.

25. Standard numbers have traditionally also been used to identify work numbers, such as the Kirchel numbers for Mozart's compositions. Consideration presently is being given to creating work identifiers for works symbolically expressed in other ways. See chapter 6.

26. Harnack and Kleppinger (1996).

27. Harnack and Kleppinger (1996). Not all these resource types are substantial enough to receive the kind of full bibliographic treatment accorded by descriptive codes like *AACR2R*.

28. Harnack and Kleppinger (1996a).

29. OCLC (1996).

30. Ibid.

Chapter 8

1. Shera (1973).

2. See, for instance, Schmitz-Esser (1991).

3. Aboutness is a difficult concept. Difficulties in attempting to determine aboutness (it is not always possible) are discussed in chapter 3.

4. Some subject languages serve also the identification objective in that they provide document addresses in the form of call numbers.

5. Alphabetico-classificatory languages are a hybrid of these, but they are derivative and seldom used.

6. Wittgenstein (1953).

7. ISO (1986a, 5–6).

8. For more elaboration, see Svenonius (1978, 1979).

9. Kaiser (1911).

10. The distinctions overlap but not entirely. Kaiser is definite on this point, observing that surface structures can be misleading. See Kaiser (1911, para. 301); Svenonius (1978).

11. C. N. Mooers (1962) introduced the term *descriptor* into the information-science terminology, using it with a restricted meaning, which — to his unhappiness — most writers, including myself, ignore.

12. Austin (1984).

13. Neelameghan (1979).

14. Austin (1976, 13).

15. See the discussion in Hudon (1998, 80 ff).

16. See, e.g., Andrykovick and Korelev (1977).

17. Austin (1984).

18. For an analysis of the relationships between the modifying and noun components of compound terms, see Jones (1971).

19. A small study was undertaken to measure the degree to which thesauri admitted compound terms. The measure used, called *coordination level,* was defined as $(a \times 1) = (b \times 2) = (c \times 3) = (d \times 4) / a + b + c + d$, where a is the number of uniterms, b the number of two-word terms, c the number of three-word terms, and d the number of four-word terms. Scores ranged from 1.1 to 1.9. While interesting, they cannot be regarded as representative or normative (Van Slype, 1976, 2:18).

20. Taube (1953).

21. Hulme (1911).

22. Cutter (1904, 69).

23. Soergel (1985).

24. Carlyle (1989).

25. Common usage, as it applies to the choice among different names for a concept, is dealt with below in the section on vocabulary control.

26. Svenonius (1984).

27. Aitchison, Gilchrist, and Bawden (1997).

28. The question of whether it is possible to combine many specialized vocabularies to form a universal vocabulary has been raised from time to time and has been answered both in the negative and the positive. See, e.g., Hutchins (1975, 13); Classification Research Group (1969).

29. Vickery (1960, 9).

30. Hutchins (1975, 77).

31. Ranganathan (1965).

32. Vickery (1975, 18, 193).

33. De Grolier (1962).

34. Bhattacharyya (1975).

35. Devadason (1986).

36. Hutchins (1975, 132).

37. Svenonius (1979).

38. As Wittgenstein (1953) observes, even terms referring to physical objects are not always clearly denotative. Is something the size of a soup bowl but having a tea-cup handle a bowl or a cup? The point being made, however, is that some terms are more clearly denotative than others; problems arise as denotations become increasingly fuzzy.

39. Austin (1984, 135).

40. Foskett (1996, 77).

41. Ranganathan (1967).

42. Luhn (1959).

43. Weinberg (1981).

44. Steinacker (1974).

45. Silvester and Genuardi (1994).

46. Spark Jones (1971); Doszkocs and Sass (1993).

47. W. S. Jevons has observed that bibliographical classification would be a good thing if it were not a logical absurdity (quoted in Sayers, 1967, 38–39, without further reference). H. L. Dreyfus (1985) explores, with a negative finding, the feasibility of structuring knowledge.

Chapter 9

1. Quoted in Cutter (1876, 535).

2. *Webster's Third New International Dictionary,* s.v. "homonym."

3. Leech (1974, 228).

4. National Information Standards Organization (1994, 3).

5. An exception to the general rule to qualify each of the resolved terms is the practice followed in the Dewey Decimal Classification (DDC) index of not qualifying the most common use of a term.

6. National Information Standards Organization (1994, 3); Chan (1990, 14).

7. Chan (1990, 14).

8. Chan (1990, 14); OCLC, Forest Press (1999, 19).

9. IFLA, Section on Classification and Indexing (1997); Library of Congress, Cataloging Policy and Support Office (1996, H430, H810).

10. OCLC, Forest Press (1996, xli–xlv).

11. International Organization for Standardization (1986, 15).

12. Despite the injunctions of Thesaurus Standards to the contrary, some thesauri do incorporate a classificatory structure that admits of perspective relationships. As will be seen in the next chapter, perspective disambiguation can also be achieved through the use of syntactic structures.

13. Freeman and Atherton (1968).

14. Markey and Demeyer (1986).

15. Liu and Svenonius (1991); Vizine-Goetz and Mitchell (1996).

16. Slamecka (1963, 224).

17. Some forays into designing lexical databases combining dictionary and thesaural information have already been made. See, for instance, Calzolari (1988).

18. Soergel (1974, 516 ff.); Piternick (1984); Bates (1986). See also the discussion in Chapter 8.

19. Vlelduts-Stokolov (1987).

20. Bhattacharyya, K. (1974).

21. Fugmann (1982).

22. See for instance Carlyle (1989); Bates (1977).

23. Tenopir (1985).

24. Not all singulars are considered equivalent with their apparently corresponding plurals in a subject language. For instance, sometimes the singular form is used to refer to a process (painting) and the plural form to things (paintings).

25. Cutter (1904, 70). The DDC uses scientific names in its schedules. It sometimes qualifies these with the corresponding common usage names; in its index it refers from common names to scientific ones.

26. This is a particularly sensitive issue when it comes to the naming of ethnic groups.

27. Williams (1968).

28. National Information Standards Organization (1994, 19).

29. Englebert (1963).

30. Personal communication from Mary K. Pietris, Chief, Subject Cataloging Division, Library of Congress, November, 1985.

31. American National Standards Institute (1980).

32. See, for instance, UNESCO, General Information Programme (1981, 39).

33. See, for instance, UNESCO, General Information Programme (1981, 39); ISO (1986, 17); National Information Standards Organization (1994, 19).

34. For instance, UNESCO, General Information Programme (1981, 39).

35. Ibid.

36. Neelamegan and Ravichandra Rao (1976); Willetts (1975).

37. Online systems may keep a record of terms frequently ORed together in searches to make them available to users in formulating their searches. See Sievert and Boyce (1983).

38. ANFOR (1981).

39. Svenonius (1983).

40. Rosch (1977).

41. Bates (1977).

42. Simon (1962).

43. Liu and Svenonius (1991).

44. In that they are used for different functions, the two types of hierarchy might usefully be distinguished as different relationships in vocabulary-control tools Svenonius (1996).

45. The likening of a classification to a tree — Porphyry's tree — is common in texts on classification.

46. In a trivial sense logical relations can be created mechanically. Computers can perform logical deduction once rules of inference are input. It can deduce that Lassie is a dog, given that all collies are dogs and Lassie is a collie. However, the deduction contains no relational knowledge that is not also present in the premises.

47. See, for instance, Willet (1988).

48. Svenonius (1992).

49. An exception is the POPSI language, which makes use of a hierarchical syntax. See Bhattacharyya, G. (1979).

50. Metcalfe (1957, 31, 226).

51. Bernier (1968, 103).

52. For instance, International Organization for Standardization (1985a); British Standards Institution (1987).

53. Quine (1980, pp. 20–46) on synonymy; Gardin (1973, p.145) on analyticity; Hutchins (1975, p. 36).

54. Gardin (1973).

55. Van Slype (1976). For ten monolingual thesauri, Van Slype computed and average richness of structure ratio of 4.79.

56. Cleverdon, Mills, and Keen (1966).

57. Svenonius (1986).

Chapter 10

1. Classification Research Group (1957).

2. Svenonius (1992, 5).

3. Kaiser (1911, sec. 45).

4. Kaiser (1911, sec. 67).

5. The difficulties attending this tripartite division of the terminology of a subject language are discussed briefly in chapter 8 and in more extended fashion in Svenonius (1995).

6. Olding (1966, 141).

7. Metcalfe (1959, 298).

8. Ranganathan (1965, 14–15).

9. See the discussion under Facets in chapter 8.

10. Austin (1976).

11. The pre- and postcoordinate distinction is unfortunate — first, because "at the time of a search" is not "post" the search (the way "pre" is before the search), and second, because there is no reason that precoordinated subject headings could not be coordinated by Boolean operators at the time of a search. The historical reasons for why the terminology became established are clarified later in this chapter.

12. Library of Congress, Cataloging Policy and Support Office (1996).

13. Chan (1990). Frequently, facets in these constructions may be left out; the order of the remaining facets is observed.

14. Library of Congress, Cataloging Policy and Support Office (1996, H1095) (p. 18, August 1997).

15. Thomas (1993).

16. Coates (1960, 50). Actually Cutter was probably the first to invoke a principle of significance order. He did it to justify term inversion.

17. Ranganathan (1989, 41).

18. Sørenson and Austin (1976).

19. Sørenson and Austin (1976).

20. Hassell (1982). This interesting study, lacking data on browsing behavior of musicians, constructs a plausible assumption about how those who are performers look for musical scores.

21. Conway (1992, 6).

22. Franz, Powell, and Drabenstott (1994).

23. Liu (1993). Though the sample used in this demonstration was limited to 1,701 synthesized numbers in the arts discipline, it is likely to be nearly or wholly representative of DDC synthetic expressions generally.

24. Creecy, Masand, Smith, and Waltz (1992).

25. Angell (1972).

26. Coates (1960).

27. Svenonius (1971).

28. Conway (1992, 46 ff).

29. Taube (1953).

30. Taube (1953).

31. Svenonius (1995).

32. Svenonius (1971).

33. Farradane (1970).

34. Crestadoro (1856).

35. Luhn (1959).

36. Craven (1986).

37. Lynch (1969); Craven (1982).

38. Massicotte (1988).

39. Massicotte (1988); Svenonius and McGarry (1991).

Afterword

1. National Library of Medicine (1999).

References

AACR2R. See American Library Association, Australian Committee on Cataloguing, British Library, Canadian Committee on Cataloguing, The Library Association, and The Library of Congress.

Abrera, Josefa, and Debora Shaw. (1992). "Frequency of Use of Cataloging Rules in a Practice Collection." *Library Resources and Technical Services* 36(2): 149–162.

Aitchison, Jean, Alan Gilchrist, and David Bawden. (1997). *Thesaurus Construction: A Practical Manual.* 3rd ed. London: Aslib.

American Library Association and The Library Association (1908). *Catalog Rules: Author and Title Entries.* American ed. Chicago: American Library Association Publishing Board.

American Library Association, Australian Committee on Cataloguing, British Library, Canadian Committee on Cataloguing, The Library Association, and The Library of Congress. (1988). *Anglo-American Cataloguing Rules,* 2nd ed. rev., edited by Michael Gorman and Paul W. Winkler. Chicago: American Library Association.

American National Standards Institute. (1980). *Guidelines for Thesaurus Structure, Construction and Use: Z39.19-1980.* New York: American National Standards Institute.

American National Standards Institute. (1985). *American National Standard for Bibliographic Information Interchange: Z39.2-1985.* New York: American National Standards Institute.

Andrykovick, P. F., and E. I. Korolev. (1977). The Statistical and Lexico-grammatical Properties of Words. *Automatic Documentation and Mathematical Linguistics* 11: 1–11.

Angell, Dick. (1972). Library of Congress Subject Headings: Review and Forecast. In *Subject Retrieval in the Seventies: New Directions: Proceedings of an International Symposium Held at the Center of Adult Education, University of Maryland, College Park, May 14 to 15, 1971,* edited by Hans H. Wellisch and Thomas D. Wilson, 143–163. Westport, Conn.: Greenwood.

Association française de normalisation (ANFOR). (1981). Règles d'Établissment des Thésaurus Monolingues (Z47-100). Paris: ANFOR.

Association for Library Collections and Technical Services. (1992). *Guidelines for Bibliographic Description of Reproductions.* Chicago: Association for Library Collections and Technical Services.

Attig, John C. (1989) "Descriptive Cataloging Rules and Machine-Readable Record Structures: Some Directions for Parallel Development," In *The Conceptual Foundations of Descriptive Cataloging,* edited by Elaine Svenonius, 135-148. San Diego: Academic Press, pp. 29–40.

Austin, Derek. (1974). *PRECIS: A Manual of Concept Analysis and Subject Indexing.* London: British Library.

Austin, Derek. (1976). "The Development of PRECIS and Introduction to Its Syntax." In *The PRECIS Index System: Principles, Applications, and Prospects. Proceedings of the International PRECIS Workshop Sponsored by the College of Library and Information Services of the University of Maryland, October 15–17, 1976,* edited by Hans H. Wellisch, 3–28. New York: Wilson.

Baker, Nicholson. (1994) "Annals of Scholarship. Discards." *New Yorker* (April 4): 64–86.

Bates, Marcia J. (1977). "Factors Affecting Subject Catalog Search Success." *Journal of the American Society for Information Science* 28: 161–169.

Bates, Marcia J. (1986). "Subject Access in Online Catalogs: A Design Model." *Journal of the American Society for Information Science* 37(6): 357–376.

Belkin, Nicholas J., et al. (1982). "ASK for Information Retrieval: Part 1. Background and Theory." *Journal of Documentation* 38(2): 61–71.

Bell, Daniel. (1976). *The Coming of Post-Industrial Society: A Venture in Social Forecasting.* New York: Basic Books.

Bernier, Charles L. (1968). "Indexing and Thesauri." *Special Libraries* 59: 98–103.

Bertalanffy, Ludwig von. (1972). "The History and Status of General Systems Theory." In *Trends in General Systems Theory,* edited by George J. Klir, 21–41. New York: Wiley Interscience.

Betz, Elizabeth. (1987). "Staff News: Online Users Group Presents Program on Visual Materials." *Library of Congress Information Bulletin* 46 (April 13): 15.

Bhattacharyya, Ganesh. (1975). "Fundamentals of Indexing Languages." In *Ordering Systems for Global Information Network: Proceedings of the Third International Study Conference on Classification Research, Bombay, 6–11 January, 1975,* edited by A. Neelameghan, 83–99. Bangalore, India: FID/CR and Sarada Ranganathan Endowment for Library Science.

Bhattacharyya, Ganesh. (1979). "POPSI: Its Fundamentals and Procedure Based on a General Theory of Subject Indexing Languages." *Library Science with a Slant to Documentation* 16(1): 1–34.

Bhattacharyya, K. (1974). "The Effectiveness of Natural Language in Science Indexing and Retrieval." *Journal of Documentation* 30: 235–254.

Bishop, William Warner. (1916). *Cataloging as an Asset*. Baltimore: Waverly Press.

Blackburn, Charles F. (1884). *Hints on Catalogue Titles, and on Index Entries, with a Rough Vocabulary of Terms and Abbreviations, Chiefly from Catalogues, and Some Passages from Journeying among Books*. London: Sampson Low, Marston, Searle, and Rivington.

Bowers, Fredson. (1949). *Principles of Bibliographic Description*. Princeton: Princeton University Press.

Bradford, Samuel Clement. (1948). *Documentation*. London: Lockwood.

Brault, Nancy. (1972). *The Great Debate on Panizzi's Rules in 1847–1849: The Issues Discussed*. Los Angeles: UCLA School of Library Service.

Bridgman, P. W. (1938). *The Logic of Modern Physics*. New York: Macmillan.

British Museum. Department of Printed Books. (1841). *Catalogue of Printed Books in the British Museum*. Volume I, edited by Sir Anthony Panizzi. London: The Trustees.

British Standards Institution. (1987). *Guide to the Establishment and Development of Monolingual Thesauri* (BS 5723: 1987). London: BSI.

Butler, Pierce. (1953). "Bibliographical Function of the Library." *Journal of Cataloging and Classification* 9(7): 3–11.

Calzolari, Nicoletta. (1988). "The Dictionary and the Thesaurus Can Be Combined." In *Relational Models of the Lexicon: Representing Knowledge in Semantic Networks*, edited by Martha Walton Evans, 75–96. Cambridge: Cambridge University Press.

Carlyle, Allyson. (1989). "Matching LCSH and User Vocabulary in the Library Catalog." *Cataloging and Classification Quarterly* 10(1/2): 37–63.

Carlyle, Allyson. (1994). "The Second Objective of the Catalog: An Evaluation of Collocation in Online Catalog Displays." Ph.D. dissertation, University of California, Los Angeles.

Carlyle, Allyson. (1999). "User Categorization of Works: Toward Improved Organisation of Online Catalog Displays." *Journal of Documentation* 55(2): 184–208.

Carlyle, Thomas. (1902). *Sartor Resartus*. Boston: Ginn. Originally published in 1831.

Carpenter, Michael. (1981). *Corporate Authorship: Its Role in Library Cataloging*. Westport, Conn.: Greenwood Press.

Carpenter, Michael. (1994). "Catalogs and Cataloging." In *Encyclopedia of Library History*, edited by Wayne A. Wiegand and Donald G. Davis, 107–117. New York: Garland.

Carpenter, Michael, and Elaine Svenonius, eds. (1985). *Foundations of Cataloging: A Sourcebook*. Littleton, Colo.: Libraries Unlimited.

Chan, Lois. (1990). *Library of Congress Subject Headings: Principles of Structure and Policies for Application.* Advances in Library Information Technology No. 3. Washington, D.C.: Library of Congress.

Chaplin, A. H. (1966). *Tradition and Principle in Library Cataloguing.* The Bertha Basam Lecture in Librarianship No. 1. Toronto: University of Toronto School of Library Science.

Classification Research Group. (1957). "The Need for a Faceted Classification as the Basis of all Methods of Information Retrieval." In *Proceedings of the International Study Conference on Classification for Information Retrieval Held at Beatrice Webb House, Dorking, England 13–17 May 1957, Appendix 2,* 137–147. London: ASLIB. Note: This was first published in memorandum form as UNESCO (IAC Doc. Ter. PAS) Document 320/5515, 26 May 1955.

Classification Research Group. (1969). *Classification and Information Control: Papers Representing the Work of the Classification Research Group 1960–1968.* London: Library Association.

Cleverdon, Cyril W. (1962). *Report on the Testing and Analysis of an Investigation into the Comparative Efficiency of Indexing Systems.* Cranfield, Eng.: College of Aeronautics, ASLIB Cranfield Research Project.

Cleverdon, Cyril and J. Mills. (1963). "The Testing of Index Language Devices." *Aslib Proceedings* 14(4): 106–30.

Cleverdon, Cyril W., Jack Mills, and Michael Keen. (1966). *Factors Determining the Performance of Indexing Systems. Vol. 1: Design, Parts 1 and 2. Vol. 2: Test Results.* Cranfield, Eng.: College of Aeronautics, ASLIB Cranfield Research Project.

Coates, Eric J. (1960). *Subject Catalogues: Headings and Structure.* London: Library Association.

Coates, Eric J. (1988). *Subject Catalogues: Headings and Structure.* London: Library Association.

Cochrane, Pauline A. (1983). "A Paradigm Shift in Library Science." *Information Technology and Libraries* 2(1): 3–4.

Coffman, Steve. (1998). "What If You Ran Your Library Like a Bookstore?" *American Libraries* 29(3): 40–47.

Comaromi, John Phillip. (1976). *The Eighteen Editions of the Dewey Decimal Classification.* Albany, N.Y.: Forest Press.

Commissioners Appointed to Inquire into the Constitution and Government of the British Museum. (1850). *Report of the Commissioners Appointed to Inquire into the Constitution and Management of the British Museum, with Minutes of Evidence.* London: Her Majesty's Stationery Office.

Conway, Martha O'Hara. (1992). *The Future of Subdivisions in the Library of Congress Subject Headings System. Report from the Subject Subdivisions Conference Sponsored by the Library of Congress, May 9–12, 1991.* Washington, D.C.: Library of Congress.

Cook, Charles Donald. (1977). "The Effectiveness of the *Anglo-American Cataloging Rules* in Achieving Standardization of Choice and Form of Heading for Certain Library Materials Cataloged in Canada, Great Britain and the United States from 1968 through 1972." D.L.S. dissertation, Columbia University.

Craven, Timothy C. (1982). "Automatic NEPHIS Coding of Descriptive Titles for Permuted Index Generation." *Journal of the American Society for Information Science* 33(2): 97–101.

Craven, Timothy C. (1986). *String Indexing.* Library and Information Science Series. Orlando: Academic Press.

Creecy, Robert H., Brij M. Masand, Stephen Smith, and David L. Waltz. (1992). "Trading MIPS and Memory for Knowledge Engineering (Parallel Automated Coding Expert Census Classification System)." *Communications of the ACM* 35(8): 48–64.

Crestadoro, Andrea. (1856). *The Art of Making Catalogues of Libraries, or, A Method to Obtain in a Short Time a Most Perfect, Complete, and Satisfactory Printed Catalogue of the British Museum Library.* London: Literary, Scientific and Artistic Reference Office.

Croghan, Antony. (1972). *A Code for Cataloguing Nonbook Media.* London: Coburgh.

Cromwell, Willy. (1994). "The Core Record: A New Bibliographic Standard." *Library Resources and Technical Services* 38(4): 415–424.

Cutter, Charles A. (1876a). "Library Catalogues." In *Public Libraries in the United States of America: Their History, Condition, and Management.* Special Report. Part 1, 526–575. Washington, D.C.: U.S. Bureau of Education. Reprinted in Monograph Series, Number 4, Urbana: University of Illinois, Graduate School of Library Science.

Cutter, Charles A. (1876b). *Rules for a Printed Dictionary Catalog.* U.S. Bureau of Education, Special Report on Public Libraries, Part II. Washington, D.C.: U.S. Government Printing Office.

Cutter, Charles A. (1904). *Rules for a Printed Dictionary Catalog,* 4th ed. U.S. Bureau of Education, Special Report on Public Libraries, Part II. Washington, D.C.: U.S. Government Printing Office.

Dahlberg, Ingetraut. (1992). "Knowledge Organization and Terminlogy: Philosophical and Linguistic Bases." *International Classification* 19(2): 65–71.

Delsey, Tom. (1989). "Standards for Descriptive Cataloging: Two Perspectives on the Past Twenty Years." In *The Conceptual Foundations of Descriptive Cataloging,* edited by Elaine Svenonius, 51–64. San Diego: Academic Press.

de Rijk, E. (1991). "Thomas Hyde, Julia Pettee, and the Development of Cataloging Principles, with a Translation of Hyde's 1674 Preface to the Reader." *Cataloging and Classification Quarterly* 14(2): 31–62.

Devadason, Francis. (1986). *Computerized Deep Structure Indexing System.* FID/CR Report No. 21. Frankfurt: INDEKS Verlag.

Domanovszky, Ákos. (1973). "Editor Entries and the Principles of Cataloguing." *Libri* 23: 307–330. Reprinted in *Foundations of Cataloging: A Sourcebook*, edited by M. Carpenter and E. Svenonius, 192–207. Littleton, Colo.: Libraries Unlimited.

Domanovszky, Ákos. (1975). *Functions and Objects of Author and Title Cataloguing*. Muenchen: Verlag Dokumentation.

Doszkocs, Tamas E. and Rivkah K. Sass. (1993). "An Associative Semantic Network for Machine-Aided Indexing, Classification and Searching." In *Advances in Classification Research*, v. 3, *Proceedings of the 3rd ASIS SIG/CR Classification Research Workshop*, edited by Raya Fidel, Barbara H. Kwasnik, and Philip J. Smith, 15-35. Medford, NJ: Learned Information, Inc.

Dreyfus, Hubert L. (1985) "From Micro-Worlds to Knowledge Representation: AI at an Impasse." In *Readings in Knowledge Representation*, edited by Ronald J. Brachman and Hector J. Levesque (71–94). Los Altos, Calif.: Morgan Kaufmann.

Drucker, Peter. (1988). "The Coming of the New Organization." *Harvard Business Review* 66: 45–53.

Dunkin, Paul. (1969). *Cataloging U.S.A.* Chicago: American Library Association.

Eddington, A. S. (1929). *The Nature of the Physical World*. Cambridge: Cambridge University Press.

The Encyclopedia of Philosophy (1967). Edited by Paul Edwards. New York: Macmillan and The Free Press.

Engelbart, D. C. (1963). "Conceptual Framework for the Augmentation of Man's Intellect." In *Vistas in Information Handling*, 1–29. London: Spartan Books.

Farradane, Jason E. L. (1970). "Analysis and Organization of Knowledge for Retrieval." *Aslib Proceedings* 22(12): 607–616.

Fattahi, Rahmatollah. (1995). "Anglo-American Cataloguing Rules in the Online Environment: A Literature Review." *Cataloging & Classification Quarterly* 20(2):25–50.

Fidel, Raya, and Michael Crandall. (1988). "The AACR2 as a Design Schema for Bibliographic Databases." *Library Quarterly* 58(2): 123–142.

Fidel, Raya, Trudi Bellardo Hahn, Edie M. Rasmussen, and Philip J. Smith, eds. (1994). *Challenges in Indexing Electronic Text and Images*. Monograph Series. Medford, N.J.: Learned Information.

Foskett, Anthony Charles. (1996). *The Subject Approach to Information*. 5th ed. London: Library Association Publishing.

Foucault, Michel. (1979). "What Is an Author?" In *Textual Strategies: Perspectives in Post-Structuralist Criticism*, edited by Josué V. Harari, 141–160. Ithaca: Cornell University Press.

Fox, Christopher, and Terry Norreault. (1980). "Indexing and the Aboutness Relation." Typescript.

Fox, Martha Sandberg. (1972). "The Amenability of a Cataloging Process to Simulation by Automatic Techniques." Ph.D. dissertation, University of Illinois.

Franz, L., J. Powell, S. Jude, and K. M. Drabenstott. (1994). "End User Understanding of Subdivided Subject Headings." *Library Resources and Technical Services* 38(3): 213–226.

Freedman, Maurice J., and S. Michael Malinconico, eds. (1979). *The Nature and Future of the Catalog: Proceedings of the ALA's Information Science and Automation Division's 1975 and 1977 Institutes on the Catalog.* Phoenix: Oryx Press.

Freeman, Robert R., and Pauline Atherton. (1968). "Audacious: An Experiment with an On-line, Interactive Reference Retrieval System Using the Universal Decimal Classification as the Index Language in the Field of Nuclear Science." In *Information Transfer: Proceedings of the Thirty-first ASIS Annual Meeting*, 193–199. New York: Greenwood.

Frost, Carolyn O. (1983). *Cataloging Nonbook Materials: Problems in Theory and Practice.* Littleton, Colo.: Libraries Unlimited.

Fugmann, Robert. (1982). "The Complementarity of Natural and Indexing Languages." *International Classification* 9: 140–144.

Gardin, J. C. (1973). Document Analysis and Linguistic Theory. *Journal of Documentation* 29:137–168.

Genette, Gérard. (1982). Palmpsestes: la Littérature au Second Degré. Paris: Editions du Seul.

Gopinath, M. A. (1970). "The Colon Classification." In *Classification in the 1970s: A Discussion of Development and Prospects for the Major Schemes*, edited by Arthur Maltby. London: Bingley.

Gorman, Michael. (1979). "Cataloging and the New Technologies." In *The Nature and Future of the Catalog: Proceedings of the ALA's Information Science and Automation Division's 1975 and 1977 Institutes on the Catalog*, edited by Maurice J. Freedman and S. Michael Malinconico, 127–152. Phoenix: Oryx Press.

Gorman, Michael. (1980). "AACR2: Main Themes." In *The Making of a Code: The Issues Underlying AACR2: Papers Given at the International Conference on AACR2 Held March 11–14, 1979*, edited by Doris Hargrett, 41–60. Chicago: American Library Association.

Gorman, Michael. (1992). "After AACR2: The Future of the Anglo-American Cataloging Rules." In *Origins, Content, and Future of AACR2 Revised*, edited by Richard P. Smiraglia, 89–94. Chicago: American Library Association.

Graham, Crystal. (1990). "Definition and Scope of Multiple Versions." *Cataloging and Classification Quarterly*, 11(2): 5–32.

Green, Rebecca. (1996). "The Design of a Relational Database for Large-Scale Bibliographic Retrieval." *Information Technology and Libraries* 15(4): 207–221.

Grolier, Eric de. (1962). *A Study of General Categories Applicable to Classification and Coding in Documentation.* Paris: UNESCO.

Guidelines for Electronic Text Encoding and Interchange. See Sperberg-McQueen, C. M., and Lou Burnard.

Hagler, Ronald (1977). "Changes in Cataloging Codes: Rules for Description." *Library Trends* 25: 603–623.

Hagler, Ronald. (1989). "The Consequences of Integration." In *The Conceptual Foundations of Descriptive Cataloging*, edited by Elaine Svenonius, 197–218. San Diego: Academic Press.

Hamdy, M. Nabil. (1973). *The Concept of Main Entry as Represented in the Anglo-American Cataloging Rules: A Critical Appraisal with Some Suggestions; Author Main Entry vs. Title Main Entry.* Research Studies in Library Science, No. 10. Littleton, Colo.: Libraries Unlimited.

Hanson, J. C. M. (1909). *A Comparative Study of Cataloging Rules Based on the Anglo-American Code of 1908.* The University of Chicago Studies in Library Science. Chicago: University of Chicago Press.

Harnack, Andrew, and Gene Kleppinger. (1996). "Beyond the MLA Handbook: Documenting Electronic Sources on the Internet." http://www.falcon.eku.edu/honors/beyond-mla (Accessed 3 July 1998).

Hassell, Robert H. (1982). "Revising the Dewey Music Schedule: Tradition vs. Innovation." *Library Resources and Technical Services* 26(2): 193–203.

Haykin, David J. (1951). *Subject Headings: A Practical Guide.* Washington, D.C.: U.S. Government Printing Office.

Heaney, Michael. (1995). "Object-Oriented Cataloging." Information Technology and Libraries 14(3): 135–153.

Helmer, John F. (1987). "Cataloging, Economics, and the Experience of Works." MLS Paper. University of California, Los Angeles.

Hirons, Jean and Crystal Graham. (1998). "Issues Related to Seriality." In *International Conference on the Principles and Future Development of AACR*, edited by Jean Weihs, 180–213. Ottawa: Canadian Library Association.

The Home Book of Quotations (1949). 6th ed. rev. Edited by Burton Stevenson. New York: Dodd, Mead.

Howarth, Lynne C. (1998). Content vs. Carrier. In *International Conference on the Principles and Future Development of AACR*, edited by Jean Weihs, 148–157. Ottawa: Canadian Library Association.

Hudon, Michèle. (1998). "An Assessment of the Usefulness of Standardized Definitions in a Thesaurus through Interindexer Terminological Consistency Measurements." Ph.D. dissertation, University of Toronto.

Hulme, E. Wyndham. (1911). "Principles of Book Classification." *Library Association Record* 13: 445–447.

Hutchins, William J. (1975). "Languages of Indexing and Classification: A Linguistic Study of Structures and Functions." Stevenage, Herts.: Peter Peregrinus.

IFLA. *See* International Federation of Library Associations; International Federation of Library Associations and Institutions.

International Federation of Library Associations. (1962). *Report: Proceedings of the International Conference on Cataloguing Principles, Paris, 9th–18th October, 1961.* London: International Federation of Library Associations.

International Federation of Library Associations and Institutions. (1987). *International Standard Bibliographic Description for Non-book Materials.* Rev. ed. London: IFLA UBCIM Programme.

International Federation of Library Associations and Institutions. (1997). *International Standard Bibliographic Description for Electronic Resources.* Frankfurt am Main: Deutsche Bibliothek; IFLA Universal Bibliographic Control and International MARC Programme.

International Federation of Library Associations and Institutions. (1998). *Functional Requirements for Bibliographic Records: Final Report. Recommended by the IFLA Study Group on the Functional Requirements for Bibliographic Records.* UBCIM Publications, New Series Vol. 19. Munich: K. G. Saur.

International Federation of Library Associations and Institutions. (1999). *Principles Underlying Subject Heading Languages (SHLs),* edited by Maria Inês Lopes and Julianne Beall for the Working Group on Principles Underlying Subject Heading Languages, Section on Classification and Indexing. A UBCIM publication. Munich: Saur.

International Organization for Standardization (ISO). (1981). *Documentation: Format for Bibliographic Information Interchange on Magnetic Tape: ISO 2709–1981.* Geneva: ISO.

International Organization for Standardization (ISO). (1985a). *Documentation: Guidelines for the Establishment and Development of Multilingual Thesauri: ISO 5964:1985 (E).* Geneva: ISO.

International Organization for Standardization (ISO). (1985b). *Documentation, Methods for Examining Documents, Determining Their Subjects and Selecting Indexing Terms: ISO 5963.* Geneva: ISO.

International Organization for Standardization (ISO). (1986a). *Documentation: Guidelines for the Establishment and Development of Monolingual Thesauri: ISO 2788.* Geneva: ISO.

International Organization for Standardization (ISO). (1986b). *Information Processing: Text and Office Systems: Standard Generalized Markup Language (SGML): ISO 8879.* Geneva: ISO.

International Organization for Standardization (ISO). (1998). Excerpts from International Standard ISO 690-2: Information and Documentation –Bibliographic References — Part 2: Electronic Documents or Parts Thereof. http://www.nlc-bnc.ca/iso/tc4sc9/standard/690-2e.htm (Accessed 3 July 1998).

IMCE. *See* International Meeting of Cataloguing Experts.

International Meeting of Cataloguing Experts (IMCE). (1970). "Report of the International Meeting of Cataloguing Experts, Copenhagen, 1969." *Libri* 20: 105–132.

ISO. *See* International Organization for Standardization.

Jeng, Ling Whey. (1987). "The Title Page as the Source of Information for Bibliographic Description: An Analysis of Its Visual and Linguistic Characteristics." Ph.D. dissertation, University of Texas, Austin.

Jewett, Charles C. (1853). *On the Construction of Catalogues of Libraries and of a General Catalogue and Their Publication by Means of Separate, Stereotyped Titles with Rules and Examples.* 2nd ed. Washington, D.C.: Smithsonian Institution.

Jolley, Leonard J. (1963). "The Function of the Main Entry in the Alphabetical Catalogue: A Study of the Views Put Forward by Lubetzky and Verona." In *Report. Proceedings of the International Conference on Cataloguing Principles held in Paris, 9th–18th October, 1961,* edited by A. H. Chaplin and Dorothy Anderson, 159–163. London: Organizing Committee of the International Conference; Clive Bingley on behalf of IFLA.

Jones, Kevin P. (1971). "Compound Words: A Problem in Post-Coordinate Retrieval Systems." *Journal of the American Society for Information Science* 22: 242–250.

Kaiser, Julius O. (1911). *Systematic Indexing.* The Card System Series, Vol. II. London: Gibson.

Kaske, Neal K., et al. (1983). *A Comprehensive Study of Online Public Access Catalogs: An Overview and Application of Findings.* Dublin, Ohio: OCLC Online Computer System.

Kintsch, W., and Van Dijk, T. (1978). "Toward a Model of Text Comprehension and Production." *Psychological Review* 85(5): 363–394.

Krikelas, James. (1980). "Searching the Library Catalog: A Study of Users Access." *Library Research* 2: 215–230.

Lambrecht, Jay H. (1992). *Minimal Level Cataloging by National Bibliographic Agencies.* UBCIM Publications, New Series, vol. 8. New York: Saur.

Langer, Susan K. (1949). *Philosophy in a New Key.* New York: New American Library.

Layne, Sara Shatford. (1989). "Integration and the Objectives of the Catalog." In *The Foundations of Descriptive Cataloging,* edited by Elaine Svenonius, 185–196. San Diego: Academic Press.

Layne, Sara Shatford. (1994). "Some Issues in the Indexing of Images." *Journal of the American Society for Information Science* 45(8): 583–588.

Layne, Sara Shatford. (1997). "Modeling Relevance in Art History: Identifying Attributes That Determine the Relevance of Art Works, Images, and Primary Text to Art History Research." Ph.D. dissertation, University of California, Los Angeles, Graduate School of Library and Information Science.

Leazer, Gregory H. (1992). "An Examination of Data Elements for Bibliographic Description: Toward a Conceptual Schema for the USMARC Formats." *Library Research and Technical Services* 36(2): 189–208.

Leazer, Gregory H. (To be published). *Items, Works, and Intertextual Networks: An Extended Design for the Organization of Information.* Personal communication.

Leech, Geoffrey. (1974). *Semantics.* Harmondsworth, Middlesex, Eng.: Penguin.

Leibniz, G. W. (1951). "Towards a Universal Characteristic." Reprinted in *Leibniz Selections,* edited by P. P. Wiener, 17–25. New York: Scribner. First published in 1677.

Library Association, The. (1973). *Non-book Materials Cataloguing Rules: Integrated Code of Practice . . .* Working Paper No. 11. Huddersfield, Eng.: National Council for Educational Technology and the Library Association.

Library of Congress. (1978–). *Cataloging Service Bulletin.* Washington, D.C.: Library of Congress.

Library of Congress. (1998). *CONSER Cataloging Manual.* Module 31: Remote Access Computer File Serials. Part 1. http://www.lcweb.loc.gov/acq/conser/mod31pt1.html#interim (1 July 1998).

Library of Congress, Cataloging Distribution Service. (1989–). *Library of Congress Rule Interpretations.* 2nd ed. Washington, D.C.: Library of Congress, Cataloging Distribution Service.

Library of Congress, Cataloging Policy and Support Office. (Various dates). *Library of Congress Classification.* Washington, D.C.: Library of Congress.

Library of Congress. Cataloging Policy and Support Office. (1996). *Subject Cataloging Manual. Subject Headings.* 5th ed. Washington, D.C.: Library of Congress.

Library of Congress, Cataloging Policy and Support Office. (1998). *Library of Congress Subject Headings.* 21st ed. Washington, D.C.: Library of Congress.

Library of Congress, Network Development and MARC Standards Office. (1998). *Providing Access to Online Information Resources.* MARBI Discussion Paper No. 54. http://www.nlc-bnc.ca/ifla/documents/libraries/cataloging/marbi54.txt (1 July 1998).

Library of Congress, Prints and Photographs Division. (1995). *Thesaurus for Graphic Materials.* Washington, D.C.: Library of Congress.

Library of Congress, Processing Department. (1946). *Studies of Descriptive Cataloging: A Report to the Librarian of Congress by the Director of the Processing Department.* Washington, D.C.: Library of Congress.

Library of Congress. Program for Cooperative Cataloging (1999). "Introduction to the Program for Cooperative Cataloging BIBCO Core Record Standard." http://lcweb.loc.gov/catdir/pcc/coreintro.html. (Accessed Aug. 21, 1999.)

Library of Congress, Serial Record Division. (1994). *CONSER Editing Guide.* Washington, D.C.: Library of Congress.

Ling Whey, Jeng. (1987). "The Title Page as the Source of Information for Bibliographic Description: An Analysis of Its Visual and Linguistic Characteristics." Ph.D. dissertation, University of Texas, Austin.

Liu, Songqiao. (1993). "The Automatic Decomposition of DDC Synthesized Numbers." Ph.D. dissertation, University of California, Los Angeles.

Liu, Songqiao, and Elaine Svenonius. (1991). "DORS: DDC Online Retrieval System." *Library Resources and Technical Services* 35(4): 359–375.

Lubetzky, Seymour. (1953). Cataloging Rules and Principles: Critique of the A.L.A. Rules for Entry and a Proposed Design for Their Revision. Prepared for the Board on Cataloging and Classification. Washington, D.C.: Library of Congress, Processing Department.

Lubetzky, Seymour. (1960). *Code of Cataloging Rules: Author and Title Entry: An Unfinished Draft.* Chicago: American Library Association.

Lubetzky, Seymour. (1969). *Principles of Cataloging. Final Report. Phase I: Descriptive Cataloging.* Los Angeles: University of California, Institute of Library Research.

Lubetzky, Seymour. (2000). "The Vicissitudes of Ideology and Technology in Anglo-American Cataloging since Panizzi and a Prospective Reformation of the Catalog for the Next Century." Paper Delivered on the Occasion of his Centennial Celebration at the Bradley Center, UCLA on April 18, 1998; in Collaboration with Elaine Svenonius. In *The Future of Cataloging: The Lubetzky Symposium,* edited by Tschera Harkness Connell and Robert L. Maxwell. Chicago: American Library Association.

Luhn, Hans Peter. (1959). Keyword-in-Context Index for Technical Literature (KWIC INDEX). Technical Report RC–127. Yorktown Heights, N.Y.: IBM.

Lynch, Michael F. (1969). "Computer-Aided Production of Printed Alphabetical Subject Indexes." *Journal of Documentation* 25(3): 244–252.

Malinconico, S. Michael. (1975). "The Role of a Machine-Based Authority File in an Automated Bibliographic System." In *Automation in Libraries: Papers Presented at the CACUL Workshop on Library Automation, Winnipeg, June 22–23, 1974.* Ottawa: Canadian Library Association.

Mann, Thomas. (1991) *Cataloging Quality, LC Priorities, and Models of the Library's Future.* Washington, D.C.: Library of Congress, Cataloging Forum.

Markey, Karen, and Anh N. Demeyer. (1986). *Dewey Decimal Classification Online a Project: Evaluation of a Library Schedule and Index Integrated into the Subject Searching Capabilities of an Online Catalog.* OCLC Research Report OCLC/OP/RR-86/1. Dublin, Ohio: Online Computer Library Center.

Maron, M. E. (1977). "On Indexing, Retrieval and the Meaning of *About.*" *Journal of the American Society for Information Science* 28: 38–43.

Massicotte, Mia. (1988). "Improved Browsable Displays for Online Subject Access." *Information Technology and Libraries* 7(4): 373–380.

Matthews, Joseph R., Gary Lawrence, and Douglas R. Ferguson, eds. (1983). *Using Online Catalogs: A Nationwide Survey: A Report of a Study Sponsored by the Council on Library Resources.* New York: Neal-Schuman.

McCallum, Sally H. (1982) "Record Linking Technique." *Information Technology and Libraries* 1(3): 281–291.

McLuhan, M. (1964). *Understanding Media: The Extensions of Man.* New York: McGraw-Hill.

Metcalfe, John. (1957). *Information Indexing and Subject Cataloging: Alphabetical, Classified; Coordinate, Mechanical.* New York: Scarecrow Press.

Metcalfe, John. (1959). *Subject Classifying and Indexing of Libraries and Literature.* New York: Scarecrow Press.

Miksa, Francis L., ed. (1977). *Charles Ammi Cutter, Library Systematizer.* Littleton, Colo.: Libraries Unlimited.

Miksa, Francis L. (1983). *The Subject in the Dictionary Catalog from Cutter to the Present.* Chicago: American Library Association.

Molto, Mavis, and Elaine Svenonius. (1991). "Automatic Recognition of Title Page Names." *Information Processing and Management* 279(1): 83–95.

Molto, Mavis, and Elaine Svenonius. (1998). "An Electronic Interface to AACR2." *Cataloging and Classification Quarterly* 26(1): 3–24.

Mooers, Calvin N. (1962). "The Indexing Language of an Information Retrieval System." In *Information Retrieval Today: Papers Presented at an Institute Conducted by the Library School and the Center for Continuation Study, University of Minnesota, Sept. 19–22, 1962,* edited by Wesley Simonton, 21–36. Minneapolis, Minn.: Center for Continuation Study.

Multiple Versions Forum. (1990). *Multiple Versions Forum Report. Report from a Meeting Held December 6–8, 1989, Airlie, Virginia, Sponsored by the Council on Library Resources, Library of Congress/Network Development and MARC Standards Office.* Washington, D.C.: Library of Congress, Network Development and MARC Standards Office.

National Education Association of the United States, Department of Audiovisual Instruction (DAVI). (1968). *Standards for Cataloging, Coding, and Scheduling Educational Media.* Washington, D.C.: DAVI.

National Information Standards Organization. (1994). *Guidelines for the Construction, Format and Management of Monolingual Thesauri: Z39.19–1993.* Bethesda, Md.: NISO Press.

National Library of Medicine. (1999). "1999 UMLS Documentation." http://www.nlm.nih.gov/research/umls/umlsdoc.html (Accessed 8/22/99.)

Neelameghan, A. (1979). "Absolute Syntax and Structure of an Indexing and Switching Language." In *Ordering Systems for Global Information Networks: Proceedings of the Third International Study Conference on Classification Research, Bombay, 6–11 January, 1975,* edited by A. Neelameghan, 165–176. FIC/CR Publication No. 553. Bangalore: Documentation Research Training Centre.

Neelameghan, A., and I. K. Ravichandra Rao. (1976). "Nonhierarchical Associative Relationships: Their Types and Computer Generation of RT Links." *Library Science with a Slant Toward Documentation* 13: 24–34.

OCLC. *See* Online Computer Library Center.

Olding, R. K., ed. (1966). *Readings in Library Cataloguing.* London: Crosby Lockwood.

O'Neill, Edward T., Sally A. Rogers, and W. Michael Oskins. (1993). "Characteristics of Duplicate Records in OCLC's Online Union Catalog." *Library Resources and Technical Services* 37(1): 59–71.

O'Neill, Edward T., and Diane Vizine-Goetz. (1989). "Bibliographic Relationships: Implications for the Function of the Catalog." In *The Foundations of Descriptive Cataloging,* edited by Elaine Svenonius, 167–180. San Diego: Academic Press.

Online Computer Library Center. (1992). *Bibliographic Input Standards.* 5th. ed. Dublin, Ohio: Online Computer Library Center.

Online Computer Library Center. (1996). "PURL Frequently Asked Questions." http://www.purl.oclc.org/OCLC/PURL/FAQ (3 July 1998).

Online Computer Library Center. Forest Press. (1996). Dewey Decimal Classification and Relative Index. 21st ed. Albany, N.Y.: OCLC and Forest Press.

Online Computer Library Center. Forest Press. (April 1999). "Editorial Rules: Dewey Decimal Classification. Print Index." Typescript.

Osborn, Andrew D. (1941). "The Crisis in Cataloging." *Library Quarterly* 11: 393–411.

The Oxford English Dictionary. 2nd ed. (The Electronic Text Project of the UCLA Library). http://etext.ucla.edu./cgi-bin/oed.

Panizzi, Anthony. (1850). "Mr. Panizzi to the Right Hon. the Earl of Ellesmere. — British Museum, 29 January 1828." In *Appendix to the Report of the Commissioners Appointed to Inquire into the Constitution and Management of the British Museum,* 378–395. London: Her Majesty's Stationery Office. Reprinted in *Foundations of Cataloging: A Source Book,* edited by Michael Carpenter and Elaine Svenonius, 18–47. Littleton, Colo.: Libraries Unlimited, 1985.

Pettee, Julia. (1936). "The Development of Authorship Entry and the Formation of Authorship Rules as Found in the Anglo-American Code." *Library Quarterly* 6: 270–290. Reprinted in *Foundations of Cataloging: A Source Book,* edited by Michael Carpenter and Elaine Svenonius, 172–189. Littleton, Colo.: Libraries Unlimited, 1985.

Pierce, Elizabeth G. (1946). "Appendix D: Testing the Value of Full Title-Page Transcription in Cataloguing." In *Studies of Descriptive Cataloging: A Report to the Librarian of Congress by the Director of the Processing Department,* 36–39. Washington, D.C.: U.S. Government Printing Office.

Piternick, Anne B. (1984). "Searching Vocabularies: A Developing Category of Online Search Tools." *Online Review* 8: 441–449.

Piternick, Anne. (1989). "Authors Online: A Searcher's Approach to the Online Author Catalog." In *The Conceptual Foundations of Descriptive Cataloging,* edited by Elaine Svenonius, 21–28. San Diego: Academic Press.

Quine, Willard Van Orman. (1980). *From a Logical Point of View.* 2nd ed. Cambridge: Harvard University Press.

Ranganathan, Shiyali Ramamrita. (1933). *Colon Classification*. Madras: Madras Library Association.

Ranganathan, Shiyali Ramamrita. (1955) *Heading and Canons: Comparative Study of Five Catalogue Codes*. Madras: Viswanathan.

Ranganathan, Shiyali Ramamrita. (1957). *Prolegomena to Library Classification*. London: Library Association.

Ranganathan, Shiyali Ramamrita. (1965). *The Colon Classification*. Rutgers Series on Systems for the Intellectual Organization of Information. New Brunswick, N.J.: Rutgers.

Ranganathan, Shiyali Ramamrita. (1967). "Hidden Roots of Classification." *Library Science with a Slant to Documentation* (4): 1–26.

Ranganathan, Shiyali Ramamrita. (1989). *Colon Classification*, 7th ed., edited by M. A. Gopinath. Bangalore: Sarada Ranganathan Endowment for Library Science.

Ravilious, C. P. (1975). *A Survey of Existing Systems and Current Proposals for the Cataloguing and Description of Non-book Materials Collected by Libraries: With Preliminary Suggestions for their International Co-ordination*. Paris: Unesco.

Rayward, W. Boyd. (1976). *The Universe of Information: The Work of Paul Otlet for Documentation and International Organisation*. FID Publication 520. Moscow: VINITI.

Rayward, W. Boyd, ed. and trans. (1991). *International Organisation and Dissemination of Knowledge: Selected Essays of Paul Otlet*. FID Publication 684. Amsterdam: Elsevier.

Rayward, Boyd. W. (1994). "Some Schemes for Restructuring and Mobilising Information in Documents: A Historical Perspective," *Information Processing & Management* 30 (2): 163–175.

Rayward, Boyd. W. (1997). "The Origins of Information Science and the International Institute of Bibliography/International Federation for Information and Documentation (FID)" (Historical Studies in Information Science). *Journal of the American Society for Information Science* 43: 283–300.

Rosch, Eleanor. (1977). "Human Categorization." In *Studies in Cross-cultural Psychology*, edited by N. Warren, vol. 1, 1–67. London: Academic Press.

Russell, Keith. W., ed. (1982). *Subject Access: Report of a Meeting Sponsored by the Council on Library Resource, Dublin, Ohio, June 7–9, 1982*. Washington, D.C.: Council on Library Resources.

Ryle, Gilbert. (1959). *The Concept of Mind*. New York: Barnes and Noble. First published in 1949.

Santayana, George. (1932). *The Life of Reason in the Phases of Human Progress*. 2nd ed. New York: Scribner's.

Sayers, W. C. Berwick. (1967). *A Manual of Classification for Librarians*. 4th ed., completely revised and partly re-written by Arthur Maltby. London: Deutsch.

Schmierer, Helen F. (1989). "The Impact of Technology on Cataloging Rules." In *The Conceptual Foundations of Descriptive Cataloging,* edited by Elaine Svenonius, 101–116. San Diego: Academic Press.

Schmitz-Esser, Winfried. (1991). "New Approaches in Thesaurus Application." *International Classification* 18(3): 143–147.

Seal, Alan. (1983). "Experiments with Full and Short Entry Catalogues: A Study of Library Needs." *Library Resources and Technical Services* 27(2): 144–155.

Seal, Alan, Phillip Bryant, and Caroline Hall. (1982). *Full and Short Entry Catalogues: Library Needs and Uses.* Aldershot, Hants, Eng.: Gower.

Shafer, Keith E., Stuart L. Weibel, and Erik Jul. (1995). "The PURL Project." In *Annual Review of OCLC Research, 1995.* Dublin, Ohio: OCLC Online Computer Library Center.

Shannon, Claude E., and Warren Weaver. (1963). *The Mathematical Theory of Communication.* Urbana: University of Illinois Press.

Shatford, Sara. (1986). "Analyzing the Subject of a Picture: A Theoretical Approach." *Cataloging and Classification Quarterly* 6: 39–62.

Shera, Jesse H. (1973). "Changing Concepts of Classification: Philosophical and Educational Implications." In *Knowing Books and Men: Knowing Computers Too,* 327–337. Littleton, Colo.: Libraries Unlimited.

Sievert, Mary Ellen, and Bert R. Boyce. (1983). "Hedge Trimming and the Resurrection of the Controlled Vocabulary in Online Searching." *Online Review* 7: 489–494.

Silvester, J. P., and M. T. Genuardi. (1994). "Machine-Aided Indexing from the Analysis of Natural Language Text." In *Challenges in Indexing Electronic Text and Images,* edited by Raya Fidel et al., 201–220. ASIS Monograph Series. Medford, N.J.: Learned Information.

Simon, Herbert A. (1962). "The Architecture of Complexity." *Proceedings of the American Philosophical Society* 106: 467–482.

Simon, Julian L. (1978). *Basic Research Methods in Social Science: The Art of Empirical Inestigation.* 2nd ed. New York: Random House.

Skrobela, Kitty. (1980). "'Best-known' vs. 'Original' in Names and Titles." *Purple Sheets* 2 PS-6(March 7): 2.

Slamecka, Vladimir. (1963). "Classificatory, Alphabetic and Associative Schedules as Aids in Coordinate Indexing." *American Documentation* 14: 223–228.

Smiraglia, Richard. (1992). "Authority Control and the Extent of Derivative Bibliographic Relationships." Ph.D. dissertation, University of Chicago.

Soergel, Dagobert. (1974). *Indexing Languages and Thesauri: Construction and Maintenance.* Los Angeles: Melville.

Soergel, Dagobert. (1985). *Organizing Information: Principles of Data Base and Retrieval Systems.* Orlando: Academic Press.

Sørenson, Jutta, and Derek Austin. (1976). "PRECIS in a Multilingual Context, Part 2: A Linguistic and Logical Explanation of the Syntax." *Libri* 26(2): 108–139.

Spark Jones, Karen. (1971). *Automatic Keyword Classification for Information Retrieval*. Hamden, Conn.: Archon Books.

Sperberg-McQueen, C. M., and Lou Burnard. (1994). *Guidelines for Electronic Text Encoding and Interchange*. Oxford: Text Encoding Initiative. Also available at http://etext.virginia.edu/TEI.html.

Steinacker, Ivo. (1974). "Indexing and Automatic Significance Analysis." *Journal of the American Society for Information Science* 25: 237–241.

Strout, Ruth French. (1956). "The Development of the Catalog and Catalog Codes." *Library Quarterly* 26 (October): 254–275.

Subramanyam, Bhagi. (1998). "Consistency of Assigned Class Numbers Derived from the Library of Congress Classification Scheme in University Libraries." Ph.D. dissertation, University of California, Los Angeles, Graduate School of Education and Information Science.

Svenonius, Elaine. (1971). "The Effect of Indexing Specificity on Retrieval Performance." Ph.D. dissertation, University of Chicago.

Svenonius, Elaine. (1978). "Facet Definition: A Case Study." *International Classification* 5(3): 134–141.

Svenonius, Elaine. (1979). Facets as Semantic Categories. In *Klassifikation und Erkenntnis*, edited by Wolfgang Dahlberg, 57–79 (Studien zur Klassifikation, Bd. 5). Frankfurt: Gesellschaft für Klassifikation.

Svenonius, Elaine. (1983). "Use of Classification in Online Retrieval." *Library Resources and Technical Services* 27: 76–80.

Svenonius, Elaine. (1984). "Information Retrieval Thesauri in the Field of Art." In *Automatic Processing of Art History Data and Documents: Proceedings of a Conference held at the Scuola Normale Superiore, September 24–27, 1984*, 33–48. Regione Toseanu: Scuola Normale Superiore and J. Paul Getty Trust.

Svenonius, Elaine. (1986). "Unanswered Questions in the Design of Controlled Vocabularies." *Journal of the American Society for Information Science* 35(5): 331–340.

Svenonius, Elaine. (1987). "Studies in Automatic Cataloging." In *Annual Review of OCLC Research, July 1986–June 1987*, 26–27. Dublin, Ohio: Online Computer Library Center.

Svenonius, Elaine. (1988). "Clustering Equivalent Bibliographic Records." In *Annual Review of OCLC Research, July 1987–June 1988*, 6–8. Dublin, Ohio: Online Computer Library Center.

Svenonius, Elaine, ed. (1989). *The Conceptual Foundations of Descriptive Cataloging*. San Diego: Academic Press.

Svenonius, Elaine. (1990a). "Bibliographical Classification." *In Library Classification and Its Functions. Proceedings of an International Conference Held June 21, 1989 at the University of Alberta*, edited by A. Nitecki and T. Fell. 21–53. Edmonton: University of Alberta.

Svenonius, Elaine. (1990b). "Bibliographical Control." In *Academic Libraries: Research Perspectives,* edited by Mary Jo Lynch and Arthur Young, 38–66. Chicago: American Library Association.

Svenonius, Elaine. (1990c). "Design of Controlled Vocabularies." In *Encyclopedia of Library and Information Science,* edited by Allen Kent, vol. 45, supplement 10, 82–108. New York: Marcel Dekker.

Svenonius, Elaine. (1992). "Bibliographic Entities and Their Uses." In *IFLA UBCIM Programme and the IFLA Division of Bibliographic Control: Seminar on Bibliographic Records Proceedings of the Seminar held in Stockholm, August 15–16, 1990,* edited by Ross Brown, 3–18. Munich: Saur.

Svenonius, Elaine. (1994). "Access to Nonbook Materials: The Limits of Subject Indexing for Visual and Aural Languages." *Journal of the American Society for Information Science* 45(8): 600–606.

Svenonius, Elaine. (1995). "Precoordination or Not." In *Subject Indexing: Principles and Practices in the 90's: Proceedings of the IFLA Satellite Meeting Held in Lisbon, Portugal, 17–18 August 1993,* edited by Robert P. Holley, Dorothy McGarry, Donna Duncan, and Elaine Svenonius, 231–255. Munich: Saur. A translation of this paper into German ("Prakoordination — ja oder nein?") has been published in *Zeitschrift für Bibliothekswesen und Bibliographie* 14(3): 279–296.

Svenonius, Elaine. (1996). "References vs. Added Entries." In Online Computer Library Center, *Authority Control in the Twenty-first Century: An Invitational Conference, March 31–April 1.* http://www.oclc.org/oclc/man/authconf/confhome.htm

Svenonius, Elaine, Betty Baughman, and Mavis Molto. (1986). "The Distribution of Access Points in a Sample of English Language Monographs." *Cataloging and Classification Quarterly* 6(3): 3–21.

Svenonius, Elaine, and Dorothy McGarry. (1991). "More on Improved Subject Displays." *Information Technology and Libraries* 10: 185–191.

Svenonius, Elaine, and Mavis Molto. (1990). "Automatic Derivation of Name Access Points in Cataloging." *Journal of the American Society for Information Science* 41(4): 254–263.

Swift, D. F., V. Winn, and D. Bramer. (1978). "'Aboutness' as a Strategy for Retrieval in the Social Sciences." *Aslib Proceedings* 30: 182–187.

Takawashi, Tadayoshi. (1989). "The Japanese No Main-Entry Code." In *The Conceptual Foundations of Descriptive Cataloging,* edited by Elaine Svenonius, 65–72. San Diego: Academic Press.

Taniguchi, Shoichi. (1996). "A System for Analyzing Cataloging Rules: A Feasibility Study." *Journal of the American Society for Information Science* 47(5): 338–356.

Taniguchi, Shoichi. (1999). "An Analysis of Orientedness in Cataloging Rules." *Journal of the American Society for Information Science* 50(5): 448–460.

Tanselle, G. Thomas. (1984). "The Arrangement of Descriptive Bibliographies." *Studies in Bibliography* (37): 1–38.

Taube, Mortimer. (1953). *Studies in Coordinate Indexing.* Washington, D.C.: Documentation Incorporated.

TEI Guidelines. (1994). *See* Sperberg-McQueen, C. M., and Lou Burnard (1994).

Tenopir, Carol. (1985). "Full Text Database Retrieval Performance." *Online Review* 2: 149–164.

Thomas, Catherine M. (1984). "Authority Control in Manual vs. Online Catalogs: An Examination of *See* References." *Information Technology and Libraries* 3: 393–398.

Thomas, Sarah E. (1993). Personal communication from Sara Thomas, Library of Congress, June 17.

Tillett, Barbara B. (1987). "Bibliographic Relationships: Toward a Conceptual Structure of Bibliographic Information Used in Cataloging." Ph.D. dissertation, University of California, Los Angeles.

Tillett, Barbara B. (1990). "Access Control: A Model for Descriptive, Holding and Control Records." In *Convergence: Proceedings of the Second National Library and Information Technology Association, October 2–6, 1988,* edited by Michael Gorman, 48–56. Chicago: American Library Association.

Tillett, Barbara B. (1991). "A Taxonomy of Bibliographic Relationships." *Library Resources and Technical Services* 35(2) (1991): 150–158.

Tillett, Barbara B. (1992a). "Future Cataloging Rules and Catalog Records." In *Origins, Content, and Future of AACR2 Revised,* edited by Richard P. Smiraglia, 110–118. Chicago: American Library Association.

Tillett, Barbara B. (1992b). "The History of Linking Devices." *Library Resources and Technical Services* 36(1): 23–36.

Tillett, Barbara B. (1995). "Twenty-first Century Authority Control: What Is It and How Do We Get There?" In *The Future Is Now: Reconciling Change and Continuity in Authority Control. Proceedings of the OCLC Symposium, ALA Annual Conference, June 23, 1995,* 17–21. Dublin, Ohio: Online Computer Library Center.

Tillett, Barbara B. (1997). "International Shared Resource File: From Authority Control to Access Control." In *Authority Control in the Twenty-first Century: An Invitational Conference, March 31–April 1.* http://www.oclc.org/oclc/man/auth-conf/confhome.htm.

Tillin, Alma M., and William J. Quinly. (1976). *Standards for Cataloging Nonprint Materials: An Interpretation and Practical Application.* 4th ed. Washington, D.C.: Association for Education and Communications Technology.

Todd, Ross J. (1992). "Academic Indexing: What's It All About?" *The Indexer* 18(2): 101–104.

United Nations Educational, Scientific, and Cultural Organization (UNESCO), General Information Programme. (1981). *Guidelines for the Establishment and Development of Monolingual Thesauri: PGI-81/WS/15.* 2nd rev. ed. Paris: UNESCO.

Van Slype, G. (1976). *Definition of the Essential Characteristics of Thesauri.* Prepared for the Commission of the European Communities. Brussels: Bureau Marcel van Dijk.

Vellucci, Sherry L. (1995). "Bibliographic Relationships among Musical Bibliographic Entities: A Conceptual Analysis of Music Represented in a Library Catalog with a Taxonomy of the Relationships Discovered." D.L.S. dissertation, Columbia University.

Verona, Eva. (1963). "The Function of the Main Entry in the Alphabetical Catalogue — a Second Approach." In International Federation of Library Associations. *International Conference on Cataloguing Principles, Paris, 9–18 October, 1961: Report.* London: Clive Bingley.

Verona, Eva. (1975). *Corporate Headings: Their Use in Library Catalogues and National Bibliographies: A Comparative and Critical Study.* London: IFLA Committee on Cataloging.

Vickery, Brian. (1960). *Faceted Classification.* London: Aslib.

Vickery, Brian. (1966). *On Retrieval System Theory.* London: Butterworths. First published in 1961.

Vickery, Brian. (1975). *Classification and Indexing in Science.* 3rd ed. London: Butterworths.

Vizine-Goetz, Diane, and Joan S. Mitchell. (1996). "Dewey 2000." In *Annual Review of OCLC Research: 1995,* 16–19. Dublin, Ohio: Online Computer Library Center.

Vlelduts-Stokolov, N. (1987). "Concept Recognition in an Automatic Text-Processing System for the Life Sciences." *Journal of the American Society for Information Science* 38 (4): 269–287.

Wainwright, Eric. (1991). "Implications of the Dynamic Record for the Future of Cataloguing." *Cataloguing Australia* 17(3/4): 7–20.

Wajenberg, Arnold S. (1989). A Cataloger's View of Authorship. In *The Conceptual Foundations of Descriptive Cataloging,* edited by Elaine Svenonius, 21–27. San Diego: Academic Press.

Waples, Douglas. (1931). "The Graduate Library School at Chicago." *Library Quarterly* 1: 26–36.

Webster's Third New International Dictionary of the English Language, Unabridged, with Seven Language Dictionary. (c. 1966). Chicago: Encyclopaedia Britannica, Inc.

Weibel, Stuart L. (1995). "Metadata: The Foundation of Resource Description." In *Annual Review of OCLC Research,* 52–56. Dublin, Ohio: Online Computer Library Center.

Weihs, Jean, with Shirley Lewis in Consultation with the CLA/ALA/AECT Advisory Committee on the Cataloguing of Nonbook Materials. (1989). *Nonbook Materials: The Organization of Integrated Collections.* 3rd ed. Ottawa: Canadian Library Association.

Weinberg, Bella Hass. (1981). "Word Frequency and Automatic Indexing." D.L.S. dissertation, Columbia University.

Wendler, Robin K. (1995). "Automating Heading Correction in a Large File: Harvard's Experience." In *The Future Is Now: Reconciling Change and Continuity in Authority Control. Proceedings of the OCLC Symposium, ALA Annual Conference, June 23, 1995*, 5–10. Dublin, Ohio: Online Computer Library Center.

Willet, Peter. (1988). "Recent Trends in Hierarchic Document Clustering: Critical Review." *Information Processing and Management* 24(15): 577–597.

Willetts, Margaret. (1975). "An Investigation of the Nature of the Relation between Terms in Thesauri." *Journal of Documentation* 31(3): 158–184.

Williams, Thyllis. (1968). *Standardized Abstracts of Dictionary Definitions*. Studies in Indexing Depth and Retrieval Effectiveness NSF GN 380/654. Chicago: University of Chicago, Graduate Library School.

Wilson, Patrick. (1968). *Two Kinds of Power: An Essay on Bibliographical Control*. Berkeley: University of California Press.

Wilson, Patrick. (1983). "The Catalog as Access Mechanism: Background and Concepts." *Library Resources and Technical Services* 27: 4–17.

Wilson, Patrick. (1989a). "Interpreting the Second Objective of the Catalog." *Library Quarterly* 59:339–53.

Wilson, Patrick. (1989b). "The Second Objective." In *The Conceptual Foundations of Descriptive Cataloging*, edited by Elaine Svenonius, 5–16. San Diego: Academic Press.

Wittgenstein, Ludwig. (1953) *Philosophical Investigations*, translated by G. E. M. Anscombe. New York: Macmillan.

Wittgenstein, Ludwig. (1971). *Tractatus Logico–Philosophicus*. London: Routledge and Kegan Paul. First published in German in 1921 and in English in 1922.

Yee, Martha M. (1993). "Moving Image Works and Manifestations." Ph.D. dissertation, University of California, Los Angeles.

Yee, Martha M. (1994a). "What Is a Work? Part 1. The User and the Objects of the Catalog." *Cataloging and Classification Quarterly* 19(1): 9–28.

Yee, Martha M. (1994b). "What Is a Work? Part 2. The Anglo-American Cataloging Codes." *Cataloging and Classification Quarterly* 19(2): 5–22.

Yee, Martha M. (1995). "What Is a Work? Part 3. The Anglo-American Cataloging Codes." *Cataloging and Classification Quarterly* 20(1): 25–46.

Yee, Martha M., and Sara Shatford Layne (1998). *Improving Online Public Access Catalogs*. Chicago: American Library Association.

Index